BUSINESS CONTINUITY PLANNING FOR DATA CENTERS AND SYSTEMS

Business Continuity Planning for Data Centers and Systems

A Strategic Implementation Guide

Ronald H. Bowman, Jr.

WILEY

JOHN WILEY & SONS, INC.

Library of Congress Cataloging-in-Publication Data:

Bowman, Ronald H., 1960-
   Business continuity planning for data centers and systems : a strategic implementation guide / Ronald H.
Bowman, Jr.
       p. cm.
   Includes index.
   ISBN 978-0-470-25861-3 (cloth)
   1. Data protection. 2. Electronic data processing—Security measures.   I. Title.
   HF5548.37.B68 2008
   658.4'78—dc22

                                                                              2008009608

Printed in the United States of America

10 9 8 7 6 5 4 3 2 1

This book is dedicated to my father Ronald Bowman, who inspired me.

CONTENTS

Preface   ix

1   How We Got Here: History of Data Centers and Current Choices   1

2   Acts of God: Mission-Critical Interruptions and Man-Made Challenges   9

3   Origins of the Business Impact Analysis   21

4   Flooding: Be Afraid, Be Very Afraid!   51

5   Data Centers Growth Velocity   57

6   Energy Use in Data Centers Globally Through 2012   73

7   Primary and Secondary Data Center Selection: Recent History   83

8   Public Sector Laws: Guidance and Consequences   97

9   Government's Role: Summary of National Infrastructure Protection Plan of 2006   101

10   Tier 4: Basis of Design   133

11   Unique Challenges of Cooling   139

12   Unique Challenges of Power   151

13   Going Green   157

14   New Methods of Effective Site Selection: Negotiation and Execution   163

15 Cyberterrorism   171

16 Need for Speed   177

17 Future of Data Center Efficiencies—Think Outside
    the Grid   181

Glossary   193

Index   199

PREFACE

The book that you are about to read has been a long time coming and is also time sensitive. I have been in the data center world for almost 20 years. Like many careers, mine began with an enthusiasm for transactional real estate and an interest in making money. In New York City in the 1980s, this meant leasing office space. At that time, and for some years to come, it was more about sales rather than true "value-added" services. For example, the president of the firm I worked for asked me to canvass Third Avenue. I promptly responded, "Which way is Third Avenue?" This kind of canvassing meant knocking on every door of each office tower (before heavy lobby security) and getting contact information on the decision maker, the relative size of the tenants, and the particular industry. After this, I would go back to the office, collate notes, transcribe them onto index cards (the database), and call the tenant to get a meeting. We would manufacture a mysterious and anonymous user who was interested in subleasing all or a portion of the space or some mysterious tenant who was moving out and wanted us to contact other tenants in the elevator bank (or building) blah blah blah, or create some other misdirection in order to get face time with the tenant. Imagine grown men and women calling this a business practice and measuring their success by how many meetings based on false requirements they could set up. These were the paper days of office leasing; the early days of leasing, when "arrogance" was a substitute for "intelligence" as salespeople and brokers strove to lease space. Fast forward to today; some overnight experts in mission-critical consulting, real estate brokerage, and construction are using similar techniques to get meetings and establish credibility. Today vendors merely have to mention "fiber" or "substation" and they get meetings with some users.

In the early days of canvassing, I would write down the number of fire stairs on each floor, the quality of the lobbies, comments about the interior: tiered, fit out, storage boxes in sight, signage, and so on. I would overcomplicate what was a con game of getting access and getting liked. I would not believe that to succeed in office leasing, all that was required was a person's name and persistence to get through the receptionist, but it was true. The techniques for getting through or finding common interests with a prospect were right out of a bad movie. Once a team member put on RollerBlades and waited for hours near a prospect's beach house; when the person came out, my partner skated by and created a chance meeting that led to our getting the work.

I was collecting data on things that were fairly meaningless for the job. I was creating detailed columns of things that did not matter to most of my industry. I was pretending my job was more important than getting names and not getting thrown out of office buildings by security or tenants themselves. (I was not in real estate yet; I was in sales.) By the way, I have been escorted out of several office buildings in New York City.

During those first few years, I learned a few things. I was successful at leasing, but I did not necessarily enjoy it. I had no passion. After doing 16 very small deals in my first year, I was almost ready to move out of the one-bedroom apartment I shared with two friends. My place was the couch (actually a love seat). I am six feet two inches tall, so you could say that I slept uphill for two years. Leasing was about getting liked, then trusted, and eventually negotiating the four corners of the lease, or what I like to call the "big four":

1. Base rent
2. Free rent
3. Landlord's work (tenant fit out)
4. Escalations

If you did not embarrass yourself on these issues, which were forged on four-function math (and a subset of 10 to 30 business points), you could get paid travel to Florida and rest on your laurels.

It was true. Better brokers had better tans. Those were the days when manicures, a good shoeshine, and custom shirts did most of the talking in meetings. What was clear to me then—and now—is that arrogance, not intelligence, ruled the day. I knew early on that if, in a meeting, a gray-haired man or woman had to revert to "in all my years" to introduce or finish a thought, he or she was weak and there would soon be an opening at the table. I was the young man at these meetings and a sponge for fun or relevant facts, construction costs, schedule issues, landlord nuances, and so on.

These were the days when fear and arrogance ruled. After these meetings, brokers and lawyers scrambled to get the intelligence to bring to the next meeting to be the "smart guy" and "own the required information or answers" they would collect from their friends or IOUs from vendors.

- How much to build the space?
- Does the equipment fit?
- Do we need approvals?

- How much or how long to cable?
- Does the landlord have off-hours air conditioning?
- How long to permit?
- What are weekend hours?
- Porters' wage versus consumer price index cost analysis

If I could get these answers to the test beforehand or have the knowledge to respond with credibility before, during, or after these meetings, I would be far more valuable to the client/customer and, more important, begin the self-esteem aspect of my career. I could actually add value and get paid for my knowledge, rather than some forced friendship or awkward collection of steak dinners, strip joints, bad golf games, and bad jokes.

Do not get me wrong. The high-risk and high-reward income did not escape me, but I never measured myself by my income. I was not trying to have a good year but start a career. I measure myself by how my wife, Maureen, son, Connor, and daughter, Ceara, are doing. I have always run my business as a program of attraction, not promotion. If you like what I am doing, grab an oar and let us row in the same direction. Promotion, however, is more like "I'm doing great, and you can do great too!" We all know people of average intelligence who have managed to make a ton of money and smart people who cannot seem to succeed.

My hope, directly or indirectly, was to be the smartest guy in the room and the smartest guy in my field. Time has showed me that at a certain level, we are all about the same. Ethics, hard work, and luck are the great differentiators. But what was my field? To this day, we have had a hard time thinking of vendors as anything but single-discipline specialists. Ever wonder where the expression "think outside the box" comes from? It is a test from a graduate school that asks how you make a triangle without starting or finishing in one or the same point and without lifting the pen off the paper (see Exhibit P.1).

The solution to the question requires the individual to plot a point outside the matrix ("the box") to connect five points inside to create the triangle.

In the old days, a vendor who knew the cost of a dropped ceiling, linear glass, and floor covering was considered a construction specialist. A vendor

x

EXHIBIT P.1 THINKING OUTSIDE OF THE BOX

who knew the conversion of tons of cooling per kilowatt of power was an electrical and mechanical engineer. A vendor who could negotiate the four corners of a lease was a leasing attorney or experienced broker.

I analyzed "acts of God" for a specific area and man-made challenges, and would articulate the history and duration of these events. Thus my specialty was odd, which made me valuable. The cornerstones of my discipline were being set, "rocketship real estate." The long-time-coming aspect of this book relates to the 25 years I have spent in real estate and the 20 years I have dedicated to data centers and trading floors, or what was called then disaster recovery and what is now business continuity.

What I can say with confidence is that the former "big four"—(1) base rent; (2) free rent; (3) landlord's work; and (4) escalations—has been transformed or eclipsed by a new "big four":

1. Power
2. Air conditioning (water)
3. Life safety/security
4. Telecom/information technology (IT)

Real estate is clearly more of a commodity than a value-add to the end goal, and the value-add to the process is far more challenging. Clients are often better informed than vendors regarding market conditions due to their more accurate and faster market reporting and multiple branch offices. Urban transportation is generally better, and hotels, restaurants, and shopping have migrated to fringe office developments and suburban office parks. Very few streets or avenues in Tier 1, or major, cities can command high rents merely because of cachet. All too often, these "trophy assets" are antiquated, with problems with power distribution and cooling to the floor; single-pane perimeter glass; elevators designed for fewer humans meaning longer peak wait times in the lobby or floor and slow door opening and closing times, and slower and more frequent floor-to-floor accelerations. This is the difference between danish and doughnut buildings. The postmodern assets of the 1980s and 1990s were designed from the outside in, and to lease, not to last. Great lobbies, interesting curtain wall, and elevator cabs loaded with millwork—these were the doughnuts: the only and best part is the outside. The forward-thinking assets, however, were designed from the inside out. The best and only part unique to the danish is the center or inside: designed from the inside out!

Today, smart buildings rule. (Smart buildings are those that can communicate with themselves.) Environmentally friendly buildings rule, and those buildings and vendors associated with forward-thinking facilities will outperform the traditional assets and vendors.

If a real estate consultant or any broker required 10 things, from getting liked to getting paid, 4 to 6 of them have been eclipsed or eliminated due to the electronic age of the online research, cable TV, electronic conferences, trade shows municipal documentation, seminars, and peer reviews.

Quickly available and abundant intellectual capital often results in a shrinking fee for the ordinary vendor (appropriate) and forces niche vendors like me to push the envelope of new "fingertip knowledge" or to reinvent ourselves to deal with the new challenges presented by the fluid landscape of data center design and implementation.

I worked for and was a lead producer in a full-service, well-known, and well-regarded real estate company in New York. There, following the creation of a niche within the country's largest real estate brokerage company to satisfy the bourgeoning mission-critical real estate growth spurred on by the Telecom Deregulation Act of 1996 and the subsequent dot-com boom, we created "the Unique Infrastructure Group." At this time, most real estate companies started "technology" groups as well. After the company's reluctance to grow concept with funds or people, I took the group off-site and grew the concept till the boom burst and the Towers fell. By 2003, I found myself at Tishman Technologies in New York City.

My road into Tishman was circuitous and purely by chance. In the early years, it was a good place to mend my soul, regroup, and sort out what was next in the overbuilt, overspent telecom world. This was a world where the future of rocketship real estate was not in doubt due to the events of September 11; it was underfunded, and would be so for some time.

Tishman Construction is a family-owned, world-class organization that is over 100 years old. It has the finest brand and one of the most extraordinary reputations in the world. There are bigger companies, certainly, but none with the vision, ownership, coaching, and players that Tishman owns. While this praise may seem over the top, I can assure readers that I have had nothing to do with the extraordinary and ongoing success of the big T. I have been with the company for a mere five years. Generations of dedicated leadership and loyal coaching and players have contributed to the philosophy and implementation of Tishman's vision.

John Tishman is a legend in the industry. His construction practices and methods of preconstruction, provisioning, and construction management are currently textbook and commonplace. Dan Tishman, our current chairman, is a visionary who is building the most significant assets in the world. He is implementing security, power, cooling, and ecological milestones by which the rest of the planet will be measured.

John Livingston, the president of Tishman Technologies, is a player coach with the great challenge of managing the assistant coaches and players. Managing a group of all-stars who have been there from 15 to 30 years is no small task.

John Krush, my partner, and I report directly to John Livingston. John Krush's vast experience in corporate account leadership has given me new sensitivity in how to approach, secure, and maintain accounts. More specifically, John has led by example to trust as a partner and has taught me how important it is to remain teachable.

This book is time sensitive because I do not see any books providing the history of how we got here. What is *here*? The changing world of business continuity, the impact of super-size events (e.g., London's Bishop's Gate bombing; the Seaport Substation outage in New York City; New York City's World Trade Center 1 and World Trade Center 2 attacks; Chicago's Loop flood; the power outages on the West Coast and the East Coast; California's fires; and the various recent hurricanes).

Early designs for mission-critical facilities were developed from military specifications. The formerly regulated telecom industry and other facilities were collectively designed by the largest spender in research and development and proven best practices: the U.S. military (or, as we commonly refer to them, "mil specs").

There was nothing wrong with mil specs, but best practices and recent solutions showed that they are no longer able to satisfy the exacting criteria of inside plants. Things were moving fast in the private sector enterprise, mainframe, and storage silos. Do not get me wrong: Our government is a huge buyer of IT kit and environmentals to support them, capacity, but recently utilization of the chip and the enterprise, mainframe, and storage areas are pushing the limits and boundaries in the private sector.

The private sector was finding new and complex ways to manipulate data and make money, lots of money. Traditional power and cooling solutions were adequate to power and cool older IBM 3084s and 3090s and tape storage components because the military and Department of Defense were using the mainframe disc storage at a similar utilization application and velocity. But soon many critical applications in the private sector or financial industry specifically required greater capacity and faster processing times to enhance batch work product and fewer touches, adjacencies, or contingencies of processing.

One would think the hospital or healthcare industry would have given us the best solutions for mission-critical solutions. Americans, who are at the epicenter of efficiency implementation, might be expected to provide solutions to sustain or prolong human life via technologies or environmentals to support life-supporting technologies; but the reality is that all too often, data centers in hospitals have too little power and cooling to support life safety systems, which are often old, not redundant, poorly maintained, and in basements (i.e., flood zones). In sum, the speed of revenue "needs" has clearly outpaced the speed of life safety support. Follow the money . . .

Why now? Why write the book now? Because we are still in the "dos" stages of IT development and implementation. In the post–September 11 world, and in the shadows of several natural and man-made disasters, the concentric circles of need and requirements that follow the concentric circles of catastrophe, loss of revenue, income, data, and life now have data points, facts, and names. In the 1980s, we sold fear. Can you imagine your facilities going down? The 1990s also gave us the deregulation of telecom and the commercial deployment of fiber optics, submersible cables, and the Internet. In addition, that decade gave us more powerful encryption, chips, and multiplexers, which force plant designers to bigger and more sophisticated solutions. The 1990s also gave us the overdesign and overspending on real or imagined problems with real or imagined solutions. Remember Y2K?

The new millennium has seen an economic downturn brought on by overdesign and underperforming telecom infrastructure, overbuilt everything "i" or "e" related in the markets. The events of September 11, 2001, showed local, state, and federal governments and multiple users how unprepared we were for a prolonged outage. This is odd because the events of September 11 were foreshadowed by the Seaport Substation outage (user generators did not work or ran out of fuel due to poor maintenance programs) and World Trade Center 1 attack (same radio systems).

In the early years of this decade, nationalism was at an all-time high. Cars were flying flags (two were better than one), flags were draped over bridges. "Get Osama" signs replaced "Baby on Board" signs. New Orleans' Mayor Nagin or Louisiana's Governor Blanco would have been perceived as successful given the circumstances. I openly resent anyone taking credit for unique follow-up or cleanup of 9/11. Everyone did his job—and more. The human spirit overcame the circumstances and allowed us to endure unspoken horrors. Scores of Americans volunteered to clean up the site, feed the workers, donate money, help families endure. However, the facts are that the radios did not work any better in the World Trade Center 2 attack than they did in the World Center 1 attack. The police and firefighters were prepared, but their equipment did not work. Police layoffs and firehouse closings were rampant. This is like sending infantrymen to war with guns but no bullets, firefighters to fight fire with hoses but no water or trucks without enough firefighters. The Port Authority sent tenants back to their desks after the first tower was struck. The list goes on. Sadly, after the first attack, the infrastructure supporting the U.S. economy was only marginally better off than before the attack.

Why this book now? We seem to be in a growth period that will last for three to five more years, driven by pent-up demand, a confluence of IT solutions, more powerful chips, and Moore's Law (i.e., the doubling of IT bandwidth every 18 months). Inside plant design—meaning the "Big Iron," uninterruptible power supply (UPS), generators, raised floor, life safety, and future-proofing of a flexible and scalable facility—we need to understand the full utilization of the chip and the servers where future chips and associated storage are going.

We have been overlectured on the challenges of hot spots, blade servers, virtualization, super-high-density rooms in Tier 3 versus Tier 4 criteria. We have not spent enough time on the future or total cost of ownership (TCO) of these facilities. TCOs have grown from hundreds of millions to $2 billion to $8 billion for larger assets, all inclusive. These data centers are meaningful. The big winners, or cost centers, for these data centers are the local and state governments; the utility, telecom transmission provider; IT equipment providers; and software providers. What is interesting and ironic is that the real estate brokers and partially trained facilities personnel who often guide the site selection and implementation process own only 10% of the total budget. The least-experienced, least-expensive cost center component—land, or property acquisition—has the biggest impact on this multibillion-dollar spend.

If you look at the sources of outages collectively being over 50% between hardware and software, then you add the human or management failure component of 10 to 20%, you can see that our model of data processing and distribution is flawed and costly. To reduce data transmissions ("touches") is to reduce or eliminate IT functions. Not a lot of IT guys are out there saying "You don't need me if you do this." Similar to provisioning "stuff" distributed by freight folks, truckers, overnight carriers and so forth, the fewer touches the greater the profitability. If overnight companies with 12 touches to get package X from point A to point B and could reduce the touches to 5 or 7, do you think this would make more sense? Well, the companies did! Similarly, the fewer data touches the better. The less kit, the better; the more kit, the greater chance of failure.

If we shift the conversation to how few times we can touch or manipulate data (fewer servers or applications) and reduce the problem of IT adjacencies and points of failure, a few things are going to happen:

- The conversation will shift from cost per square foot to cost per application by way of kilowatts and cooling.
- Fewer touches mean faster movement and less energy, which means a smaller carbon footprint.
- Fewer touches mean more meaningful single points of failure, which means we better get it right!
- Virtual mainframe solutions will slow but not stop our insatiable appetite and associated power and cooling.
- Direct current power, cogeneration, and lower-carbon-footprint solutions are needed now. The Environmental Protection Agency has been unable and too willing to lead the charge. It has just determined that the states *cannot* supersede the federal government's standards and goals. If that had been the case with smoking, we would still have plenty of secondhand smoke around us.

We are still working with arrogance in favor of intelligence paradigm; that's why I'm writing this book now.

1

HOW WE GOT HERE: HISTORY OF DATA CENTERS AND CURRENT CHOICES

Data center processing capabilities were designed to do multiple and complex equations, transactions, executions, and storage. The limitations of the mainframe are often the abilities and brain trust of the information technology (IT) director/operator in using the mainframe, and the bandwidth to the mainframe often limits its use. For example, one mainframe properly utilized can collapse 10,000 to 20,000 square feet of legacy servers and white space. This is not only one big single point of potential failure but one remarkably efficient use of space and environmentals.

The utilization of the mainframe is often 50% or less, which is not a good return on investment (ROI). The protocols of the mainframe functions are not as nimble as those of enterprise systems, unless the programmers are confident and fluent. Older mainframes were nine feet by five feet wide, broken into modules (5 to 11 modular components). A minimum of three feet had to be left for service accessibility on all sides. Mainframes had fixed power from whips and were fixed to plumbing for cooling; they did not easily move once they were set. In the 20-year total cost of ownership model, the 20-year environmentals would service three to four IT life cycles of equipment with nonsevere (low-velocity) increases of power distributions or cooling.

Mainframes were expensive, and they did a myriad of complex functions simultaneously. They cost millions of dollars, old and new, and it took an act of Congress or multiple senior executive signatures to authorize the purchase and installation and growth of mainframe installations. The downside of mainframes were:

- Very expensive IT spend
- Very expensive and exacting environmentals (installation) to operate 24/7

1

- Difficult to move into a live data center (monolithic)
- Expensive to maintain vendor-driven costs, vendors on-site (licensed engineer required)
- Migration or upgrade challenges
- Tape storage a challenge
- Bandwidth of telecom connectivity (blend of copper and fiber inside plant and outside plant)

Plenty of the mainframe computers were placed in vertical assets in urban environments in the 1980s. They stayed urban because companies wanted them to be near or close to fiber optics central offices and the IT personnel, who in the old days stayed at headquarters for political and public transportation reasons.

As we will discuss later, in the 1990s, data centers became populated with just-in-time solutions precipitated by a flurry in overspending. Financing of kit was easy. If a piece of kit could provide marginal or a few added features, it was sold and provisioned. Tactical solutions eclipsed strategic solutions. Money was abundant for IT spending. The leasing terms for the new, most relevant equipment were almost silly. To please shareholders, vendors were making it too easy to get the equipment out the door. Users were unsure of the solutions they were buying. The total cost of ownership models were thrown out the window. The question at that time was: What is a data center?

My introduction to the world of data centers came on the heels of the futuristic high-rise development working for a rock star, high-rise developer and a few prewar renovations developers in the cast-iron and SoHo areas of lower Manhattan, for assets meant to lease, not to last.

My boot camp (following the above work), for the world of acronyms or mission-critical facilities was an eight-story concrete grain warehouse on a pier. The LeFrak Organization (Sam and Richard LeFrak) added eight stories of steel to turn it into a 15-story office building (no thirteenth floor), named Newport Center I. (It was renamed Newport Financial Center [NFC], a name I suggested in a naming contest).

A Japanese publishing company (Recruit, USA) came to New York in the mid- to late 1980s. The chairman went up in a helicopter, pointed to the building, and told the broker to buy it. When they found that 111 Pavonia Avenue in Jersey City, New Jersey, was not for sale, they leased it.

The NFC was one of the largest, most dynamic and forward-thinking developments in America's history. Recruit deserves all the credit. The company missed the market by 18 months, but it was brilliant nonetheless. Newport rivals the turnarounds of Boston's Faneuil Hall, Baltimore's Inner Harbor, and London's Canary Wharf. Sam LeFrak was a visionary who created the LeFrak City housing development in New York. He saw the value of the views from New Jersey to New York and realized that Manhattan as an island had limits. New Jersey's PATH train, which was cleaner and less expensive than the New York City subway and connected to the New York City subway system, enhanced the sale of NFC. Sam's son Richard would carefully craft and successfully implement the multiuse and mature development that we now see. Richard's visionary qualities are eclipsed only by his humility. Although the LeFraks were best known for the development of the masses and not the classes, their greatest assets are not real estate but the relentless efforts and loyal human infrastructure that keep the machine running. (Mike Sabet, the on-site development manager, is a good example of this.) Like Sam, the Japanese saw an opportunity to leverage the close proximity to the city and decided to develop the land as they did in Japan: developing mission-critical assets on the fringe of an urban environment. Businesses in New York were moving in the same direction. There was a movement to get back-office operations out of Manhattan to the boroughs of New York and New Jersey to support the boom of the mid-1980s (remember the age of excess, "bright lights, big city"?). Development that characterizes this time is the Staten Island "Teleport" (satellite farm with office building on low-cost real estate), Paine Webber in Weehawken, New Jersey, and Newport in Jersey City. Manhattan was moving back-office operations, call centers, and noncritical functions to Connecticut, New Jersey, Queens, Brooklyn, and warm-weather points in the South.

Recruit wanted to take a business plan developed in Japan and export it to the United States, to the undisputed financial capital of the world: New York City. Jersey City would do. The concept was "shared infrastructure."

I will take a circuitous route in defining just what a data center is via the shared infrastructure concept because the brain trust and intellectual capital was great, among multiple users, and because the importance of human infrastructure, documentation, and proactive preventive maintenance was highlighted with a co-op of users and their inherent best practices and unique requirements.

The shared concept delivered by the Japanese was based on the challenges of cooling mainframe computers. IBM was dominant in the early 1980s. Its "big iron," or mainframe, computers were being spit out of Ulster, Kingston, and Poughkeepsie in New York State and elsewhere as fast as they could be made.

In Japan, due to the challenges of expensive or unavailable real estate in urban environments (specifically Tokyo and Roppongi, respectively), businesses realized that these data centers were going to have to be vertical assets and that a shared "heartbeat," or critical cooling system, could be far more efficient and economical. By more economical, I mean that users would not have to acquire a relatively small data center space and the associated relatively huge expense and delay associated with land acquisition, and the protracted and expensive design and construction required for a 15- to 20-year asset. For small users, this may not be the best use of valuable resources of money, time, and talented in-house staff.

Cooling the mainframe was the challenge. The mainframe is fixed (but modular) for a long time; even in the 1980s, this meant for a period of five to seven years. As we know, "necessity is the mother of invention." The decision to build data centers vertically was then, and is still, a concern because of possible water flow from floors above to a data center, and could force an outage. Mixing water and electricity is traditionally a bad idea. Also, another tenant or user could force an interruption within a shared asset and could create a security breach or evacuation. Mainframes had water on the floor and in the equipment.

The compromise was *shared infrastructure*. The benefits were:

- Lower capital expense-entry barrier
- Faster to market
- Maintenance performed by experts in their core business
- Clustered IT and facilities vendors led to economies of "buy," improving service-level agreements
- Modular moves, adds, and changes

Traditional data center components often were an afterthought for corporate facilities. Many times they were placed in odd and nonstrategic locations:

- Basement locations were problematic due to their proximity to piping (water, steam, etc.) and flooding.
- Top-floor locations were liable to roof flooding, and expensive long power and fiber runs.
- Locations under or contiguous to cafeterias on second floors led to smoke and water flow issues.
- Locations with center core assets were problematic due to building services running through the data center.

In the 1980s, data centers were underfunded and poorly maintained with a host of single points of failure. At the time, we were still living in the paper age of transactional work and batch work. Storage was requested but rarely required, and enforcement was archaic. Consequences of noncompliance of storage had rare enforcement consequences. There was no "hammer" to speak of.

In vertical assets, data centers were often placed in odd or unusual locations. Cooling and power upgrades were brought to the white space under the most challenging and circuitous routing and conditions.

Outside plant upgrades or power had to be worked out with the utility. That meant the utility dictated how much and how long to make proposed improvements. Then easements with the landlord du jour had to be satisfied, often requiring additional real estate for a substation or step-down or step-up transformers of power in a basement. Then a vertical right-of-way had to be mapped out with paper drawings. (There were no "as-builts," so a time-consuming and dirty process of climbing into shaftways, elevator risers, and duct banks needed to be verified before a landlord would allow the work; then charge by the linear foot to run and maintain the distribution and usage of new risers, decommissioned elevators, etc.)

The same challenges were waiting for the cooling component of the data center for the placement of cooling towers, or DX units, the conduits to serve the source of the air-handling units and computer room air-conditioning units.

The raised floor to underside of dropped ceiling was challenging but not a showstopper due to the lower density of heat dissipation and respective cooling needed. Getting the mainframe—a piece of equipment the size of a small car—into the building, up the freight car, down the hall, in the tight turns was always an interesting challenge. Although the mainframe was built in modular units, and most were designed to make it through a 30-inch doorway, moving the mainframe from the truck to its designated footprint was often an arduous process. Face it, servers are cheaper and faster to place in cabinets.

Today these data center design and implementation challenges for vertical assets within urban environments seem humorous. Yet this was the situation until the crash of 1987 and the economic slowdown that lasted until 1991. IT spending was dramatically reduced and the moves, adds, and changes during these years were generally required, not merely requested.

So why were data centers not given the reverence that we give them today? What has changed?

- Data centers were tied at the hip to large office installations due to the human infrastructure; both IT and facilities management are needed to make these things happen. Large office installations were driven to public transportation services and prestigious addresses.
- The only diverse and redundant telecom infrastructure in the regulated world of telecommunications that served with large bandwidth

solutions based on multiple business and large human populations to serve. Follow-the-money infrastructure is built around fast and economical penetration of markets. At the time, most businesses and dense human populations were urban. Meaningful telecom facilities serviced meaningful billing opportunities. While by law they had to bring services to rural or suburban areas, diverse, scalable, burstable, and synchronous optical networks (SONET) did not exist or were prohibitively expensive and challenging to build, operate, and maintain. (My first T1 was $1,500 a month in Jersey City.)

- Access to large power substations or near large telecom infrastructure (central offices) was in urban environments, not just in New York City but in most parts of the country.

To sum up, data centers of the 1980s and the early 1990s often were underfunded afterthoughts of the corporate world. Chief financial officers (CFOs) often were in charge of the go/no go decisions for large capital spending, and the IT executive or chief information officer did not have a place at the table to speak for or on the behalf of the data center. Neither the CFO nor the chief executive officer knew the difference between a mainframe or main gate, kilovolt ampere or British thermal unit. These important disciplines were far down the food chain with poor corporate visibility and were largely undercompensated. They were viewed as taskmasters at best, rarely acknowledged or appreciated for their long hours or years of dedicated service. These were the data center warriors.

Besides having low power, data centers had low cooling standards and were monolithic and not nimble in design. Big box in, add a box, big box out (usually in pieces), storage tapes in, storage tapes out. There was no regulation other than peers or best practices. Power moves were limited to the distance of the whips or seal-tight conduit from the power distribution unit or junction box.

Users would move when the lease expired, and the same madness would continue over and over until 1996, and the era of telecom deregulation. There was no real, compelling reason to change the model. To state the obvious:

- There were no extraordinary events outside of the periodic hurricanes or tornadoes. (Data centers in these regions had no excuse.)
- Earthquakes with meaningful destruction were limited to California. (Most financial institutions and exchanges are in the Northeast.)
- Floods, although national and often underreported, had not had catastrophic consequences in urban environments. Suburban employees had been inconvenienced, but there were no marked events of extensive

duration and great financial loss to power, telecom, the exchanges, national economy, or security.

Because no meaningful consequences had interfered with the U.S. economy, there were few or no drivers to improve the design, installation, or maintenance of the data centers of the 1980s or early 1990s.

These events were noteworthy largely because of the loss of lives; they had no impact on data center siting (locations), design, implementation, or maintenance:

- 1938: The Great Hurricane (i.e., the "Long Island Express") killed 50 people.
- 1985: Hurricane Gloria touched down on the Atlantic coast as a category 2 storm, with winds under 65 miles an hour.
- 1992: Hurricane Andrew killed 23 people and inflicted $43.7 billion in damages. The losses to homes and some businesses were so great that 11 insurance companies went bankrupt.
- 1995: A heat wave killed over 750 people in Chicago.
- 2003: During a heat wave, 35,000 Europeans died. The United Nations predicts urban deaths in the United States to double by 2020 thanks to global warming.
- 2005: In a 52-day period, hurricanes Katrina, Rita, and Wilma caused approximately $20 billion in damages and approximately 1,500 lives were lost. These are 100% new. What is noteworthy is that seven of the top ten most powerful hurricanes in 154 years of record keeping happened between 2004 and 2005.

It is ironic that heat waves traditionally kill more Americans than any other national disaster.

Now that we have identified the general reason or causes to spend the money and time to design, build, and maintain a data center based on traditional acts of God, we can articulate the choices available since the early 1990s.

Currently there are three choices for data centers:

1. **Stand-alone data center.** Such centers are built as greenfield single- or multistory single-purpose assets. Some are found in multitenanted and multistory buildings, but they are not preferred. Some stand-alone data centers can also be 100% new or augment existing centers (warehouse, manufacturing, etc.). Most users start out by trying to save time or money by improving an antiquated asset or partially improved asset with some of the improvements in place for a data center.

2. **Shared infrastructure, multitenanted asset.** This center is a single-purpose and often multistory asset with inside plant improvements that often include emergency power service generator only, uninterruptible power supply, battery, and rectifiers for clean, computer-grade power, air-cooled, DX, dry coolers, security, monitoring, and maintenance. Tenants take largely unimproved space by service provider, inclusive of maintenance, et cetera, all at a premium and expense. Users can buy 100 KVA of uninterruptible power supply and 200 kilowatts of generators. Tenants can buy 40 tons of heating, ventilation, and air conditioning. They also can buy "hot hands," or modified services, for fixed or "cross-connect fees" in a protracted menu. Services are à la carte. Users need to make sure services will be in place during the full term of the lease or licensing agreement to ensure that the asset does not run out of infrastructure capacity. This is a buyer-beware program. The devil is in the details of the service-level agreements (SLAs). No one should expect compensation for lost revenue or brand damage due to outage. Compensation comes in the form of future free rent or minimal setoffs. In fact, SLAs are really little more than facility descriptions; more often than not, the sales staff does not know the difference between the two.

3. **Collocation-caged environments.** These centers often are multi-tenant or telecom assets in which there is shared improvements of generators, uninterrupted power supply, air conditioning, and often cabinets and IT equipment. The services are sold by the cabinet, power circuits, cross-connects, IT circuits, and pretty much everything you look at you pay for. The "hot hands" for all IT work is priced by task or duration of tasks per month (e.g., five hours per month). Like the shared infrastructure model, this is also a buyer-beware program.

These choices can satisfy mission-critical needs in urban environments, where cross-connectivity or layer-one, layer-two, and layer-three solutions can have choice and various architecture. The TELCO assets have the confluence of facilities- and nonfacilities-based fiber optics with a plethora of optic multiplexing and manipulating to suit users' needs with competitive prices based on multiple vendors and, therefore, competition.

2

ACTS OF GOD: MISSION-CRITICAL INTERRUPTIONS AND MAN-MADE CHALLENGES

Real threats for data centers are regional acts of God, which can be memorialized "on-line" to the trained eye:

- Hurricanes in Florida
- Earthquakes in California
- Snow in western New York
- Droughts in Texas
- Tornadoes in the Midwest

Do not kid yourself; there are data centers in all these locations.

When it comes to siting, or locating, data centers, imagined or unlikely events take up most steering committee strategy meetings. Similar to the phenomena that anyone who has bought a house is an overnight expert in commercial real estate, quite often everyone on the data center siting steering committee is a siting expert. Every data center manager, operator, engineer, or information technology (IT) professional is an expert in acts of God; more interestingly, often all are overnight experts in human intervention (terrorism) or man-made disasters (e.g., highways, railroads, nuclear facilities, commercial air fields, fixed base operations, waste facilities, etc.). In fact, however, there are few experts in either field. There are and were mature professionals with relevant history and experiences. Many are patient and wise enough to study historical data on acts of God and possibilities or relevance of an act happening to a specific site. The passion and emotion erupts when the consequences of business impact analysis are announced and we work to ensure that such adverse events do not happen at a site.

These user observations told in war stories are useful for vendors to identify unique sensitivities. Ongoing meetings are useful and helpful regarding the possibilities or what-if scenarios of the data center operations. We, as experts, try to manage the data to suit user applications in the relevant part of the world. For this reason, not all the what-if scenarios make it into the data center budget. If every data center had to incorporate each and every risk, no one could afford to build one. If we experts were free to do as we liked, we would all build and manage a bulletproof facility with redundancy and every reasonable component, including water and fuel reserves, to survive a prolonged outage. In the 1980s and 1990s, we used to discuss perceived fear, what the lawyers would call "the parade of horribles." It is a nice phrase, almost like "let's go to the parade of horribles" after we go to the beach.

Data center siting experts and data center strategic planners often have strong beliefs about risks, beliefs that, once formed, change very slowly and are extraordinarily persistent even in the face of contrary evidence. Changing opinions on acts of God or human intervention is like turning a ship; it takes miles and careful navigation. According to Vincent Gabello of the Center for Risk Communications at Columbia University, "At a very base level, the user applies his or her own common sense and services of what he likes and filters. The so-called fight-or-flight instincts take over at a very basic level, and a gut check is now incorporated on risk assessment for the data center." The gut check is really a multiple of the number of personalities in the steering committee and their cumulative experiences. Since the expression is not found in corporate governance or documentation or as part of the action plan in the Patriot Act, we use other criteria, which are a bit more exacting.

By minimizing the regional predictable risks and exaggerating the unlikely ones, we expose ourselves to the unlikely and overlooked but likely. The devil is in the details here. Acts of God and man-made challenges are all-consuming in sorting out where to and where not to site a mission critical facility. Vendors and users need to be sensitive to the relevant recent history of both natural and man-made events and need to pay close, unemotional, and detailed attention. One municipality in New Jersey, for example, had over 250 gas main breaks and 17 forced evacuations. Nevertheless, this area was short-listed for a data center. Just so we are clear: Evacuations are bad for data centers.

The "anger range" and detailed approach brought to a siting can be counterproductive to the focus on money. Again, we need to leave out emotion as much as possible when weighing and leveling events. An event or condition can be disregarded if it is not relevant to this location or how that story or loss applies to you. Anger equals fear. Fear is false evidence appearing real.

The "anger range" generally encompasses feelings, not facts. We owe it to the process to stay on or as close to facts as we can.

Today, most media outlets are far too concerned with sensationalizing acts of God. We are almost disappointed if a rainstorm, snowstorm, or flood does not live up to its horrific potential. Reporting is often not accurate on some level of cost, lost lives, and time needed to make improvements. The anecdotes are universal: "They said it would last for two days"; "They said the death toll would reach 25 people."

The main reason the media often gets the story wrong is that they are on tight deadlines; frequently there is no time to check a story's sources. After the first World Trade Center bombing, I was called to the NBC studios to give a live interview regarding a "substation failure" (explosion). By the time I took the subway, I learned it was a bomb. The interview went on, but the focus shifted to the loss of life and the willful act. My contribution as the infrastructure guy was relevant to redundant systems for unique and trophy assets. In the early 1990s, this was a noteworthy topic.

One example of the blind-leading-the-blind model is the government following the media as it relates to catastrophic events; this is one source of our misguided confidence in the government, in those whose job it is to protect us. According to James Walsh in *True Odds: How Risk Affects Your Every Day Life*: "Government's decision makers also get their information from the media more than any place, so the government is no better about assessing risk than the average person."[1] Think about it. These are not high-pay-grade jobs; frankly, these people are just like you and me. Maybe they live closer to relevant data points for historical weather, but not much more.

In the following, I will identify, weight, level, and score 11 main, obvious, or easier man-made challenges:

1. **Highways.** The first thing to identify is the orientation of a candidate property. Routes ending in odd numbers run north–south; routes ending in even numbers run east–west. For example, routes 95 and 1 run north–south; routes 46 and 40 run east–west. This information is relevant for prevailing winds for highway shut, snow drifts, and so on. The next thing is to identify if these routes are intrastate traffic (within the state) or interstate (between states). Traffic between states often is busier and roads often are four lanes; intrastate traffic often is less heavy and only and two lanes. Four-lane traffic anticipates truck traffic. This is good and bad. The good news is the routes are designed and built with wide turns and strategic turns in place to prevent mindless driving and require a minimum of concentration. The exits (where

most accidents take place) are well thought out and often are away from topographical challenges. The traffic often moves faster, and that increases risk with smaller vehicles between trucks and specifically trucks hauling hazardous materials (hazmats). Intrastate traffic can be two lanes and have more turns and expensive topographic challenges. Traffic lights and stop signs on intrastate traffic increase risk. What we are looking to do is minimize the risk of an accident that is accompanied by an evacuation of up to 1,500 feet as the first response is diagnosing the conditions and up to 3,000 feet as the second ring of evacuation is established. The roads are safer by movement than the trains. However, there are more deaths during road evacuations than during rail evacuations. What is to be avoided at the roads are lights and stop signs; curves; stepped up or down; bridges; railroads; flooding or surge potentials; and land protection from high winds, snow, and debris. These conditions increase risk overall.

2. **Railroads.** Railroads are looked at in terms of existing freight and passenger traffic as well as future traffic. I look at the railway as a right-of-way (ROW) that has inherent benefits and challenges. The first consideration is the existing traffic. The CSX or freight companies do not have to reveal what cargo is on the rails. Common sense and my experience say that most hazmats or undesirable freight are shipped in the evening, under cover of darkness. During the evening, there is not as much competing traffic, and stops or slowdowns are minimal. The freight companies, big and small, get two to four times their usual fees to haul explosives or hazmats. I often have to stay at the freight yard or freight lines to determine the time and frequency of traffic of relevant rail. One data center site acquired in New Jersey had a freight train hit an electrical substation contiguous to rail; the substation burned for three days, forcing a regional evacuation. This is the worst-case scenario. The data center user did not and does not know this. We also look at the potential for passenger lines to take freight or more passenger lines. Even though there may be only a minimal risk of traffic increasing, fiber optic and power service during the two- to five-year construction period will likely be disrupted and catastrophic failure of services may result. Power and fiber are often buried or on poles in the railroad ROW. Railroads make a good deal of money for renting space in their ROWs. The distance of evacuation is fairly similar from the first responder of 1,500 to 3,000 feet of ringed evacuation. Before acquiring space on or near a railway, it is wise to walk the ROW. ROW maintenance usually can be classed as really

good and proactive or really not good. There is not a lot of in between, and a layperson is more than qualified to make that call.

3. **Gas lines.** There are gas lines in more parts of urban candidate properties. The one- to two-inch-diameter distribution lines are designed and built for swift and nondisruptive access for residences and businesses. These are the lines that are most frequently hit, forcing evacuations. There are often gas and nonliquid petroleum products. The gas has no smell unless an ammonia or sulfur additive is mixed to the gas. The transmission lines have with more volume and catastrophic potential. The 18 to 36/42 inches lines or "war lines" are the ones with the potential for meaningful and longer-term damage. The evacuation rings are similar for first responders, but winds often play a larger role for evacuation and greater distances. Most gas line hits result from construction: backhoes in backyards or construction on the shoulder of a road. Gas line proximity can and will be a benefit for the cogeneration plants of ordinary and mission-critical facilities.

4. **Airfields.** In viewing candidate properties, I consider that among the possible disasters, the chances of an aircraft crashing into a mission-critical facility are remote. However, over the past 20 years, many data centers have been located near airfields because most airfields were designed with military specifications of power and communications in mind. These sites often have redundant power and fiber in place to support the airfield. The distance of 15 to 20 Euclidean miles from the take-off and landing point of the airfield come from the reasonable distance the airfield has the pilot come off the instrument flight rating to visual flight rating to land the aircraft. Day or night, the decision to line up the approach comes at about 15 miles away from the tower. Given other approaches, the number of aircraft or movements of the commercial airport or fixed based operation, we can make intelligent decisions on how much risk is associated with a candidate property. Sites in a flight path will not score well. Sites contiguous to flight paths will score better.

5. **Snow/Ice.** I consider these challenges in terms of net results to users. Some parts of the world are more susceptible to ice than snow. However, both ice and snow make roads impassable. They both add weight to distribution and transmission lines. They both can cause trains and cars to crash into poles or towers, creating interruptions. They both can cause freezing issues at the transfer stations. One misleading fact is that areas of high snow frequency and ice accumulation are often better at removing or mitigating the resultant damages. When snow

and ice storms hit Texas or Georgia, for example, a mess generally ensues. Citizens are not familiar with driving in this weather, and local governments are ill prepared to cope. In many cases they just wait for snow and ice to melt. However, sometimes, not always cities like Syracuse or Buffalo, New York, and other areas of frequent accumulation know how to drive in such conditions, and localities are prepared to cope. In general, it is better to stay away from such areas.

6. **Droughts.** The frequency of drought is often overlooked in the site selection process. Recently it has gotten more attention due to the drought in Georgia affecting the Atlanta market. As data center users and particularly in high-density power conversation, the cooling requirements and source of cooling have taken higher visibility. Texas used to be eliminated from data center siting consideration due to droughts and wildfires; recently this is no longer the case. I have often looked into the alternative aquifer scenario to find the pressure is a variable and the water restrictions that a utility enforces often apply to the aquifers as well. For water-cooled assets, the answer is all too often the need to surface store water and treat it for use in mission-critical facilities.

7. **Wildfires.** Similar to droughts in that they often occur during an extraordinarily dry season and spread swiftly, wildfires make roads impassable for lengths of time. Wildfires burn and interrupt power substations, power lines, and telecommunication lines that are required for mission-critical facilities. The mean time to repair an asset following a wildfire is longer than for snowstorms and high winds. Often miles of infrastructure need to be replaced or repaired under the most extraordinary conditions.

8. **High winds.** The high-wind concerns of data center users relate to hurricanes or tornadoes. Over the past 10 years, there have been fewer hurricanes from the Florida coast to Maine, but the ones that have occurred have been stronger. The year 2005 was the warmest on record with the most damage done on record: $85 billion. Depending on your brand of global warming, fewer but stronger storms are forecast. What does that have to do with high winds...plenty. I recommend looking at the wind history in the local region and identifying the high, low, and frequency of wind storms. Apply a debris factor to design, and build a facility to withstand a meaningful and prolonged outage. Do not overdesign, but assume that windows will blow out or be broken, and the internal environment will lose pressure and may cause an evacuation. There will be no controlled ambient air

for heating or cooling. Assume that roof- or earth-mounted equipment needs to be properly secured and *not* merely by gravity. Most damage done in big windstorms is done by wind lift, not horizontal winds.

9. **Earthquakes.** International and U.S. seismic zones are well known and fairly well documented. The idea is to stay 60 to 100 miles away from such areas, not only for issues related to immediate earth movement but because in the event of a quake, the outside plant infrastructure improvements of power, telecom, roads, and others will not be usable. When unique design, site work, and improvements to mitigate damage from earth movement are considered, the cost to build properly in seismically sensitive areas are about 24 to 27% higher than in nonseismic areas. Although the data centers are built to withstand a quake, services that feed them are not. The centers may be fine, but the substation or central office may be out for some time.

10. **Lightning.** Lightning often accompanies rainstorms with frequent high winds and tornado activity. Although siting in a tornado alley is not recommended, there are data centers in that part of the world. When siting in a high-lightning-strike part of the world, preventive improvements consist of putting up lightning rods or domes to capture energy and bring it to earth directly with as few 90-degree turns as possible to prevent catastrophic damage and outages inside the asset due to electrical surges and resets. Lightning, like earthquakes and other acts of God, can damage outside-plant telecom and power improvements, and the region should be considered closely as well as the design.

11. **Nuclear facilities.** There are 103 nuclear facilities in the United States with one being built in the Tennessee Valley Authority network and two being considered in Texas. The dynamics of nuclear power and benefits are discussed later in the book. The relevance of nuclear facility proximity to a data center site is based on the unlikely event of a leak of plutonium and contaminated water. The immediate kill zone of contamination established by the Nuclear Regulatory Commission is 18 Euclidean miles. Potassium tablets are given out to residents within this ring. The other kill zone is 50 Euclidean miles for livestock and agriculture. The idea is to be out of the kill zone, because even though the chances of interruption are small, the risk still exists. It is good to be in a nuclear footprint, due to shortages of coal- and gas-fired generating plants. The cost for power provided by nuclear generating plants is often more reasonable. The point is to be near, not in, the kill zone.

		Site A			Site B		
		Site Score:	39%	252	**Site Score:**	51%	328
	Weighting	**Description**	**Rating**	**Score**	**Description**	**Rating**	**Score**
Available White Space	3	To be built; 20,000 data center space available, space in mountain. 18–24 months for delivery	4	12	9,000 sf white space	4	12
Price	2	$45 per sf per month per annum	0	0	$25 per sf per month	1	2
Existing Total Project Sq Footage	4	3,000,000 sq ft	4	16	31,500 white space	1	4
Zoning (If rezoning is required what is the impact?)	4	As-of right	1	4	As-of right	4	16
Description	3	All land in mountain; horizontal, 34 feet to ceiling; multistory in mountain	3	9	Multistory; multitenant	0	0
Water and Water Storage Second Source (high-level study of well and aquifers)	5	Surface storage	1	5	Surface storage	4	20
Sewer to satisfy data center (and runoff)	4	In place; pumps and pumping required	0	0	As-of right	4	16
Security Setbacks: berming, etc.	4	In mountain, multiple tenants	0	0	Triple fail-safe in place, multiple users	2	16
Accessible Public Transportation (access for vendors and home office, not daily commutation)	2	None	0	0	None	0	0

EXHIBIT 2.1   INVENTORY MATRIX OF CANDIDATE PROPERTIES *(continued)*

		Site A			Site B		
		Site Score:	39%	252	**Site Score:**	51%	328
	Weighting	**Description**	**Rating**	**Score**	**Description**	**Rating**	**Score**
Soil Conditions (benefits and drawbacks of solid or rock foundations)	3	Dolomite mountain	2	3	Data center In building	1	3
Human Resource Depth (other companies nearby, college/ universities)	4	TBD	0	0	Atlanta	4	16
Proximity to Current Data Center Operations	5	301 miles	2	10	389 miles	2	10
Sales Tax (local/state)	5	7.23	1	5	0%	4	20
Installation Costs (local labor)	3	Within 5% of existing	2	0	10% over existing	0	0
Power Plant/Rough Order of Magnitude Pricing	3	8 miles	1	3	No cost	4	12
Cost per kWh (peak/off peak)	5	4.9	0	0	Included	4	20
Tariffs (other)	3	2%	0	0	2.5%	0	0
EDC Benefits (local)	4	None in place	0	0	None in place	0	0
State (incentives)	4	None	0	0	None	0	0
Telco Transmission Costs	5	Century Tel; Lycor, Empire State: TBD	0	0	Verizon, ATT: TBD	0	0
Power/Electricity: 150 watts/sf (capability/ scalability: 30 megawatts capability from each substation. Day 1 power of 5 MW from each substation)	5	150 watts per sq ft. plant in design	2	10	168 watts per sq ft.	4	20
Diverse Electrical Feeds from Separate Substations (route distances for	5	2 substations in place	4	20	2 feeds; 1 substation	3	15

EXHIBIT 2.1   INVENTORY MATRIX OF CANDIDATE PROPERTIES   *(continued)*

	Weighting	Site A			Site B		
		Site Score:	39%	252	Site Score:	51%	328
	Weighting	**Description**	**Rating**	**Score**	**Description**	**Rating**	**Score**
each—aerial or terrestrial, note highway, railroad, or other ROWs that create risks)							
Facilities Fiber and Telecom (3 facilities-based providers, separate ROWs)	5	3 in place	1	5	2 in place	0	0
Longitude/Latitude		Confidential	0	0	confidential	0	0
Generators (Department of Environmental Protection, Environmental Protection Agency)	3	3 generators in place; 60-day permitting	0	0	6 generators; 2.5 megawatts ea. 90-day permitting	4	12
Fuel Storage (potential challenges of service storage or buried)	4	Surface; none in place	1	4	In place; 2 days	3	12
Floodplain: 100/500 (portion or percentage of acreage in flood zone as well as access roads in flood zone)	5	In mountain: 500 year	4	20	500 year	4	20
Earthquake	4	In mountain, near fault	2	8	Nonseismic	4	16
Tornado/Hurricane (highlighting sensitiveness to disruption of OSP services: power poles, power towers, etc.)	4	In mountain, none	4	16	Some risk	2	8
Wildfires	3	In mountain	4	12	Some risk	2	6
Landslide Possibilities	3	In mountain	4	12	None	4	12
Drought	2	Water pumping may be issue	1	2	Currently	0	0

EXHIBIT 2.1   INVENTORY MATRIX OF CANDIDATE PROPERTIES *(continued)*

		Site A			Site B		
		Site Score:	39%	252	**Site Score:**	51%	328
	Weighting	**Description**	**Rating**	**Score**	**Description**	**Rating**	**Score**
Snow/Ice (relevance to power lines, fiber optic lines, and road access/accidents)	4	Roads and power risk	1	4	Low risk	3	12
Lightning Activity	4	In mountain, none	4	16	Some risk	3	12
Composite Risk (overall)	4	Average	2	8	Moderate	2	8
Distance from Railroad, Freight and Passenger (minimum of 3,000 linear feet)	4	In mountain, 52 miles	4	16	22 miles	0	0
Regional Declared Disasters (within past 10 years)	3	14	0	0	22	0	0
Nuclear Power Plant Proximity (minimum of 18 linear miles/shaded to 50 miles downwind of potential event)	3	In mountain, 75 miles	4	12	37 miles	1	0
Highway Proximity (minimum of 3,000 feet 4-lane highway)	4	1 mile to Route 65	1	4	3 miles to Route 104	1	4
Airport Proximity (minimum of 15 linear miles from FBO or commercial airfield)	4	32 miles to FBO	0	0	15 miles— commercial airport	1	4
Hazardous Facilities (minimum of 5 linear miles from contaminated soil or water)	4	Other tenants	1	4	Gas storage, 7 miles	0	0

EXHIBIT 2.1   INVENTORY MATRIX OF CANDIDATE PROPERTIES *(continued)*

This list is a high-level summary of what to look for in the field during a mission-critical siting tour. It is not complete, but it is a good start. You need to apply some common sense to the criteria and realize that there is no perfect site. Every site has some issues. That is why we weigh the categories for importance and score them on field conditions inspected as well as data retrieved.

Exhibit 2.1 provides a matrix of inventory properties.

NOTE

1. James Walsh in *True Odds: How Risk Affects Your Every Day Life* (Merritt Publishing, 1996).

3

ORIGINS OF THE BUSINESS IMPACT ANALYSIS

The fact that we live in an open society is an inherent risk. Our borders are porous, our water and agriculture are accessible, and our information technology (IT) infrastructure is littered with single points of failure. We lull ourselves into a false sense of security by thinking that great America must be able to outdesign, outmanage, guard, mandate, and legislate our nuclear arms with the best-trained military personnel in the world. This is obviously not the case. We cannot defeat an entity we cannot see beyond or within our borders. We have found it challenging to declare and to win a war on a noun or adjective (e.g., the war on drugs). Without borders, uniforms, or structure, it is hard to measure effectiveness of such a war. (Cyberthreats are discussed in Chapter 15.) Zero risk or 100% security is unobtainable in any society, and the lower the security, the more open the society. The goal is to mitigate risk to a reasonable level given the data, field or location, and resources available. We do not design earthquake criteria in nonearthquake zones; you get the idea.

We live in an open society. This is good news and it is also bad news.

Let me articulate the more obvious acts of God that site selectors, consultants, and their end users are concerned. Exhibit 3.1 is a work product that is often used to guide us through the site selection process. The idea is to weigh the category based on the user's sensitivities and our experiences with siting, building, and outbuilding of data centers (man-made hazards to follow, highways, airports, nuclear facilities, etc.).

The composite risk map shown in Exhibit 3.2 includes the unlikely and frequent acts that may influence a decision to site a data center nationally. Note that the dark area is a good siting location, but heavy snow and ice is

Mag: Magnitude
Dth: Deaths
Inj: Injuries
PrD: Property Damage
CrD: Crop Damage

232 event(s) were reported in Collin County, Texas between 12/31/1997 and 12/31/2006

Location or County	Date	Time	Type	Mag	73 Dth	30 Inj	0 PrD	0 CrD
1 TXZ091>095–100>107–115>123–129>135–141>148–156>162–174>175	1/4/1998	4:00 PM	Excessive Rain	N/A	0	0	0	0
2 McKinney	1/4/1998	4:22 PM	Hail	0.75 in.	0	0	0	0
3 Allen	1/4/1998	4:25 PM	Hail	1.00 in.	0	0	0	0
4 Branch	1/4/1998	4:30 PM	Hail	1.00 in.	0	0	0	0
5 McKinney	1/4/1998	4:40 PM	Flash Flood	N/A	0	0	0	0
6 McKinney	1/4/1998	4:45 PM	Flash Flood	N/A	0	0	0	0
7 Blue Ridge	1/4/1998	4:50 PM	Flash Flood	N/A	0	0	0	0
8 Princeton	1/4/1998	5:52 PM	Flash Flood	N/A	0	0	0	0
9 Prosper	1/4/1998	9:09 PM	Flash Flood	N/A	0	0	0	0
10 Blue Ridge	1/4/1998	10:00 PM	Lightning	N/A	0	0	20K	0
11 TXZ091>095–100>107–115>123–129>135–141>148–156>162–174>175	1/5/1998	5:00 PM	Excessive Rain	N/A	0	0	0	0

22

#	Location	Date	Time	Event	Magnitude			Property Damage	
12	Murphy	1/21/1998	4:25 PM	Hail	1.00 in.	0	0	0	0
13	TXZ091>095-100>107-115>123-129>135-141>148-156>162-174>175	2/25/1998	5:00 PM	Severe Tstm	N/A	0	0	0	0
14	Anna	2/25/1998	7:39 PM	Hail	0.75 in.	0	0	0	0
15	Prosper	2/25/1998	7:40 PM	Hail	0.75 in.	0	0	0	0
16	TXZ018>020	3/7/1998	7:00 PM	Blizzard	N/A	0	0	0	0
17	McKinney	3/16/1998	7:05 PM	Tornado	F1	0	0	200K	0
18	Celina	4/16/1998	12:30 AM	Hail	1.75 in.	0	0	0	0
19	Desert	5/2/1998	9:28 PM	Hail	1.00 in.	0	0	0	0
20	Anna	5/2/1998	9:35 PM	Hail	0.75 in.	0	0	0	0
21	McKinney	5/8/1998	8:25 PM	Hail	1.00 in.	0	0	0	0
22	McKinney	5/8/1998	8:25 PM	Tstm Wind	53 kts.	0	0	0	0
23	Frisco	5/8/1998	8:35 PM	Hail	1.75 in.	0	0	0	0
24	Frisco	5/8/1998	8:35 PM	Tstm Wind	61 kts.	0	0	100K	0
25	McKinney	5/8/1998	8:50 PM	Tstm Wind	61 kts.	0	0	100K	0
26	McKinney	5/8/1998	8:53 PM	Hail	0.75 in.	0	0	0	0
27	Melissa	5/8/1998	8:54 PM	Hail	1.75 in.	0	0	0	0
28	McKinney	5/8/1998	8:57 PM	Tstm Wind	52 kts.	0	0	0	0
29	Frisco	5/8/1998	9:26 PM	Hail	0.75 in.	0	0	0	0
30	McKinney	5/8/1998	9:54 PM	Hail	1.75 in.	0	0	0	0
31	McKinney	5/8/1998	9:55 PM	Hail	1.75 in.	0	0	0	0
32	Plano	5/27/1998	1:30 AM	Tstm Wind	0 kts.	0	0	0	0

EXHIBIT 3.1 ACTS OF GOD MATRIX *(continued)*

Mag: Magnitude
Dth: Deaths
Inj: Injuries
PrD: Property Damage
CrD: Crop Damage

232 event(s) were reported in Collin County, Texas between 12/31/1997 and 12/31/2006

Location or County	Date	Time	Type	Mag	73 Dth	30 Inj	0 PrD	0 CrD
33 Celina	6/4/1998	7:00 PM	Tstm Wind	0 kts.	0	0	0K	0
34 TXZ091>095-100>107-115>123-129>135-141>148-156>162-174>175	7/1/1998	12:00 AM	Drought	N/A	0	0	0	0K
35 TXZ091>095-100>107-115>123-129>135-141>148-156>162-174>175	7/1/1998	12:00 AM	Excessive Heat	N/A	32	0	0	0
36 Royse City	7/17/1998	3:47 PM	Tstm Wind	0 kts.	0	0	1K	0
37 TXZ001>020	8/1/1998	12:00 AM	Drought	N/A	0	0	0	0
38 TXZ001>020	9/1/1998	12:00 AM	Drought	N/A	0	0	0	0
39 TXZ001>020	10/1/1998	12:00 AM	Drought	N/A	0	0	0	135.0M
40 Melissa	10/2/1998	6:00 PM	Tstm Wind	0 kts.	0	0	5K	0
41 Blue Ridge	10/2/1998	6:20 PM	Hail	1.00 in.	0	0	0	0
42 Princeton	10/2/1998	6:40 PM	Tstm Wind	0 kts.	0	0	5K	0

# Location	Date	Time	Type	Magnitude				
43 Blue Ridge	10/2/1998	7:15 PM	Tstm Wind	0 kts.	0	0	2K	0
44 Plano	11/9/1998	11:10 PM	Tstm Wind	50 kts.	0	0	0	0
45 Central Portion	12/4/1998	1:00 AM	Flash Flood	N/A	0	0	0	0
46 Nevada	12/4/1998	1:00 AM	Flash Flood	N/A	0	0	0	0
47 TXZ091>095–098 >107–115 >123–129>135–141 >148–156>162– 174>175	12/22/1998	12:00 AM	Ice Storm	N/A	6	0	0	0
48 Frisco	2/6/1999	7:54 PM	Hail	1.75 in.	0	0	0	0
49 Celina	2/6/1999	7:55 PM	Tstm Wind	0 kts.	0	0	1K	0
50 Farmersville	2/6/1999	8:50 PM	Hail	0.75 in.	0	0	0	0
51 Celina	4/3/1999	5:11 AM	Hail	1.00 in.	0	0	0	0
52 Plano	4/26/1999	8:00 AM	Tstm Wind	0 kts.	0	0	0K	0
53 Weston	5/4/1999	12:10 PM	Hail	1.00 in.	0	0	0	0
54 Celina	5/9/1999	11:40 PM	Tstm Wind	0 kts.	0	0	0K	0
55 McKinney	5/9/1999	11:40 PM	Tstm Wind	0 kts.	0	0	0K	0
56 Plano	5/9/1999	11:45 PM	Tstm Wind	0 kts.	0	0	0K	0
57 Lavon	5/17/1999	3:33 PM	Flash Flood	N/A	0	0	0	0
58 Wylie	5/25/1999	6:18 PM	Hail	1.00 in.	0	0	0	0
59 Plano	6/8/1999	7:00 PM	Flash Flood	N/A	0	0	0	0
60 TXZ091>095–098 >107–115>123–129 >135–141>148–156 >162–174>175	8/1/1999	12:00 AM	Excessive Heat	N/A	3	0	0	0

EXHIBIT 3.1 ACTS OF GOD MATRIX (*continued*)

Mag: Magnitude
Dth: Deaths
Inj: Injuries
PrD: Property Damage
CrD: Crop Damage

232 event(s) were reported in Collin County, Texas between 12/31/1997 and 12/31/2006

Location or County	Date	Time	Type	Mag	73 Dth	30 Inj	0 PrD	0 CrD
61 Allen	10/9/1999	6:00 AM	Lightning	N/A	0	0	5K	0
62 Plano	12/12/1999	8:00 AM	Lightning	N/A	0	0	30K	0
63 TXZ091>095–098 >107–115>123–129 >135–141>148–156 >162–174>175	1/25/2000	12:00 AM	Winter Storm	N/A	4	0	0	0
64 Wylie	2/25/2000	10:35 PM	Tstm Wind	61 kts.	0	0	0	0
65 Lavon	2/25/2000	11:17 PM	Hail	0.75 in.	0	0	0	0
66 Lavon	2/25/2000	11:17 PM	Tstm Wind	52 kts.	0	0	0	0
67 Lavon	2/25/2000	11:30 PM	Tstm Wind	0 kts.	0	1	40K	0
68 Plano	2/25/2000	11:40 PM	Tstm Wind	61 kts.	0	0	0	0
69 Plano	2/25/2000	11:45 PM	Tstm Wind	0 kts.	0	0	2K	0
70 Prosper	3/2/2000	6:10 PM	Hail	1.75 in.	0	0	0	0
71 Plano	3/2/2000	6:15 PM	Hail	1.00 in.	0	0	0	0
72 Plano	3/2/2000	6:24 PM	Hail	1.75 in.	0	0	0	0
73 McKinney	3/2/2000	6:29 PM	Hail	1.00 in.	0	0	0	0
74 Allen	3/2/2000	6:30 PM	Tstm Wind	0 kts.	0	0	25K	0
75 Farmersville	3/2/2000	6:50 PM	Hail	1.00 in.	0	0	0	0

Location	Date	Time	Event	Magnitude				
76 Plano	3/10/2000	10:45 AM	Hail	0.75 in.	0	0	0	0
77 Plano	3/10/2000	12:30 PM	Lightning	N/A	0	0	25K	0
78 Wylie	3/16/2000	9:28 PM	Hail	0.75 in.	0	0	0	0
79 Murphy	5/12/2000	4:25 PM	Tstm Wind	0 kts.	0	0	10K	0
80 Parker	5/12/2000	4:40 PM	Hail	0.75 in.	0	0	0	0
81 Frisco	5/27/2000	4:20 PM	Tstm Wind	57 kts.	0	0	0	0
82 Royse City	5/27/2000	4:30 PM	Tstm Wind	0 kts.	0	0	1K	0
83 Wylie	5/27/2000	4:50 PM	Hail	0.75 in.	0	0	0	0
84 Wylie	5/27/2000	4:50 PM	Tstm Wind	61 kts.	0	0	0	0
85 Farmersville	6/4/2000	2:15 AM	Flash Flood	N/A	0	0	0	0
86 Murphy	6/11/2000	12:55 PM	Flash Flood	N/A	0	0	0	0
87 Wylie	6/15/2000	2:00 AM	Flash Flood	N/A	0	0	0	0
88 TXZ001>020	7/1/2000	12:00 AM	Drought	N/A	0	0	0	0
89 TXZ091>095–098 >107–115>123–129>135–141>148–156>162–174>175	7/1/2000	12:00 AM	Excessive Heat	N/A	8	0	0	0
90 TXZ001>020	8/1/2000	12:00 AM	Drought	N/A	0	0	0	0
91 TXZ091>095–098 >107–115>123–129 >135–141>148–156 >162–174>175	8/1/2000	12:00 AM	Drought	N/A	0	0	0	0
92 TXZ091>095–098 >107–115>123–129 >135–141>148–156 >162–174>175	8/1/2000	12:00 AM	Excessive Heat	N/A	5	0	0	0

EXHIBIT 3.1 ACTS OF GOD MATRIX (continued)

Mag: Magnitude
Dth: Deaths
Inj: Injuries
PrD: Property Damage
CrD: Crop Damage

232 event(s) were reported in Collin County, Texas between
12/31/1997 and 12/31/2006

Location or County	Date	Time	Type	Mag	73 Dth	30 Inj	0 PrD	0 CrD
93 TXZ001>020	9/1/2000	12:00 AM	Drought	N/A	0	0	0	0
94 TXZ091>095–098 >107–115>123–129 >135–141>148–156 >162–174>175	9/1/2000	12:00 AM	Drought	N/A	0	0	0	0
95 TXZ091>095–098 >107–115>123–129 >135–141>148–156 >162–174>175	9/1/2000	12:00 AM	Excessive Heat	N/A	5	0	0	0
96 TXZ001>020	10/1/2000	12:00 AM	Drought	N/A	0	0	0	64.0M
97 TXZ091>095–098 >107–115>123–129 >135–141>148–156 >162–174>175	12/12/2000	6:00 PM	Winter Storm	N/A	0	0	0	0
98 TXZ001>020	12/25/2000	6:00 PM	Heavy Snow	N/A	2	0	40K	0
99 TXZ091>095–098 >107–115>123–129 >135–141>148–156 >162–174>175	12/25/2000	12:00 AM	Winter Storm	N/A	0	0	0	0

	Date	Time	Event	Magnitude			
100 TXZ091>095–098 >107–115>123–129 >135–141>148–156 >162–174>175	12/31/2000	12:00 AM	Winter Storm	N/A	0	0	0
101 TXZ091>095–098 >107–115>123–129 >135–141>148–156 >162–174>175	1/1/2001	12:00 AM	Heavy Snow	N/A	0	0	0
102 TXZ009>010–013 >015–018>020	1/27/2001	12:00 PM	Winter Storm	N/A	0	0	0
103 Countywide	2/16/2001	1:34 AM	Flash Flood	N/A	0	0	0
104 Countywide	2/16/2001	3:51 AM	Flash Flood	N/A	0	0	0
105 Plano	2/16/2001	12:24 AM	Lightning	N/A	0	750K	0
106 Princeton	2/24/2001	11:20 AM	Tstm Wind	0 kts.	0	50K	0
107 Plano	3/11/2001	2:40 PM	Hail	0.88 in.	0	0	0
108 TXZ002>005–007 >020	4/11/2001	4:17 AM	High Wind	57 kts.	0	0	0
109 McKinney	5/6/2001	1:28 AM	Flash Flood	N/A	0	0	0
110 Plano	5/6/2001	6:22 PM	Hail	1.00 in.	0	0	0
111 Plano	5/6/2001	6:43 PM	Hail	3.00 in.	0	0	0
112 Allen	5/6/2001	7:00 PM	Hail	1.00 in.	0	0	0
113 TXZ011>020	5/20/2001	10:45 PM	High Wind	36 kts.	0	0	0
114 McKinney	5/28/2001	12:08 AM	Tstm Wind	57 kts.	0	0	0
115 Countywide	6/14/2001	6:45 PM	Tstm Wind	58 kts.	0	0	0
116 McKinney	6/14/2001	7:00 PM	Tstm Wind	61 kts.	0	0	0

EXHIBIT 3.1 ACTS OF GOD MATRIX *(continued)*

Mag:	Magnitude
Dth:	Deaths
Inj:	Injuries
PrD:	Property Damage
CrD:	Crop Damage

232 event(s) were reported in Collin County, Texas between 12/31/1997 and 12/31/2006

Location or County	Date	Time	Type	Mag	73 Dth	30 Inj	0 PrD	0 CrD
117 Frisco	9/5/2001	2:05 PM	Tornado	F0	0	0	0	0
118 Celina	9/5/2001	2:30 PM	Tornado	F1	0	0	30K	0
119 Melissa	9/18/2001	6:05 PM	Tstm Wind	73 kts.	0	0	0	0
120 Celina	10/10/2001	10:51 PM	Tstm Wind	52 kts.	0	0	0	0
121 Frisco	10/12/2001	7:30 PM	Tstm Wind	0 kts.	0	0	50K	0
122 McKinney	10/12/2001	8:20 PM	Tstm Wind	52 kts.	0	0	0	0
123 TXZ091>095-100 >105-107-115 >123-129>134-141 >147-156>161-175	11/27/2001	12:30 PM	Ice Storm	N/A	0	0	0	0
124 TXZ001>020	1/30/2002	6:00 AM	Winter Storm	N/A	0	0	0	0
125 TXZ092>095-101 >107-117>123- 130-133	2/5/2002	5:00 AM	Winter Storm	N/A	0	0	0	0
126 TXZ005-010- 015-019>020	2/5/2002	12:00 AM	Heavy Snow	N/A	0	0	0	0
127 TXZ091>095-100 >106-115>119-129 >132-141	3/2/2002	2:15 AM	Winter Storm	N/A	0	0	0	0
128 Blue Ridge	4/16/2002	11:15 PM	Hail	0.75 in.	0	0	0	0

129 McKinney	4/29/2002	3:00 PM	Lightning	N/A	0	1	0	0
130 McKinney	5/9/2002	11:10 PM	Hail	0.75 in.	0	0	0	0
131 Celina	8/25/2002	2:26 PM	Tstm Wind	52 kts.	0	0	10K	0
132 McKinney	8/27/2002	5:50 AM	Tstm Wind	52 kts.	0	0	5K	0
133 Melissa	10/19/2002	2:05 AM	Flash Flood	N/A	0	0	25K	0
134 Frisco	12/30/2002	1:30 PM	Hail	1.75 in.	0	0	0	0
135 Plano	12/30/2002	2:30 PM	Flash Flood	N/A	0	0	0	0
136 Plano	12/30/2002	2:30 PM	Hail	1.00 in.	0	0	0	0
137 TXZ091>095–100 >107–115>123–129 >135–141>148–156 >162–174>175	2/24/2003	11:20 AM	Winter Storm	N/A	0	0	15.0M	0
138 Plano	4/5/2003	10:16 PM	Hail	2.00 in.	0	0	0	0
139 Plano	4/5/2003	10:32 PM	Hail	3.00 in.	0	0	0	0
140 Plano	4/6/2003	1:00 PM	Hail	1.00 in.	0	0	0	0
141 Plano	4/6/2003	12:55 PM	Hail	1.00 in.	0	0	0	0
142 Blue Ridge	5/13/2003	5:22 AM	Hail	1.00 in.	0	0	0	0
143 Farmersville	5/24/2003	9:20 PM	Tstm Wind	52 kts.	0	0	20K	0
144 Nevada	5/24/2003	9:30 PM	Hail	0.75 in.	0	0	0	0
145 McKinney	5/24/2003	10:47 PM	Hail	1.00 in.	0	0	0	0
146 McKinney	5/24/2003	10:47 PM	Tstm Wind	52 kts.	0	0	0	0
147 Frisco	6/11/2003	9:55 PM	Tstm Wind	52 kts.	0	0	5K	0
148 Allen	6/14/2003	4:23 PM	Hail	1.50 in.	0	0	0	0

EXHIBIT 3.1 ACTS OF GOD MATRIX *(continued)*

Mag: Magnitude
Dth: Deaths
Inj: Injuries
PrD: Property Damage
CrD: Crop Damage

232 event(s) were reported in Collin County, Texas between 12/31/1997 and 12/31/2006

Location or County	Date	Time	Type	Mag	73 Dth	30 Inj	0 PrD	0 CrD
149 Plano	6/14/2003	4:40 PM	Hail	1.00 in.	0	0	0	0
150 Frisco	7/1/2003	1:50 PM	Tornado	F0	0	0	0	0
151 Celina	7/2/2003	4:15 PM	Hail	0.75 in.	0	0	0	0
152 Anna	7/22/2003	3:46 PM	Hail	0.75 in.	0	0	0	0
153 McKinney	7/22/2003	4:22 PM	Hail	1.00 in.	0	0	0	0
154 Plano	7/22/2003	4:45 PM	Hail	0.75 in.	0	0	0	0
155 Plano	8/22/2003	4:10 PM	Tstm Wind	61 kts.	0	0	0	0
156 Plano	8/22/2003	4:30 PM	Tstm Wind	61 kts.	0	0	2K	0
157 McKinney	8/26/2003	2:38 PM	Tstm Wind	52 kts.	0	4	15K	0
158 Frisco	8/26/2003	2:58 PM	Tstm Wind	61 kts.	0	0	5K	0
159 McKinney	8/26/2003	3:30 PM	Lightning	N/A	0	0	300K	0
160 TXZ091>095–102>106–118>119	2/14/2004	1:00 AM	Heavy Snow	N/A	0	0	0	0
161 Nevada	3/4/2004	3:20 PM	Tstm Wind	60 kts.	0	0	75K	0
162 Lavon Res	3/4/2004	3:35 PM	Tornado	F1	0	2	150K	0
163 Farmersville	3/4/2004	3:41 PM	Tstm Wind	61 kts.	0	0	250K	0
164 McKinney	6/2/2004	6:32 PM	Tstm Wind	50 kts.	0	0	2K	0
165 McKinney	6/5/2004	4:35 PM	Hail	1.75 in.	0	0	0	0
166 Frisco	6/19/2004	1:22 PM	Hail	0.88 in.	0	0	0	0

			Winter Weather/mix					
167 TXZ091>095–100 >107–115>123–129 >135–141>148–156 >162–174>175	12/22/2004	12:01 AM	Winter Weather/mix	N/A	0	0	0	0
168 Plano	1/12/2005	5:15 PM	Hail	1.25 in.	0	0	0	0
169 Wylie	2/22/2005	11:21 PM	Hail	1.00 in.	0	0	0	0
170 Blue Ridge	2/23/2005	12:15 AM	Hail	0.75 in.	0	0	0	0
171 Westminster	2/23/2005	12:25 AM	Hail	1.75 in.	0	0	0	0
172 TXZ001>020	3/15/2005	5:00 AM	Heavy Snow	N/A	0	0	0	0
173 Plano	4/5/2005	3:50 PM	Hail	1.00 in.	0	0	0	0
174 Frisco	4/5/2005	4:00 PM	Hail	0.88 in.	0	0	0	0
175 Frisco	4/5/2005	4:12 PM	Hail	0.75 in.	0	0	0	0
176 Frisco	4/5/2005	4:14 PM	Hail	1.00 in.	0	0	0	0
177 McKinney	4/5/2005	4:50 PM	Tstm Wind	58 kts.	0	0	0	0
178 Anna	4/5/2005	4:58 PM	Hail	1.75 in.	0	0	0	0
179 Blue Ridge	4/5/2005	5:50 PM	Hail	1.00 in.	0	0	0	0
180 TXZ091>093–101>104	5/1/2005	12:00 AM	Drought	N/A	0	0	0	60.0M
181 Plano	5/25/2005	12:30 PM	Hail	0.75 in.	0	0	0	0
182 Allen	5/25/2005	12:38 PM	Tstm Wind	50 kts.	0	0	0	0
183 TXZ091>095–101 >107–118>120–123	6/1/2005	12:00 AM	Drought	N/A	0	0	0	60.0M
184 Farmersville	6/13/2005	10:52 PM	Hail	0.88 in.	0	0	0	0
185 TXZ091>095–100 >107–115>123–129 >135–141–143 >148–159–161	7/1/2005	12:00 AM	Drought	N/A	0	0	0	60.0M

Exhibit 3.1 Acts of God Matrix *(continued)*

Mag: Magnitude
Dth: Deaths
Inj: Injuries
PrD: Property Damage
CrD: Crop Damage

232 event(s) were reported in Collin County, Texas between 12/31/1997 and 12/31/2006

Location or County	Date	Time	Type	Mag	73 Dth	30 Inj	0 PrD	0 CrD
186 Princeton	7/15/2005	3:53 PM	Tstm Wind	55 kts.	0	0	0	0
187 TXZ092>095–102>107–117>123–131>134	8/1/2005	12:00 AM	Drought	N/A	0	0	0	60.0M
188 Wylie	8/4/2005	4:37 PM	Tstm Wind	52 kts.	0	0	1K	0
189 Plano	8/15/2005	7:45 PM	Flash Flood	N/A	0	0	0	0
190 TXZ001>020	8/28/2005	12:00 AM	Drought	N/A	0	0	360K	230.0M
191 TXZ091>095–100>107–115>123–131>134	9/1/2005	12:00 AM	Drought	N/A	0	0	0	60.0M
192 TXZ094–094–104>105–107–148	9/24/2005	9:30 AM	Tropical Storm	N/A	0	0	40K	0
193 Princeton	9/28/2005	6:35 PM	Tstm Wind	50 kts.	0	0	15K	0
194 TXZ091>095–100>107–115>123–131>134	10/1/2005	12:00 AM	Drought	N/A	0	0	0	60.0M
195 TXZ091>095–100>107–115>123–129>135–141>148–156>162–174>175	11/1/2005	12:00 AM	Drought	N/A	0	0	0	120.0M

Location/Zone	Date	Time	Event	Mag				
196 TXZ004>005–009>010–014>015–019>020	11/15/2005	3:06 AM	High Wind	39 kts.	0	0	1K	0
197 TXZ091>095–100>107–115>122–129>135–141>148–156>162–174>175	12/1/2005	12:00 AM	Drought	N/A	0	0	0	120.0M
198 TXZ091–093>095–101>105–107–116>119–121>123–130>135–145>146–148–156>159–174	12/7/2005	7:00 AM	Winter Storm	N/A	0	0	0	0
199 TXZ001>020	12/17/2005	8:00 PM	Winter Weather/mix	N/A	5	15	139K	0
200 TXZ091>095–100>107–115>123–129>135–141>148–156>162–174>175	1/1/2006	12:00 AM	Drought	N/A	0	0	0	1.0B
201 TXZ091>095–100>107–115>123–129>135–141>148–156>162–174>175	2/1/2006	12:00 AM	Drought	N/A	0	0	0	300.0M
202 TXZ103>104–118>119–121–131>132–134–144>145–156–159	2/18/2006	3:30 AM	Winter Weather/mix	N/A	0	0	0	0
203 TXZ091>095–100>107–115>123–129>135–141>148–156>162–174>175	3/1/2006	12:00 AM	Drought	N/A	0	0	0	200.0M

Exhibit 3.1 Acts of God Matrix (continued)

Mag: Magnitude
Dth: Deaths
Inj: Injuries
PrD: Property Damage
CrD: Crop Damage

232 event(s) were reported in Collin County, Texas between 12/31/1997 and 12/31/2006

Location or County	Date	Time	Type	Mag	73 Dth	30 Inj	0 PrD	0 CrD
204 Frisco	3/13/2006	1:11 AM	Tstm Wind	61 kts.	0	0	0	0
205 Countywide	3/19/2006	3:00 PM	Flash Flood	N/A	0	0	0	0
206 TXZ091>095–100 >107–115>120–129 >134–141>145–156 >157–159	4/1/2006	12:00 AM	Drought	N/A	0	0	100.0M	0
207 TXZ011>020	4/6/2006	1:00 PM	High Wind	40 kts.	0	0	0	0
208 TXZ104–118 >119	4/7/2006	4:35 PM	Strong Wind	N/A	0	0	60K	0
209 TXZ091>095–100 >107–115>120–129 >134–141>145– 156>157–159	5/1/2006	12:00 AM	Drought	N/A	0	0	0	100.0M
210 Melissa	5/9/2006	9:04 PM	Hail	1.75 in.	0	0	5K	0
211 Anna	5/9/2006	9:26 PM	Tornado	F0	0	0	0	0
212 Anna	5/9/2006	9:33 PM	Tornado	F0	0	0	30K	0
213 Anna	5/9/2006	9:37 PM	Tornado	F3	2	6	1.0M	0
214 TXZ092>095–102 >107–116>123–130 >135–143>148–157 >162–174>175	6/6/2006	12:00 AM	Drought	N/A	0	0	0	100.0M

215 TXZ104	6/16/2006	3:20 PM	Strong Wind	N/A	0	0	2K	0
216 TXZ104	6/25/2006	11:00 AM	Wildfire	N/A	0	0	17K	2K
217 TXZ091>095–100 >107–115>123–129 >135–141>148–156 >162–174>175	7/1/2006	12:00 AM	Drought	N/A	0	0	0	100.0M
218 TXZ091>095–100 >107–115>123–129 >135–141>142–142 >148–157>162–174>175	8/1/2006	12:00 AM	Drought	N/A	0	0	0	100.0M
219 McKinney	8/12/2006	4:10 PM	Tstm Wind	50 kts.	0	0	0	0
220 Plano	8/22/2006	4:45 PM	Tstm Wind	40 kts.	0	0	15K	0
221 McKinney	8/22/2006	5:10 PM	Tstm Wind	50 kts.	0	0	0	0
222 McKinney	8/23/2006	5:00 PM	Tstm Wind	50 kts.	0	0	0	0
223 Plano	8/27/2006	3:30 PM	Tstm Wind	50 kts.	0	0	5K	0
224 TXZ091>095–100 >107–115>123–129 >135–141>148– 156>162–174>175	9/1/2006	12:00 AM	Drought	N/A	0	0	0	80.0M
225 Frisco	9/17/2006	4:30 AM	Tstm Wind	50 kts.	0	0	5K	0
226 TXZ091>095–102 >107–117>123–130 >135–144>148– 159>161	10/1/2006	12:00 AM	Drought	N/A	0	0	16.0M	16.0M

Exhibit 3.1 Acts of God Matrix *(continued)*

Mag: Magnitude
Dth: Deaths
Inj: Injuries
PrD: Property Damage
CrD: Crop Damage

232 event(s) were reported in Collin County, Texas between 12/31/1997 and 12/31/2006

Location or County	Date	Time	Type	Mag	73 Dth	30 Inj	0 PrD	0 CrD
227 TXZ104	10/31/2006	10:00 AM	Strong Wind	N/A	0	0	2K	0K
228 TXZ091>095–100 >107–115>123– 129>135–141>148– 156>162–174>175	11/1/2006	12:00 AM	Drought	N/A	0	0	0K	36.8M
229 TXZ003–003 >013–013>014– 014–014>015– 015–018>020	11/14/2006	2.05 PM	High Wind	62 kts.	0	0	0K	0K
230 TXZ095–104 >105–117>119– 129–131–146–148– 157>159–174	11/15/2006	6:00 AM	Strong Wind	N/A	0	1	270K	0K
231 TXZ091>093– 100–102>104–116– 118>119–129	11/29/2006	6:00 PM	Winter Storm	N/A	0	0	40K	0K
232 TXZ001–003 >005–007>020	11/29/2006	11:00 PM	Heavy Snow	N/A	0	0	0K	0K

EXHIBIT 3.1 ACTS OF GOD MATRIX (continued)

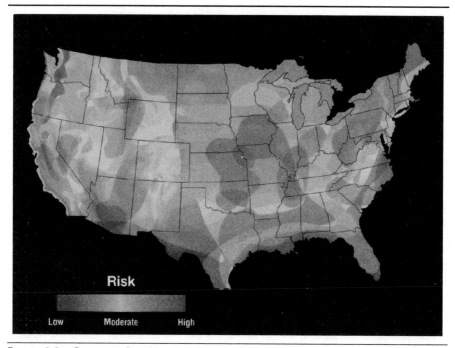

EXHIBIT 3.2 COMPOSITE RISK MAP

in the Northeast and seismic activity is in the far West cause problems. The detailed maps in Exhibits 3.3 through 3.6 provide more guidance.

Lightning strikes are not good for power plants, telecommunications, transportation, and mission-critical facilities in general. They happen everywhere and are *not* escapable. The idea is to minimize the exposure. Note that Florida has heavy or frequent strikes but has many data centers for various other reasons. Exhibit 3.3 shows a map of lighting activity.

Seismic activity can be disruptive to the asset but, as important, it can be disruptive to the outside plant (OSP) that services the asset. If the asset is fine but humans cannot make it to the facility, a company may suffer the same business interruption even though it invested up to 125% more in improvement costs in anticipation of the event. Note that California is seismically active but has many data centers (see Exhibit 3.4).

Snowfall and ice are dangers to the Northeast visually and statistically, but keep in mind that those states that receive the most snowfall are the best able to cope with it (see Exhibit 3.5). Texas and Georgia are two states that seem to suffer whenever there is snow, due to their unfamiliarity in handling it.

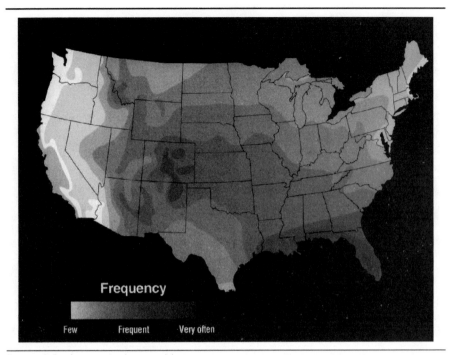

EXHIBIT 3.3   LIGHTNING ACTIVITY MAP

After power generation was deregulated from distribution, the maintenance of tree trimming is no longer a priority in regional companies operations. Unfortunately, snow and ice on trees in rights-of-way is a leading cause of interruptions. When vetting a power company, I look for any accumulations in ROWs during helicopter tours.

Areas subject to tornadoes and hurricanes (see Exhibit 3.6) are obvious regions to avoid when considering where to locate mission-critical facilities. Again, from an acts-of-God point of view, the asset being considered can be fortified and will likely be fortified to withstand the 200-mile-per-hour wind with the aggregate of large debris that can break (e.g., walls, roofs, and OSP improvements) See Exhibit 3.7. The telecommunications and power infrastructure as well as passable transportation becomes tantamount to the services. Humans have to be willing *and* able to make it to work under these extraordinary conditions. The damage from such events often comes from wind lift, which means that *everything* needs to be belted down and secured. Mission-critical gear, including the "big iron" of chillers and generators, need to be within enclosures to keep debris out of fans' motors and allow adequate fresh air intake.

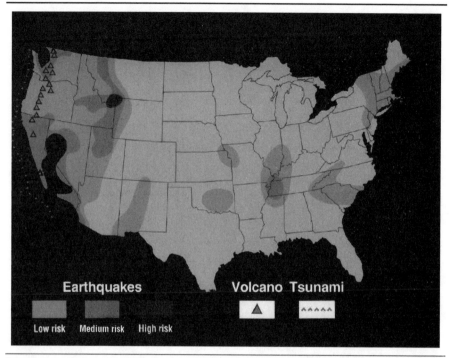

EXHIBIT 3.4   SEISMIC ACTIVITY MAP

Exhibit 3.8 provides guidance for design and development of OSP infra-structure improvements. When accessing a region and the history of high wind activity; most weather recordings are memorialized with the Fugita scale in mind for integrity of improvements and survivability of same. It is important to remember that the tenant or user needs to consider the survivability of the power and fiber improvements affected by high winds and not just the survivability of a perimeter wall!

Exhibit 3.9 shows man-made, or human, challenges that impact data center sitings. The radio frequency (RF) can impact the information technology (IT) communication and integrity. The less RF the better. The man made or human challenges of site planning, building department, and permitting concerns vary by region and state. Time and schedule unknowns are the enemy of a smooth and effective project program. We assess the familiarity of a building department with mission-critical improvements and the time or schedule impact they can have in the overall planning. The length of time it takes the building department to review plans and issue permits can vary by over 12 months. Remember, time is money. Gas lines are more prevalent

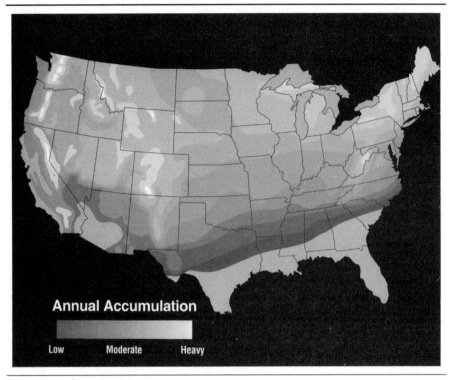

Annual Accumulation

Low   Moderate   Heavy

EXHIBIT 3.5   SNOWFALL MAP

in urban regions than in rural ones and are considered a potential for risk or evacuation in the unlikely event of a backhoe damaging a line. In such cases, first responders often evacuate 1,500 to 3,000 feet surrounding the break. Gas line damage is more prevalent in some regions than others.

The topic of flooding generally gets a good deal of attention during steering committee meetings. Often the committee is made up of heads of IT, facilities, real estate, risk management, human resources, legal, and executive personnel. The concerns of water within the data center are fairly obvious; readers of this book presumably understand that water and electricity do not mix. Water above an active data center floor or above the environmentals that support the data center is an ongoing concern and to be avoided at all costs. Overflow in bathrooms, pantries, fire sprinklers, and roofs are common sources of water and outages. That is why vertical and multistory assets are generally not preferred for data centers unless they are uniquely designed with special consideration given to vertical surfaces of conduits,

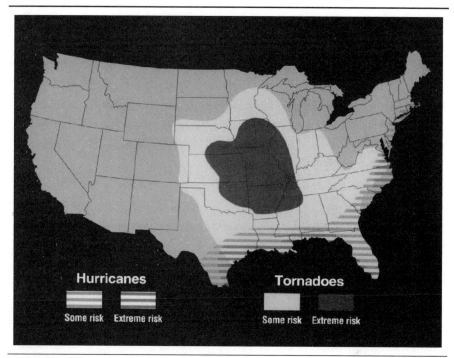

EXHIBIT 3.6 TORNADOES AND HURRICANES MAP

drains, water, damming, or containment, where appropriate. Internal flood conditions appear to outweigh external flood conditions as a source of interruption in mission critical-facilities. Once water flow is identified, the first responder's primary consideration is to mitigate risk, cut the power on or near the water flow, and cut or stop the water flow in the data center. Water flow is the source of most data center interruptions that are human and inside plant related. According to Contingency Planning Resources,[1] "flooding or burst pipes account for 16% of prolonged outages which are outages over one hour." Given that over 90% of all outages last less than one hour, you might wonder what the big deal is. The big deal is that it takes a considerable amount of time to reset a system once it has been interrupted or once power to the source has been cut due to the water flow or evacuation. In addition, if not restarted by authorized manufacturers' representatives. Plenty of kit and environmental equipment will operate, some will not operate, or will violate warranties. There are real-world and tangible amounts of money lost due to outages and interruptions. In addition, there are some intangible results, such

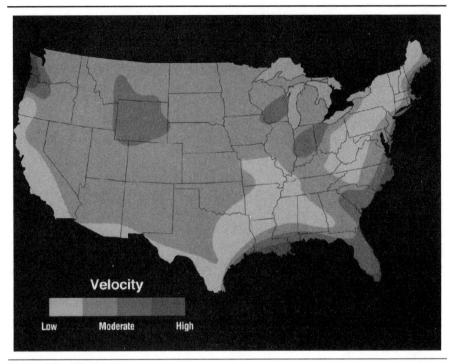

Velocity

Low   Moderate   High

EXHIBIT 3.7 WIND MAP

as damage to a company's brand image and the ability and willingness of other companies to do business with a firm that takes a hit due to carelessness, human intervention, or overall outage.

One of the more unrecognized or stealthy problems attributed to the loss of power or service interruption to a single piece of equipment is its position in the total system solution and in manipulating data. Failure of one piece of equipment likely impacts other pieces of equipment and applications. It is very rare to find one piece of equipment functioning as a self-contained processing and storage solution. If the front end of a solution is negatively impacted, then the back end will be impacted as well.

Often lost or unrecognized costs are accelerated or coefficient costs associated with bringing a piece of equipment or system back online for a host of well-documented reasons:

1. To do so would breach the manufacturer's services warranties unless the manufacturer is on site. Many service-level agreements from equipment providers require trained and authorized manufacturers, employees, or certified vendors to work on the equipment, including starting it

F-Scale Number	Intensity Phrase	Wind Speed	Type of Damage Done
F0	Gale tornado	40–72 mph	Some damage to chimneys; breaks branches off trees; pushes over shallow-rooted trees; damages signboards.
F1	Moderate tornado	73–112 mph	The lower limit is the beginning of hurricane wind speed; peels surface off roofs; mobile homes pushed off foundations or overturned; moving autos pushed off the roads; attached garages may be destroyed.
F2	Significant tornado	113–157 mph	Considerable damage. Roofs torn off frame houses; mobile homes demolished; boxcars pushed over; large trees snapped or uprooted; light object missiles generated.
F3	Severe tornado	158–206 mph	Roof and some walls torn off well constructed houses; trains overturned; most trees in forest uprooted.
F4	Devastating tornado	207–260 mph	Well-constructed houses leveled; structures with weak foundations blown off some distance; cars thrown and large missiles generated.
F5	Incredible tornado	261–318 mph	Strong frame houses lifted off foundations and carried considerable distances to disintegrate; automobile-size missiles fly through the air in excess of 100 meters; trees debarked; steel-reinforced concrete structures badly damaged.
F6	Inconceivable tornado	319–379 mph	These winds are very unlikely. The small area of damage they might produce would probably not be recognizable along with the mess produced by F4 and F5 wind that would surround the F6 winds. Missiles, such as cars and refrigerators, would do serious secondary damage that could not be directly identified as F6 damage. If this level is ever achieved, evidence for it might only be found in some manner of ground swirl pattern; it may never be identifiable through engineering studies.

EXHIBIT 3.8   FUJITA SCALE

up. In reality, users cannot wait four hours or longer to get a factory or equipment representative on-site. (The premium for business interruption insurance goes up significantly after two hours.) If the water flow or interruption came from an act of God, say flood or tidal surge, then obviously the service provider will be delayed in reaching the site. (This is another reason why backup services should not be located

Existing Condition	Weight	Condition	Score	Total	Condition	Score	Total
Natural Gas Lines: transmission distribution (minimum of 3,000 linear feet from pressurized transmission lines)	4	8 inch line 5 miles	2	0	10 inch line 2 miles	0	0
Electronic Interference (minimum of 2 linear miles from point to point or panel system)	3	In mountain	4	12	RF and cell tower 2,000 feet	1	0
Building Department Process Case	2	90-day permit	1	0	90-day permit	1	0

EXHIBIT 3.9   MAN-MADE CHALLENGES

within 40 to 60 miles of a primary system.) Once a manufacturer's representative is on-site, the actual work can take time. Spinning the disc up or down takes time, and if the circuit board is burned out or fried, the service person must have the replacement parts, boards, circuits, and cabling available to remedy the problem.

2. The adjacencies that one piece of equipment have with another also increase repair costs. Failure of one piece of kit often impacts the overall success of the data manipulation.

For every 15 minutes of downtime due to flooding or other event, it takes between one and ten hours to recover documentation, execute trades, settle trades, and store information. Data center users can process or clear $2 to $4 trillion a day in financial instruments. Due to the tremendous sums involved, it is vital to think through possible flooding scenarios. By averages only, continuity disaster resources have established these losses by industry:

- Financial brokerage services: $7,840,000 per hour, $130,667 per minute
- Credit card sales: $3,160,000 per hour, $52,667 per minute
- Media pay-per-view: $182,000 per hour, $3,050 per minute
- Airline reservations: $108,000 per hour, $1,800 per minute

As you can see, there is a lot at stake. In Chapter 9, we discuss more completely the corporate governance view and government's role in a well-thought-out business impact analysis (BIA). Through a BIA, a company can look at the financial significance of an event, short or long term, and give it a value.

Common sense prevailing, if a company does not lose a significant amount of revenues due to a service failure, it is less likely to commit the money and time to design, build, and maintain a significant facility, primary, active-active, triangulated, or geoplexed. If a company will lose a significant amount of money due to a service failure, whatever the length, and its brand is likely to be damaged, it will establish a one-time operating budget large enough to deal with these losses over a period of time, the human infrastructure to recover losses, and continuity of business viewed as critical, possible, or even likely.

The BIA is effective if these guidelines are followed:

- Establish and document business unit by business unit, including expense-only centers such as facilities, legal, human resources, and so forth.
- Realize that the BIA is a tool for business continuity, not data retrieval. To that end: how to maintain and protect the company's human infrastructure, data, brand, and facilities.
- The business continuity planning (BCP) plan that flows from the BIA template must be tested and updated regularly.

These guidelines are not rocket science. Nevertheless, you cannot believe how many folks think they can pick and choose rather than following these time-tested and effective guidelines.

Companies morph or reinvent themselves every three years; the risk management view should change also. Business units may be sold or acquired; people come and go. Recent or relevant acts of God or human intervention may impact the plan. A host of things can happen that could add time and expense or reduce it.

The company BCP should describe in detail the people and call tree protocols. It should also provide a summary flowchart of fail-safe procedures complete with names of people to contact, multiple numbers for them, details and pictures of appropriate action, and change management methods of procedures, if appropriate.

A strategy for all companies needs to include:

- A declaration point (memorialized and agreed to)
- Recovery point objectives
- Recovery time objectives
- Action plan based on a short list of scenarios (long term, short term)

Often users engage the services of a vendor to assist in the BCP process and execute in anticipation of the event. What I have learned is that exclusive of the fees that users pay (the fees are all over the charts for organizational or consulting services), users themselves do most of the heavy lifting for the final deliverable and its testing and maintenance.

The fees to organize and develop a user's program run from $25,000 to $2 to $3 million. You generally get what you pay for. However, I have noticed that with proprietary software programs, users are tied to the vendor for disproportionate fees to value. Users have to populate and update the programs or pay a significant multiplier to the vendor to do so.

I am not sure this is wrong, but the "sell" is deceiving. Users should make the call on their recovery time objectives, recovery point objectives, and so forth. These are user-dollar decisions. However, the outrageous fees associated with an overzealous insurance policy need to be checked. Point-and-click programs for activation and recovery are oversold; rarely are they as good as advertised or even understandable by users. Most executive or midlevel managers are not technically savvy enough to execute or augment in real time, let alone under stress. These programs seem to be priced by the pound rather than content when printed. I do not mean to oversimplify the tricky business of planning and implementing BCP; but pricing should fall in line with value, man-hour effort, or intellectual property. Since some commoditization has occurred in this space to make BCP companies fight for their work, it seems the larger-user companies are afraid *not* to write the big check because of the perception that there is something behind the man and the curtain that will save them during an event (e.g., vendors, elves, hobbits, equipment, etc., will parachute into critical footprints "just in time").

If we understand that over 90% of the data center requirements are 10,000 square feet or smaller and that similarly 90% of all traditional real estate users are 10,000 square feet and smaller, it is clear that most of the BCP marketplace is small.

Recently compliance with Sections 302 and 404 of the Sarbanes-Oxley Act (SOX) has been the largest driver for implementing BCP programs. As a result, there are plenty of small to medium-size vendors to choose from to help coordinate, develop, document, and implement a BCP program.

SOX compliance at the large user level and job security often influence the overbuying of ineffective programs with shared or dedicated footprint scenarios. I am not saying that big is bad among service providers. As with other services, it often comes down to the humans supporting the program and nonusurious fees to implement understandable and usable plans. Particularly with electronic point-and-click solutions, pricing should reflect value. The construction analogy I often use is designing a trading floor of 1,000 traders; we are designing one trader 1,000 times or four units 250 times. I understand that egress, power, cooling, pantries, bathrooms, conference rooms, and other adjacencies have impact and add value, but should the service meet the fee or at least get close? The punch line is that it is a market. When vendors are busy, the price goes up, and when it is slow, users have leverage.

Finally, as we get better and better fiber that is able to handle more and faster bandwidth to the home infrastructure in place (more bandwidth that is reliable); and telecom providers deploy the "triple play" of fat pipe data, video, and voice in bundled packages to the home; the more critical services we can leverage the larger footprints (with fewer single points of failure).

Consider that 80% of all critical documents are stored on our e-mails and e-mail servers and that most passwords and access codes continue to be placed under keypads or on Post-it Notes attached to a computer screen at the office or home! We are doing much better currently—remotely.

This chapter does not concern truly mission-critical users with terabits of data flowing through their collective electronic veins on a daily basis. In this post–September 11, 2001, world, there is a right pricing and right sizing to BCP planning and implementation, and remote or home solutions can be a part of successful planning and implementation.

NOTE

1. Contingency Planning Resources, 2006.

4

FLOODING: BE AFRAID, BE VERY AFRAID!

One of the first questions users or tenants have been trained to ask during the site selection process is: What parts of the asset's land are within the 100-year floodplain? Is the candidate's property on an area of frequent and documented flooding (regardless of source)? The question is a good one, but it is misleading. To the layperson, it implies that a flood occurs once in a 100-year period. Since the useful life of an asset is generally 13 to 20 years, siting a data center within the 100-year topology almost sounds like a safe bet, right? Wrong!

Here are a few things that these tax/topography maps and data do not consider:

- The roads, highways, and airfield to access the asset may be partially or entirely impassable due to flash floods, tidal surge, still water, high winds, and fallen trees.
- The services that feed the asset may be under water. These services include:
  - Utility substations
  - Telecom central office
  - Power (buried)
  - Telecom fiber/copper
  - Generator plant
  - Buried fuel/water
  - Buried facilities to asset
- Hundred-year storms occur far more regularly than stated and should be treated with a high level of seriousness.

The second misleading statistic or data point is the 500-year topology or flood rings as indicated on tax maps, by the Federal Management Emergency Agency, and others. Unless the data center ring or topology sites the landing point of Noah's Ark, this ring should be fairly high above sea level, but it is not. The line delineations really consider more how much surface area needs to fill before I get wet mentality.

First, most weather records over 100 years old are a bit sketchy. Although some date back 154 years or so, there is no legitimate, well-documented 500-year story for the United States. Second, if the water has pushed past the 100-year ring, then the roads, trains, and rights-of-way that provide functionality to the data center are likely to be partially flooded and therefore not passable.

What is a flood? Flooding takes place in low-lying areas during prolonged rain of a day or more. Thunderstorms cause flooding generally if the downpour is over an inch per hour. According to the U.S. Geological Society (USGS), "Flash floods occur within six hours of a rain event, dam, or levee failure." Due to the "sealing" of land for parking and new construction or new improved properties in urban areas, the runoff can be two to six times greater than the normal water flow during previous areas. Flooding is caused by slow-moving thunderstorms and tropical storms, and is generally driven by the duration of the storm and soil conditions.

The term "100-year storm" came from the mathematical equation based on early data that a storm had a 1 in 100 chance of occurring in any one year. "Ten or more years of data is required to perform a frequency analysis," says the USGS. Common sense prevailing, the more data there are, the better the confidence in the results. These are no more than "frequency analyses." They cannot predict. If you are like me and notice that we have had more than one 100-year storm every three years, you might wonder why they are called 100-year storms.

When performing a site analysis, you should use the flooding map, and other maps, for guidance only. Gather more specific information at a local level for history and for specific disasters; these data should give the source, duration, and amount of dollar volume lost or damage and cumulative deaths per event.

Hundred-year storms and flood levels are determined by stream flow and watershed or outlet locations between points A and B. This is the catch, The USGS maintains a gauging station, where conditions are measured and recorded continuously by electronic instruments to an accuracy of 1/100 of a foot. This information is gathered by satellite and telephone telemetry and transmitted to USGS computers. Can you have a 100-year storm one year after another? Yes. The expression comes from the complex polynomial equation that will spit out the chances of an event hitting again given the algorithmic equation based on the last 10 years of data. It is also a hell of a way for meteorologists to gain the audience's attention when a large storm or an expected storm surge is coming.

Surprisingly enough, some media and politically hyped stories actually contain elements of truth. Coverage of the rising sea level threatening our shores, low-lying regions, and plenty of critical infrastructures become a critical infrastructure/key assets story, a human story, an urban story, and an ecology story. You know when Anderson Cooper and Larry King are doing segments on the ecological angle of flooding—we are late; or in real estate terms; if you want to know what happened six months ago in Manhattan real estate—pick up today's daily newspapers.

Interestingly enough, the coastline sea level has been rising by 1 to 1.25 millimeters per year for the past 100 to 150 years (again, data is a little sketchy that far back), according to the Metropolitan East Coast Assessment. According to the Bush administration, the sea level is expected to rise up to three feet over the next century. That is approximately .36 inches a year, or 7.2 inches over 20 years, what we called the total cost of ownership (TCO) window for new data centers. (I use 20 years as a TCO model due to the useful life of environmental equipment.) A seven-plus-inch swing in sea levels for data centers I am working with now will have a meaningful impact on siting the asset and will contribute largely to the "parade of horribles" conversation in the steering committee. With 50% of Americans living within 100 miles of our coastlines, and an extraordinarily large number of people living in the port cities of New York, Philadelphia, Boston, Baltimore, Miami, New Orleans, San Francisco, and Los Angeles, the concentric circles of challenges are overwhelming. In New York City alone, the five boroughs have over 80 bridges and tunnels connecting them; most entrances or exits for these bridges and tunnels are on or below sea level. Twenty bridges surround Manhattan alone. Like New Orleans, many parts of the United States will have to adjust to the rising water levels and build levees and dams to displace water and keep communities and infrastructure in our urban centers safe and dry. Louisiana, New Orleans, and Hurricane Katrina make a good case study.

When the French claimed the southern coast of the United States hundreds of years ago, the territory that became the Louisiana Purchase was above sea level. Since that time it has sunk an inch every year, not because the levees broke but because they *worked*. The levees were put in place at the river's edge to protect the cities. The levees held, and prevented the river from depositing new dirt and sediment along the river's edge. "That's why in Louisiana, 50 acres of land turns to water daily. Every ten months, an area of land the size of Manhattan joins the Gulf of Mexico" according to Mike Tidwell, author of *The Ravaging Tide*,[1] and why "landmasses the size of Rhode Island have been subtracted from southern Louisiana" annually since World War II. The scars of the rising coastline and sinking land are abundant.

According to the Environmental Protection Agency (EPA), a two-foot rise in coastal seawater can eliminate 43% of the coastal wetlands. Obviously, homes and businesses within reach of the 7 to 24 inches are at risk. In New York City, plenty of waste treatment facilities are located on the East River, Harlem River, and Hudson River. My son and I recently had the pleasure of swimming around Manhattan in a 28.5-mile race. We can say with confidence that the water is significantly dirtier near the waste stations (I will spare you the details). If these stations become at risk to flooding and tidal movements, imagine the disruption that a catastrophic failure would cause. Have you imagined what the sewage system in New York City, looks like at 8 AM with 12 million people flushing at the same time? Briefly, the waste is flushed or pumped using gravity to holding stations at the water's edge and moved by barge to treatment facilities, where it is scrubbed and expelled. If the stations went underwater, we would have one large regional hazardous materials site.

Most of our primary potable water mains in the United States are over 100 years old. Combined with the fact that the pressure of new coastal floodwater is creeping into the ground pressure, it is clear that the United States is facing a sinkhole of water and sewer main breakage issues like we have never seen before. Until recently, New York City had over 250 water main breaks every year. Remember, water and power do not mix. Almost every time there is a water main break, there is a power or telecom interruption.

Again, consider the new rise in coastal sea levels and the EPA's projection (exclusive uprising water) "that unless cities invest more into repair and replacement, their water and sewer systems, nearly half of the water system pipes in the United States, will be in poor, very poor, or life elapsed standings by 2020." Cities and municipalities traditionally spend the second greatest amount of their budget on water and sewer. (Education traditionally is number one.) Without federal assistance, the negative effects of cascading sewer and water pipeline failures will significantly impact our urban environments within 5 to 10 years. Consider these recent examples:

- After a sinkhole swallowed a 40-foot sewer repair truck the day after Christmas, the tank's crew crawled to safety muddy and mystified in Seattle in 2004.

- In 2006, a two-year-old boy disappeared into a sinkhole in Irving, Texas. Authorities thought he had been kidnapped. He was missing for days but eventually was found in the sewer system.
- In December 2006, firefighters in Brooklyn rescued a woman carrying groceries who fell into a hole that opened up just beneath her on the sidewalk.
- In Hershey, Pennsylvania, a damaged store drain caused a six-foot-deep sinkhole in Hersey Park, nearly sinking a New Year's Eve celebration.

Get the point? Rising sea levels coupled with sinking landmasses equate to infrastructure risk. And remember that half the population of the United States is within 100 miles of a coast and two-thirds of them are within 20 miles of the coast. A hundred million people reside in our urban infrastructure.

Now that we have established that our land is sinking and the water is rising, you may buy into the fact that the well-documented melting ice caps, glaciers, Greenland, et cetera, is a result of carbon dioxide (CO_2) emissions. The CO_2, acting like a blanket around Earth, holds the heat from the sun and heats the air and, hence, the water. Heat expands and makes molecular structures larger; cold reduces molecular size, making water smaller. It is not so much that the huge ice caps are melting and contributing to the ocean mass, but rather that the water is heating and expanding, which makes it larger. Because the oceans are warmer, they are causing not more, but more intense, storms and hurricanes, which in turn create problems for mission-critical facilities.

According to the *Journal of Science*, storms of categories 1 through 3 or winds up to 165 miles an hour went down while storms of 165 to 250 miles an hour went up. In the 1970s, we had 10 category 4 to 5 storms; and in the 1990s, we had 18. We have fewer but stronger storms.

The year 2005 was the warmest year on record; it also included the most category 4 to 5 storms. See the relationship? Not more storms, but stronger storms. These facts will guide site searchers for mission-critical facilities away from flood-prone areas and areas that accumulate storm surge. The number-one cause of most hurricane damage is not from the high winds or what the storm eats, but rather storm surge, the tidal and high-water events that accompany the storm's high winds or rain. In the twentieth century, there were 167 named hurricanes. Of those 167 storms, one-third made landfall in Florida. In other words, 110 storms landed between the Gulf of Mexico and

New York. And we now know that these storms will be stronger, creating mind-boggling damage. In 2005, $85 billion in insurance claims were made, a new outdoor record.

NOTE

1. Mike Tidwell, *The Ravaging Tide: Strange Weather, Future Katrinas, and the Coming Death of America's Coastal Cities* (Free Press, 2007).

5

DATA CENTERS GROWTH VELOCITY

I have already discussed the data center of the 1980s and 1990s. During that time, I effectively predicted 30 to 70% growth over 10 to 13 years. That means if users needed (day 1 and future) 100,000 square feet of white space, they would plan for 130,000 to 170,000 square feet total (inclusive of environmentals to support the white space). That figure was based on existing velocity of growth for white space. Power densities were 15 to 25 watts a foot, and cooling was fairly static. Moore's Law, although in place at this time, did not anticipate the more powerful chips associated with cooling configurations until years later. More recently, particularly following the phenomena of Y2K and the terrorist events of September 11, there has been accelerated growth and interest in large data centers. The "mega–data center" had lost its place (90% of all data centers are less than 10,000 square feet). The cost and time required to design the 50,000 to 100,000 square feet of white space was and is overwhelming. It often made sense to augment human space or office space within a strategic asset rather than taking the time and expense to secure, design, improve, and maintain a large data center. Operating expenses over 15 to 20 years are staggering, and are the justification many users give for not designing a large data center. Data centers are not their core competency or core business; why should they pour $3 to $10 million a year into just the maintenance of a noncore business?

More recently, and largely in the shadows of the events of September 11, various white papers and regulations (which we will discuss in Chapter 8) regarding data centers have been taking a more centralized approach from a human, equipment, and a real estate cost point of view. Information technology (IT) service topology delivery inspired a move to a more centralized model. Collapsing multiple sites into fewer sites is a target-rich environment for cost savings. Some reasons to migrate out of existing or legacy "spoke-and-wheel" data centers are:

- They are too close to the primary facility.
- The infrastructure is outdated in power, cooling, and telecom infrastructure and is no longer able (even with retrofits) to satisfy new power and air-conditioning requirements.

According to Gartner, "server rationalization, hardware growth, and cost containment" are "driving the consolidation of enterprise data processing sites into larger data centers." Underutilized and oversupplied servers became financially imprudent to manage and maintain. Gartner discussed the rise of distributed computing and other trends, which led them to the deduction that large data centers were on the decline. The rise of distributed computing and other trends drove decline into large data processing sites that characterize the era of mainframe dominance. Now, however, data centers are rising in importance. There is a real and palpable relationship between lost revenues and downtime between the negative cascading of power in California, the regional outage in New York, and the events of September 11. When these events are coupled with corporate governance concerns and new legislation, companies recognize how much money they will lose by the moment in the event of a catastrophic or prolonged outage. (See the company business impact analysis in Chapter 3.) There are a number of main drivers associated with interest in larger data centers; they include server rationalization, cost containment, improved security and business continuity (a new corporate discipline), growth in hardware, and containing software. Current reasons for unique focus and interest in larger data centers include:

- Now more than ever, users are looking for IT solutions to reduce human costs or overall operating expenses, effectively trying to create their own "special sauce" to become more efficient in data processing, trading, clearing, and storing data (cost containment).
- Revised and ongoing, there has been continued interest in reducing the footprint of various legacy or antiquated data centers. As a result, many users have reduced the number of sites and placed equipment in larger sites.
- The need to improve security and a business continuity plan (BCP), what used to be disaster recovery interest, has led to a new and unique interest in security. No longer is triple fail-safe security satisfactory for most data centers (triple fail-safe, human, closed-circuit television, and proximity). Corporate governance is establishing a new level of criteria

for possible IT, intervention, human intervention, and cyberterrorism. It is common sense to recognize that with fewer assets to protect, there will be less risk of interruption.

- Another reason for the growth in larger data centers is the hardware requirements. In the past few years, we have seen large server deployments (blade [multiple servers] deployments of 55% in 2006 and 2007). Anybody who had a $250,000 signing authorization had these blades or the multiple servers were rolled into data center and were often underutilized. Coupled with the server deployments, the storage ability of new solutions for various equipment providers has increased significantly, which requires physical space. For nonfinancial and financial companies, storage has been tantamount to productivity due to the Health Insurance Portability and Accountability Act and new generally accepted accounting principles (GAAP) requirements created by the Sarbanes-Oxley Act; records need to be kept for a minimum of seven years. Implementation is slow. In 2007, I went to an emergency room and was provided with two pages of 30 detailed name and address stickers for various files. My visit was recorded with over 30 user groups or companies, providing a redundant paper trail that is both cost inefficient and a waste of real estate space.

The reduced number of data centers and a company's willingness to invest in multiple footprints have resulted in fewer and more meaningful data centers. These data centers are now often broken into simple squares or rectangles commonly referred to as cells, pods, or data halls to satisfy redundancy requirements inside the plant or inside the envelope. The topology of the mega–data center or multiple data centers has been reduced to an active-active (both in the same region), active-passive (one outside of the region), or geoplexed footprint scenario (out of region and out of the likely area subject to the act of God).

These new, enlarged data centers aim to scale size the white space and power/cooling capability as well as human infrastructure to enhance functionality of the hub or server locations within the organization and create centers of extraordinary human infrastructure and best practices to be deployed elsewhere around the country. One of the goals is to have the least amount of redundancy of hardware and infrastructure across multiple sites by concentrating capital, human intellectual capital, and operating expenses into a smaller number of sites and then making those sites as meaningful and redundant as reasonable. Not only can hardware costs run rampant, but unused software licensing costs and taxes thereon can run into the tens of millions of dollars. By leveraging buying power and considering the economic incentives of new deals for sales taxes for kit, utility, and telecom transmission cost; and human employee tax benefits, this kind of model can be adapted, with the result scaled to create the most cost-effective, cost-efficient deployment of physical and cyberassets. This is important and a new way for corporate executives and real estate brokers to leverage users' spend. There is no reason for users to occupy a footprint where the cost per kilowatt-hour (kWh) is $0.13 to $0.15 or even $0.22 per kWh and there is full sales tax on equipment when users can move to a footprint of $0.3 to $0.5 per kWh with limited or no sales tax. The difference is staggering for large users; it can mean $300 to $400 million over 20 years.

Another compelling reason to go to the large or main data center scenario is the use of virtualization to improve asset utilization and virtual capacity planning. Quite often user efficiency is somewhere between 8 and 25% of modeled capacity. Emerging virtualization technologies, particularly in server and storage equipment, offer the best asset utilization potential. "Solutions providers" are growing at an extraordinary rate; currently there exist between 240,000 to 260,000 such providers. These data center operators "manage your mess for less," according to ad campaigns. Their average time in the business is just over 10 years; the average duration of client relationship is almost 8 years, and the average number of customers is 180. Solution providers manage a balanced menu of services:

- Hardware: 26%
- Software: 25%
- Services: 49% (everything else)

Solutions providers' velocity of growth is good. For every three clients they gain, they lose just one. This is a positive churn and indicates that there is some product loyalty, which in a commoditized world is good for all of us.

These hardware and software technologies can also improve operational and operating expense processes, driving down telecom, human infrastructure, and hardware cost. Although virtualization does leave some risk in terms of inflating data, it does provide a meaningful cost savings and footprint savings scenario.

This server proliferation or virtualization has helped the IT industry to shift from higher-priced mainframes to lower-cost servers. It also has contributed to an exponential increase in the number of multiple servers deployed by financial institutions and ordinary user groups.

The blade surge has had an impact on value-added resources (VARs) in the deployment and utilization of the kit:

- 14% of VARs sold blades in 2007.
- 20% of VARs plan to sell blades in 2008.
- Represents a 45% increase for 2007 *leading all* technologies.

The blade server shipments have been recently documented to the measure growth and velocity, which has caused a buzz regarding the environmentals. (Note that several customers and clients are moving toward the multi-"U" topology and away from the blade and heating and cooling challenges—less expensive, easy in and easy out.) Projected growth of the blade technology and pricing is:

- 2006: 620,000 blades shipped—average selling price $4,189
- 2007 (estimated): 856,000 will ship—average selling price $3,967
- 2011 (estimated): 2.4 million will ship—average selling price $3,605

In comparison, overall server shipments were:

- 2006: 7.8 million
- 2011 (estimated): 11.3 million

This has also been combined with customers' historical interest in deploying a single special application over a single server while not risking other encryption over critical applications. This is like a family of four being the sole occupants of a 40-key hotel and living there indefinitely. Virtualization techniques and applications have compelling financial and human infrastructure reasons for adoption; such adoption is taking place only slowly, however.

The server processes have continued to evolve according to Moore's Law, and they continue to double in density every 18 months. Although the benefits to the IT user group have enabled them to run bigger-bandwidth applications and scenarios and to work in batches, they have also resulted in a massive increase in power consumption due to the more powerful chips and cooling requirements and environmental expenses. Keep in mind as we discuss the new, larger data centers, and the unique time and capital effort it takes to design, build, and maintain such unique facilities, that they are built with Tiers 3 and 4 in mind. A brief discussion of the tiering models is worthwhile so we know what the object is.

Tier 1. Single path of power and cooling. No redundant components. Less than 28.8 hours of downtime per year (satisfactory for noncritical users, form infrastructure requirements for most telecoms).

Tier 2. Single path for power and cooling distribution and redundant components. Less than 22.0 hours of downtime per year (common design-build
scenario for telecoms postderegulation, insurance companies, credit card
companies, and media outlets).

Tier 3. Multiple power and cooling distribution paths but only one active
redundant component currently maintainable. Less than 1.6 hours of
downtime per year (traditionally military specifications grew out of the
enterprise and the mission-critical phenomena postderegulation). The
motto of this tier is two is one, one is none.

Tier 4. Multiple active power and cooling distribution paths, redundant components, all tolerant. Less than 0.4 hours of downtime per year. In Tier 3
and 4 scenarios, our architectural suggestions are not offered. These
assets can actually be vertical. Except from conventional wisdom of
making these tiers horizontal, there exist compelling reasons—namely
cost savings and efficiencies—for having the white spaces on the second floor and the environmentals to serve the white space fed from
directly below the white space.

Exhibit 5.1 provides an easy-to-understand summary of the tiering differences commonly discussed today. Most of the data center world is working
between a Tier 2 and Tier 3 infrastructure for concurrent maintainability
goals. Tiers 1 and 4 are becoming more uncommon.

The most important point about the tiering models is the difference between
Tiers 2 and 3. This is a defining moment. The price difference between these
tiers is significant and largely due to the fact that Tier 3, by definition, is
concurrently maintainable. Concurrent maintenance requires the systems to
be shut off in portions of the asset so a certain area can have an anticipated outage, an unanticipated outage, or a predicted scheduled maintenance.
Therefore, the incremental investment for dual electrical mechanical systems
to meet the concurrent maintainability and fault-tolerant criteria causes a
significant increase in capital expense. Tiers 1 and 2 are practically linear.
There is backup for anticipated outage but bypasses and some redundancies
in general give them their linear design.

The costs and the cost benefits of the various tiers are fluid. In addition to
modified descriptions of tiers like "Tier 4 light" or "Tier 3 on steroids," the
pricing gymnastics are often "real time" with scheduling and challenging lead
times and interests. In effect, the cost of copper has gone up 100% in the last
five years. Believe it or not, materials go up approximately 1% per month.
They never go down, but they sometimes remain flat. Therefore, costs of
switch gear, uninterruptible power supply modules, cabling, and labor have

	Tier 1	Tier 2	Tier 3	Tier 4
General Premise	Basic: Susceptible to disruption from both planned and unplanned activity. Urgent situations will require frequent shutdowns.	Redundant components: They are slightly less susceptible to planned and unplanned activity. Maintenance of critical power path will require shutdown.	Concurrently maintainable: Allows for planned site infrastructure activity without disrupting computer operations. Unplanned activities errors in operation or spontaneous failures will still cause a disruption.	Fault Tolerant: Provides site infrastructure the capacity to permit any planned or unplanned activity without disruption to the critical load. Fault-tolerant functionality provides the ability of the site infrastructure to sustain one worst-case unplanned failure or event with no critical load impact.
#Delivery Paths	Only 1	Only 1	1 active 1 passive	2 active
Redundant Components	N	N+1	N+1	2N or S+S
Support Space to Raised Floor Space	20%	30%	80–90%	100%+
Initial Watts per Square Foot	20–30	40–50	40–60	40–80
Ultimate Watts per Square Foot	20–30	40–50	100–150	100–150+
Raised Floor Height	12 inches	18 inches	30–36 inches	30–36 inches

EXHIBIT 5.1 TIERING (continued)

	Tier 1	Tier 2	Tier 3	Tier 4
Floor Loading (pounds/sf)	85	100	150	150+
Utility Voltage	208,480	208,480	12–15kV	12–15kV
Months to Implement	3	3–6	15–20	15–20
Year First Deployed	1965	1970	1985	1995
Construction $/Raised sf	$650	$850	$1,850	$2,250+
FY2004 Projected Cost to build 100,000 sf raised floor data center environment				
Annual Predicted Downtime Due to Site Limitations	28.8 hours	22.0 hours	1.6 hours	0.4 hours
Site Availability	99.671%	99.749%	99.982%	99.995%
Augment existing 50,000–100,000 sf of white space	50 watts $650 psf	100 watts $850 psf	100 watts $2,700 psf	150 watts $3,500 psf
Colocation (up to 20,000 sf)	$150 psf per annum w/o electricity & setup	$350 psf per annum w/o electricity & setup	$550 psf per annum w/o electricity & setup	None available
Greenfield 50,000–100,000 sf of white space	$650 psf	$1,200 psf	$2,200 psf	$2,800 psf

Exhibit 5.1 Tiering *(continued)*

increased significantly. The cost of lead has increased similarly, so wet cell batteries are remarkably expensive. See Exhibit 5.2 for terms of pricing and tiering.

Again, if the shelf life of this book is three to five years, we anticipate that the pricing models in the exhibit will be outdated within 18 months. In 2006, China bought 80% of the world's supply of concrete. Do you think that had an impact on supply and demand? Currently India and China consume 80% of all energy, and only half of the population of these countries has plumbing and lighting. China builds a city containing 8 million people—a city equivalent to New York City—every three years. Its population is literally dropping their hand tools and walking to the cities and getting work. The point here is that renewable energy and finite resources are impacting our ability to site, design, and build mission-critical facilities.

The dirty little secret of building a larger data center is not only the capital expense for the meaningfully designed and built mission critical infrastructure that takes an act of Congress to get through the Steering Committee, but the operating expenses to maintain the same are equally onerous. As most data center managers will explain, beyond software costs, their major concern has been driving down operating expenses. Data center managers are trying to achieve better utilization by driving down utility waste from electrical distribution and cooling. To satisfy the explosive growth of the enterprise and storage environments, an extraordinary number of raw processors and supersized chips on the data center floor and disc space capacity are being managed within the footprint. This unique growth has come at an operating cost that has become a major focus of the industry. Beyond the hot aisle, cold aisle, and hot spot seminars held around the country every quarter, a unique focus is now bringing down the operating expense of the data center.

Total cost of ownership (TCO) models once reserved for the hardware or IT discipline of the data center environment have migrated into the facilities. Once again, the private sector is looking to the public sector for guidance and forecasts regarding the extraordinary power usage of these data centers. It is fairly clear at this point for consultants like myself to sort out various parts of the country with acceptable tolerances of acts of God, human intervention, and to identify level and score regions of the country with meaningful, reliable, and relatively cost effective power distribution (not only the capital expense to build, but the operating expense to maintain same). Following most deregulation scenarios or breakups, the first operating expense to be discounted is maintenance and management. The first thing to leave the utility sector was the human infrastructure (or heavy lifters) that once maintained

Total Cost of Ownership

Project Fortress—Confidential

	Site 1		Site 2		Site 3	
	Cost	Notes	Cost	Notes	Cost	Notes
Property Acquisition	$17,700,000	108 acres	$5,900,000	68 acres	$4,000,000	92 acres
Utility and Sales Tax Unique to Region: See matrix by utility	$179,475,600		$207,755,350		$186,860,337	
Upcharge Local Labor: See labor rates	E $18.35/P $16.59/M $16.85/L $12.25/C $14.53	plus $1,600,000	E $22.60/P $14.77/M $18.27/L $10.58/C $16.83	plus $5,500,000	E $22.60/P $14.77/M $18.27/L $10.58/C $16.83	plus $5,500,000
Seismic	$0		$0		$0	
IT Transmission Costs and Sales Tax Unique to Region	$202,460,555		$234,775,471		$278,664,418	
Total	$399,636,156	Baseline	$448,430,823 $48,794,667	—	$469,524,758 69,888,602	—

EXHIBIT 5.2 TIERING AND COST PER SQUARE FOOT MATRIX

this critical footprint (generators, transmission, and substations) now between 30 and 60 years old in many parts of the country.

Unfortunately, it comes down to a base level of maintenance of rights-of-way, tree trimming, snow removal, upgrade software controls, and network operating control center maintenance storage of spare parts and management. Ask a utility the costs of primary and reserve power, the number of transformers at the substation, and the source of transmission power. Location of the spare parts has become more important than history of outages. Who manufactures your spare parts? Where do you warehouse them? How many trucks do you have? Can I go up in a helicopter and identify your rights-of-way? Allow me to level and score your tree trimming and maintenance procedures.

On the heels of deregulation and due to the explosive growth of the data center market segment, President Bush on December 8, 2007, signed into law HR 5646, to study and promote the use of energy-efficient computer servers in the United States. The Environmental Protection Agency (EPA) worked with computer makers to recommend that the government adopt new incentives to handle the problem of rising power consumption and computer data centers. The EPA had six months to submit the study. It determined that power consumption for data centers unique to mission-critical environments accounts for approximately 2.9% of our total usage in the United States (equal to the annual consumption of the state of Michigan or the energy for every television in the country to be run at the same time).

These mega–data centers generally are sited in rural or "cornfield" scenarios on the bubble of urban environments. These locations are chosen because generally that is where the confluence of meaningful power service, humans, manufacturing, legacy factory, and/or distribution centers meet, significant telecommunications (fiber optic scalable, burstable, and synchronous optical networks [SONET]) networks to service multiple humans or commercial development. Managers of these data centers want to site them near urban locations, not too rural. The utility needs of a 30- to 60-megawatt data center will be similar to the power needed to light up a small town. Although data centers have few well-paying jobs, they provide hundreds of jobs (up to 300 at times) with evergreen construction and vendor support on-site or nearby. The greatest benefit to the local and state government is in the sales, real estate, and personal property taxes, which vary dramatically from state to state.

Data center equipment is composed of hardware or servers coupled with the software to make it cost efficient and profitable. Analysts expect the server market in the United States to grow from 2.8 million units, or $21 billion, in 2005, to 4.9 million units, or $25 billion, in 2009, a rate of almost 50% in five years, according to a recent IDC forecast. This is consistent with Moore's Law. The history and future of Moore's Law and Gordon Moore's legacy are well known and worth reviewing.

In 1965, Intel cofounder Gordon Moore predicted the economics of the next four decades of computer power. This is and was extraordinary. His theory was tucked away in an essay in an April issue of *Electronics* magazine. (An original copy of this issue recently sold for $10,000.) Moore said that the transistor density of integrated circuits at minimum would double roughly every 18 months. Over the years, there have been spikes and dips in the model based on the economy and commercially deployed equipment. However, today what has become known as Moore's Law is commonly taken to mean that the cost of computing power halves every year. The cornerstone of what Moore articulated in the article has drifted into all components of the mainframe and enterprise environments and trends in hard disc capacity over the past few decades—our ability to manipulate and store data. Commercially deployed technologies of broadband, video, audio, and fat bandwidth to satisfy the thirst for processing force growth in processing power. The commercial analogy I use for the increase in chip breakthroughs is the trickle-down benefits of adjacent processing in PDAs (personal digital assistants) and cell phones that were made in battery technology. Eight to ten years ago, our phones were small with multiple functions, but when fully utilized they only lasted 15 to 20 minutes. When batteries became lighter and lasted longer, the PDAs in phones began to sell. This is the same with the enterprise environment. When the chips got faster, technology got cheaper and became more commercially viable.

The good news here is that the cost to manipulate data or encryption— effectively, the chips—is now coming down in price. However, the cost to build Tier 4 environmentals has gone up nearly 100% in the last ten years. One noted industry consultant has indicated that the cost per processor has fallen 29% per year in three years; as a result, the IT budget will buy 2.7 times more processors and 12 times more processing power. However, the cost to manage the environmentals—cooling, fire suppression, and power distribution—has gone up 20 to 35% over the same time. We are collectively being forced out of our comfort zones of the AC uninterruptible power supply power plants and cogeneration to slow the "hockey stick" price increase models for Tier 3 and Tier 4 environmentals. (See Chapter 17.)

Recently a study conducted by the Data Center Users Group found that 96% of current facilities are projected to be at capacity by 2011. This opinion may be guided by the fluid dynamic of hardware, software, and virtualization. These predictions are not straight line. Technology moves too swiftly.

The data center life cycle is shrinking. Aggressive corporate growth plans, along with the use of new, more powerful server technologies, are pushing data centers to their limits. A host of facilities in urban environments and legacy facilities designed for 35 to 50 watts per square foot are maxed out; although they may have the physical space to add more equipment, they lack the power and cooling capacity to support that equipment! This fact has put a host of facilities managers, engineers, and IT consultants out of work or have annoyed some users.

The challenge of consulting the super-data center dynamic of how much, how long, where, how to make the data center scalable, flexible, and versatile is extraordinary, however, to "future-proof" what we call "rocketship real estate" is challenging and often protracted. Consultants need to take look at the velocity of growth of hardware, add-ons, utilization at the cabinet; incorporate anamolic growth, such as acquisitions, layoffs, antiquated hardware, and software storage networks; and then project and chart high-velocity, low-velocity, and projected mathematical growth. Most projections based on full utilization of kit will show "hockey stick" growth over three to five years and arching downward or slowing in the velocity of growth due to the server, mainframe, and storage chip capacity efficient utilization and a reduced footprint.

Exhibit 5.3 shows models for growth. A relevant history and velocity of growth is critical before a user gets over-vendored into overdesigning an infrastructure based on organic and anomolic growth patterns.

At this point, the steering committee coupled with their host of war stories can make contributions to where they think the company is going. The only way companies are going to overcome the obstacles of running out of power, cooling, and footprint is by designing for higher densities and employing adaptive IT infrastructures that will have greater flexibility to adapt to industry changes.

I am not necessarily an advocate for the 200- to 250-watt-per-square-foot environments. Except for exclusive, super-high, or compartmentalized environments, these are not commercially viable. In these small, super-high rooms, if one cooling component fails, the environments will overheat within a matter of seconds, not minutes. Generally designers of such data centers install additional air-handling units for the just-in-case scenario. Thus they effectively use up the floor space that you expected to "save." To move to super-high, super-perforated tiles that you anticipated to use in front of your

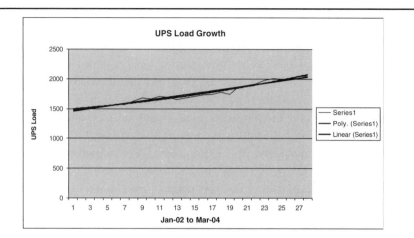

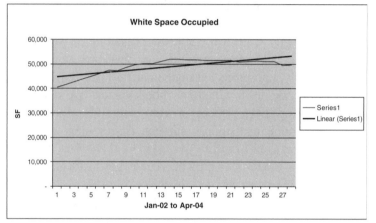

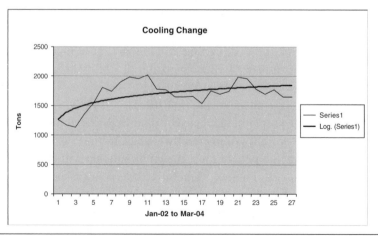

EXHIBIT 5.3   MODELS FOR GROWTH

cabinets effectively have a speed of about 125 to 175 miles an hour which eliminates all dresses in the environment, and goggles, not glasses may be standard issue. These data centers are not necessarily practical. Spreading high loads over low-load densities appears to lessen the risk of this model. Furthermore, these densities are rarely met. One large utility in New Jersey has not seen densities over 65 watts per square foot; one large data center landlord has seen densities between 45 to 65 watt per square foot. Let us assume growth. Let us provide room for equipment growth, *but let us be reasonable!*

The super-high scenarios are being commercially deployed with not only a hot-aisle/cold-aisle configuration but with a spreading of load. Until recently, data center managers wanted to line up servers, mainframe, and storage networks by discipline or by faceplate. This was generally done for appearances with similar results as the "Redcoats" during the Revolutionary War. This may look good, but it is not efficient. As one would come into the data center, this blue kit was over here, and that black kit was over there. Looked great...did not always make sense coupled with the fact that over 50% of data center managers do not know, within 24 hours of a move, what equipment is coming into the center and what the new loads will be. Circuiting and conductoring is often done on the fly by in-house electricians.

Rolling out equipment like soldiers is that it is not commercially viable. A 0.5-kilowatt (kW) cabinet should probably sit next to a 10-kW cabinet to blend the heat distribution. Beyond 6 kW (by average per cabinet), unique cooling solutions need to be provided.

Because most data center users do not know of what equipment is being rolled into the environment when, this means it has generally not made it through the lab or the testing bins to apply the special applications. The speed to market has eclipsed data center functionality (how close to substation, fiber, or outside plant issues). Effectively, whips and power circuits with cooling are expected to be in place to anticipate unknown server distribution. This ongoing turf war duplicates the friction between the IT and facilities groups going on since the 1990s. More functional and effective companies have put down their weapons, eliminated the silos, and learned to work together.

One financial institution that I have worked with was the biggest blade buyer in the country in 2006. On average, it was receiving 30 blades per week. Although the utilization of these blades was under 15%, they were being commercially deployed to satisfy user groups that did not want to share resources. Once fixed in place, the blades would grow vertically (within the chassis/cabinet) and not horizontally (taking more floor space).

This is a more mature view of growth from the point of view of load density and balancing. Equipment utilization is the cornerstone of effective data center management. Getting business units to share physical equipment and take that back to the profit and loss statement is far from easy, but it is well worth the effort and associated savings. Companies are working feverishly to create a better, faster, cheaper mouse trap; they are now working hard to reduce operating expenses without reducing or compromising the integrity of the plant.

6

Energy Use in Data Centers Globally Through 2012

The Environmental Protection Agency (EPA) has presented the greatly antic-ipated report in response to the request from Congress stated in Public Law 109431; the report effectively states what everyone already knew: Data centers are growing, power consumption is extraordinary, and the existing utilities' infrastructure to satisfy the growth, redundancy, scalability, and burstability is in danger. What is the danger? The danger is the possibility of negative cascading for failed substations much like the Northeast regional outage that began in Ohio on November 16, 2003.

Exhibit 6.1 shows the negative cascading that can happen if a substation fails. Most portions of the network are being asked to accept 100% load "under anger" seamlessly. This would require all major components of the utility network station system nationally to be 100% redundant contiguous to 100% redundant networks nationally, which is cost prohibitive. In telecom terms, companies do not build assuming all clients will use the network at the same time. They assume 10% static utilization. This is similar for utility companies, which assume all businesses and homes do not turn the lights on at the same time. It was when the government owned or operated the power network and we paid for it; now is prohibitively expensive. With shareholders and customers paying for improvements, redundancy and scalability become negotiable.

The EPA study provides information on the cost of data centers to the federal government and shows opportunities to reduce these costs. Of the 61 billion kilowatt-hours (kWh) used per year in the United States, data centers use approximately 2% of the total electric consumption nationally. The total cost of power—that would be the utility bills for these unique data center components—is about $4.5 billion a year. That is what the country is

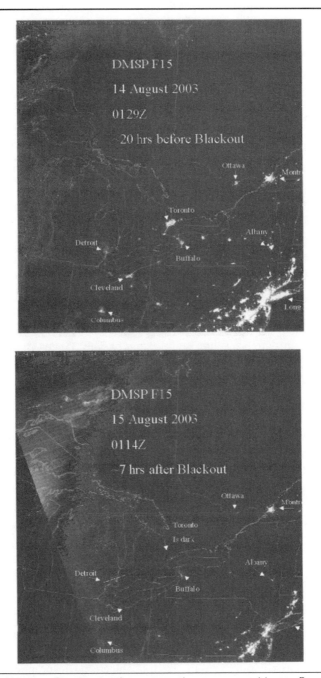

EXHIBIT 6.1   NATIONAL OCEANIC AND ATMOSPHERIC ADMINISTRATION MAPS OF BEFORE AND AFTER NORTHEAST REGIONAL OUTAGE

paying in utility bills; approximately 75% of that is waste, which amounts to over $3 billion for not using cogeneration or being more efficient. It is counterintuitive for the U.S. government to reduce this too much because most of these utilities bills are taxed at the municipality's tax rate, with the taxes supporting schools and the hospital, fire, and state infrastructure (between 4 and 9% state to state).

The federal government is not a neophyte in the world of data center design, construction, and operation. The government, federal servers and mainframes, software, and data centers account for approximately 6 billion kWh, or 10%, of the electric use (nearly $455 million annually). The government alone could save over $300 million annually via alternative methods.

In 2000, the cost to the nation of annual electric use was approximately $30 billion; it is expected to be approximately $120 billion in 2010 (a 400% increase in 10 years!). The data point here is the year 2006 for relevant data. If we take the existing or current velocity of power consumption and forecast it without the complex polynomial equation, we will hit just over $120 billion in kilowatts per year in 2012. Except for Moore's Law, these straight-line relationships generally hold. Effectively we need to apply anamolic growth, a current efficiency trends scenario, or do a better job. We can improve the operating scenario by applying free cooling, off-hour processing, better utilization at the server, best-practice scenarios, the exchange of best ideas for how to apply power consumption and cooling scenarios to unique super-sized chips and storage scenarios, as well as state-of-the-art scenarios that effectively have an extraordinary capital expense or up-front cost which provide the best return on investment.

The main findings of the EPA study are that:

- Data centers consumed about 60 billion kilowatts in 2006.
- The energy consumption of servers and data centers has doubled in the past five years and is expected to almost double again in the next five years to more than 100 billion kWh, costing about $7.4 billion annually. Remember, that amount is taxable. This data point is consistent with most large data centers running out of white space by 2011.
- Federal servers and data centers alone account for approximately 6 billion kilowatts or $450 million a year.
- Existing technologies and strategies could reduce the typical server energy by 75% by some estimates. This number is subject to a host of improvements introduced to the data center component. However, big users are reluctant to change. (Remember "flywheel technology" and how that was supposed to take us out of the purchase of uninterruptible

power supply [UPS] modules and battery footprints?). Free cooling, thermal storage, direct current (DC) plants, and cogeneration are all commercially viable with well-documented field hours of successful operation.

The total cost of operating expense model for these larger data centers should not be lost sight of. Designers and planners recognize the capital expense to protect the user group from an unplanned, short- or long-term outage. The determination of how much infrastructure to apply to protect a server has doubled in price. As indicated earlier in the book, acts of God are becoming not more frequent but more violent, and the outside plant infrastructure of the deregulated utilities is less reliable; effectively two or three 9s in most footprints or regions. Currently, a five or six 9s solution requires a Tier 3 or Tier 4 infrastructure, which is now running on a greenfield scenario between $2,200 and $2,850 per usable square foot, or $700 to $1,000 per square foot over the total envelope. (A large variable is expansion space under the roof and the size of the day 1 and future human component.) The costs are rising quickly. Local labor, applicable taxes, and competition among trades and equipment manufacturers could mean a 10 to 20% difference in the total cost of occupancy before considering utility, sales, personal property, and income taxes.

That is the algorithm on which most users are now focusing. As we level and score various acts of God and human intervention scenarios in a footprint, we then apply the telecommunications transmission costs (last mile with tax) and utility rate (incorporate percentage growth and tax) with history of outage and come up with a "leveled" scenario for how much to spend on a certain footprint. (See Exhibit 6.2 for an example of circuit reliability, source, and duration form.)

In certain parts of the country, six and seven 9s scenarios exist from single circuits from the substation. Given acts of God, this would encourage a user to spend less on the inside plant to satisfy asset reliability. However, nationally, the ugly truth is that most circuits are becoming less reliable due to deregulation and poor system maintenance. Again, common sense prevailing, we want to be closer to transmission, primary lines, or substation. Increased distance increases risk. A bridge crossing adds more risk, as does a river crossing. Boring under a highway adds even more risk. You get the point. Yes, our power grids are somewhat fluid with buy/sell agreements seemingly across tariff footprints, but maintenance and the human and equipment infrastructure are still unique and specific to footprints. Effectively, the utilities have become generation companies and wire services (accounts receivable/accounts payable).

SUMMARY

Circuit 3551:

Over 10 years, Trip Falls Circuit 3551 was available 99.98140% of the time (three 9s availability). Circuit 3551 experienced approximately 1 hour and 44 minutes of downtime per year.

EXPLANATION

Circuit 3551:

From June 1 1997 to May 31st 2005 (8 years), Circuit 3552 was down for 13 hours and 2 minutes, equaling 782 minutes of downtime or 46,920 seconds of downtime over the 8 years.

13 hours × 60 minutes/hour	=	780 minutes
+ 2 minutes	=	782 minutes
× 60 seconds/minute	=	49,920 seconds

Method:

To find out the circuit's availability over the 8-year period:

1. Relate the circuits' downtime to the 8 year period with a common unit (seconds).
2. Determine what percentage of 8 years the circuits were down.
3. Subtract this percentage from 100% to find the availability of each circuit.

There are 252,288,000 seconds in 8 years. (8 yrs × 365 days/yr × 24 hours/day × 60 minutes/hour × 60 seconds/minute = 252,288,000 seconds in 8 years).

Circuit 516:

Circuit 3551, with 46,920 seconds of downtime, was available 99.98140% of the time.

Fraction of downtime:

$$46,920 \text{ sec}/252,288,000 \text{ sec} = 0.00018598$$

Convert to percent:

$$100\% \times 0.00018598 = 0.018598\% \text{ downtime}$$

Subtract from 100% for availability rate:

$$100\% - 0.018598\% = 99.98140\% \text{ availability}$$

The circuit has three 9s availability.

As a fraction of 8 years, Circuit 3551 experienced approximately 1 hour and 44 minutes of downtime per year.

EXHIBIT 6.2 CIRCUIT RELIABILITY, SOURCE, AND DURATION *(continued)*

Sidenote: Downtime

Downtime per year is a more intuitive way of understanding the availability of a circuit. This table compares availability and its corresponding downtime.

Availability	Downtime
90% (one 9)	36.5 days/year
99% (two 9s)	3.65 days/year
99.9% (three 9s)	8.76 hours/year
99.99% (four 9s)	52 minutes/year
99.999% (five 9s)	5 minutes/year
99.9999% (six 9s)	31 seconds/year

EXHIBIT 6.2   CIRCUIT RELIABILITY, SOURCE, AND DURATION *(continued)*

A generation service is just that. Due to the cost of fossil fuels and gas, the cost to run and operate a generating facility and buy and sell across tariff footprints is a very thin-margin business.

Today, with the tighter margins under which companies are operating, there is little money available to maintain the wire networks. Redundancy is not built in at substations on speculation where most humans have left or migrated from. Power providers have not yet recovered from the scars of the dot-com boom and "trust me, heavy power loads are coming." (They are wise to charge for their time and designs to sort out the dreamers from the users.) Take, for instance, the cities of Rochester, Syracuse, Albany, and Buffalo in northeastern New York state. This area was once a very productive, blue-collar, light-manufacturing part of the country. Now most of those jobs have moved South, and utility networks there have lost profitability. One would think being within 100 to 200 miles of Niagara Falls, the major source of generation in upstate New York, the cost per kWh would be down in the $0.4- to $0.5-per-kW range. However, primary and transition rates at the local utility are between $0.12 and $0.14 per kWh. This is counterintuitive considering that the utility is next to a nearly free, renewable generation system. But if you consider that Buffalo was the twenty-second largest city in the United States in 1993 when the Buffalo Bills were invited to play in the AFC (American Football Conference), and in 2006, it was the sixty-sixth largest city in the country. Fewer humans in businesses are footing the bill for the static or constant cost to run that utility footprint. In simple terms, it is cheaper to split a dinner check ten ways than four ways.

Not to mislead the reader: If a user ends up in North Carolina, South Carolina, or Tennessee where there are known nuclear facilities that still have some capacity, that power is sold into the grid nationally. Approximately 19% of the nuclear energy developed in the United States goes into the national grid; however, 40% of the nuclear facilities are in the Northeast and are regional players.

Consistently green or ecologically friendly sources of power, such as wind and solar, account for less than 2% of the national consumption. However, these sources are growing at an accelerated rate.

As London and New York continue to slug it out for the title of financial capital of the world, the challenges, concerns, and interests and mission-critical facilities (rocketship real estate) are consistent.

Similar to the economic cold the world catches when New York sneezes, London, continental Europe, and Asia are realizing extraordinary growth in data center consumption and needs (aka "Economic Jet Lag"). Research indicates that half of the U.K. data center owners and operators aim to build new facilities in 2007, up from slightly less than 10% in 2006. This situation

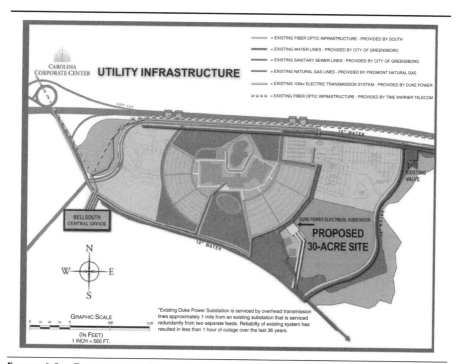

EXHIBIT 6.3   CONFLUENCE OF EXTRAORDINARY POWER AND FIBER OPTICS *(continued)*

EXHIBIT 6.4   CONFLUENCE OF EXTRAORDINARY POWER AND FIBER OPTICS *(continued)*

reflects the hockey-stick velocity of growth mentioned earlier and the inability of existing legacy environments to satisfy heat densities and cooling challenges.

Equally interesting are the perceptions of U.K. user groups and facility owners regarding what will happen in their data centers. Only 1.5% strongly agree that they can understand and predict what will happen; 21% slightly agree; and 32% do not agree. Approximately 4% neither agree nor disagree, 28% strongly agree, and 14% strongly disagree that they can predict what will go on in their centers.

To further emphasize the globalization of mission-critical facilities, the uninterruptible power supply market grew by almost 12% in the first half of 2006. Remember, recent and relevant data indicate a doubling of consumption over the next few years prior to 2011. That acceleration of growth is extraordinary and create the concentric circles of concern for unique power distribution and cooling solutions. Exhibit 6.3 is one of the best examples of the confluence of extraordinary power, fiber optics, and potable water. Like other candidates, it sits on the bubble of an urban environment and was designed to military specifications years ago. The outside plant infrastructure still has use, and the surrounding human infrastructure, local-state incentives, and a utility with a disproportion of nuclear generation with substation on-site make it truly unique and valuable.

7

PRIMARY AND SECONDARY DATA CENTER SELECTION: RECENT HISTORY

Establishing and implementing unique criteria for data center selection is not a new idea. The idea for a mission-critical facility has grown more exacting over the past ten years and even more so over the past three years. In the northeastern United States, the financial capital of the world, the data center and business continuity site often was located within 10 miles of headquarters or the primary site. The proximity was established largely to be close to synchronous encryption to the critical data within 26 route kilometers (18 miles) and to be close enough so the managers or business heads could oversee implementation and maintenance effectively.

It was rare that the primary data center was geographically remote from a second site or that a business continuity site would truly be remote (over 80 miles away). Currently there are over 40 business (active/active) continuity sites in Jersey City, New Jersey, just 1.5 Euclidean miles from lower Manhattan and 6 to 8 Euclidean miles from midtown Manhattan, where the primary data centers and headquarters are located. What we witnessed from the events of September 11, 2001, other than the catastrophic loss of life, is that commercial transportation on bridges, tunnels, and most waterways were effectively stopped, unless escorted by official vehicles. Companies received police escorts to various sites for fuel and temporary generator distribution. If possible at all, it was extraordinary to get a human or critical human infrastructure to a second site or a primary site ("under anger") under these conditions, and time-sensitive executions were delayed. I personally drove a truck for two days to expedite the provisioning process; I was able to do this because I had security clearance at bridges, tunnels, and the tenant's highly secure space.

Few official documents specify where to site data centers. This information is not provided in Securities and Exchange Commission (SEC) white papers of October 12, 2007, and April 7, 2003; the National Association of Securities Dealers rules of 3510 and 3520; sections 302 and 404 of the Sarbanes-Oxley Act 2002; or the Public Company Accounting Oversight Board's Standard No. 2 or Statement of Accounting Standards 70, to name a few. Collectively they provide a few suggestions and guidelines. In essence, they tell companies to:

- Have a brief continuity plan.
- Update and document the plan if significant changes occur in the company or process.
- Test the plan annually.

These laws and bodies did put information technology (IT) in "the game" but the teeth were still missing!

We will discuss recent and relevant legislation and acts in Chapter 8. What are looming large are the tiered designations of Tier 1 and Tier 2 and their accountability to the private sector. The SEC applies these tier designations to users, recognizing that not all companies have or should have the resources to comply on all levels:

- **Tier 1 Designation.** Two-hour recovery time objective.
- **Tier 2 Designation.** Four-hour recovery time objective (everyone else).

Furthermore, the SEC has cited a $75 million market capitalization as a threshold for the size of operation designation of tiers. Effectively, the U.S. government told businesses to comply with Sarbanes-Oxley as of June 15, 2004. About $75 million is the total market capitalization exposure in the market; that generally means a greater capital expense to build greater operating expenses to SEC reporting companies. This was their attempt that one size of compliance and documentation did "not" fit all.

When we think of Sarbanes-Oxley, we think of the "bad guys." We think about large companies taking money from hardworking investors and manipulating the books so when investors reach retirement, there is little or nothing left. However, the concentric circles of Sarbanes-Oxley have drifted into business continuity planning, document retention, and corporate governance. The difference between recent legislation and Sarbanes-Oxley is that negative consequences now have teeth. In other words, if there is noncompliance by the chief executive officer or the chief financial officer, *jail time* is possible, if not likely. Again, this was structured for the bad guys.

As we discuss interruptions and consequential damages, the overwhelming evidence of recent and large interruptions include, but are not limited to, the first World Trade Center attack, the Seaport Substation outage, the Chicago Loop flood, the second World Trade Center attack, the eastern regional blackout, and several 100-year storms in the last 10 years.

If you wanted to drill just a little deeper, you would find that the cause of most data center outages is simply human intervention and willful misconduct and sabotage. These events account for almost 90% of short-term outages and 80% of long-term outages. Of the outages, 70% are caused by humans, 21% are human error, and 9% are management or process related. These numbers are inclusive of information technology and data centers.

In this book, we spend most of our time considering outside plant (OSP) and some inside plant (ISP) consequences of planned or unplanned outages. What we have learned about recent acts of God and human intervention is that although we can make assets bulletproof, storms can make roads impassable. Telecommunications systems that were designed and maintained by the U.S. government for some 40 years ago have been overlooked, and overbooked. The legacy infrastructure is undermaintained or antiquated in many parts of the country. These legacy systems were not built with the same levels of redundancy or burstability as those currently being built in the private sector. There is a site in Greensboro, North Carolina, which is the best available in the United States: its design ISP and OSP is to military specifications—it has six 9s on one feeder and seven 9s on the other.

Regarding the human component of continuity, if personnel were designated to go to recovery solution sites but were either unable or unwilling to participate, the corporate user needs able to get "willing" employees to execute or perform. Remote solutions increase people's willingness to work, respond, and rise to the occasion. An employee who is focused on the welfare and quality of life of immediate family members is not going to be responsive or effective. This was the thinking that developed from white paper 2. Recovery needs to be far enough from an event that people can treat it as a media event, not a personal event. If too close, ISP improvements may not operate properly due to local events or because generators run out of fuel and roads are impassable.

Site selection for the stand-alone or bunker scenario has become more exacting. The unsettled part of the process is that it has a level of interest in direct relationship to current events and, particularly, media coverage. As a result, these consequences are permanently etched into our minds:

- When the first World Trade Center attack happened, Manhattan was no longer a viable location for a second site.

- When the second World Trade Center attack occurred, regional selection was employed away from lower Manhattan.
- When the dirty bomb concern was peaking (remember anthrax), the plume of radioactivity reaching a 25- to 40-mile radius around the city made that area undesirable. The Nuclear Regulatory Commission "kill zone" is equivalent to 18 Euclidean miles.
- When the aircraft crashed in New York, airplane flight-path approaches and take-offs were of unique concern.
- Nuclear power plants were determined to be vulnerable. Forty-mile rings of potential radioactivity were placed around them, and the areas to the east of all rings are considered at high risk due to prevailing winds. Historically, potassium iodide pills have been distributed to humans living within an 18-mile ring of nuclear reactors and wastewater (the kill zone).
- When the regional power outage occurred, its extended duration was realized. The outage highlighted the inconvenience to humans of not being able to access public transportation, automatic teller machines, and sustenance elements.

Because of the reality of recent events and the media spin on them, as well as users' own war stories, a floating emphasis on possible outages has had an impact on recent legislation, rules, and compliance for business continuity.

Information technology (IT) governance helps ensure that IT supports business goals, optimizes business investment in IT, and appropriately manages IT-related risks and opportunities. These ISP controls with ISP and OSP infrastructure improvements increase survivability of data and human life under extraordinary circumstances.

The solution we employ is a weighted matrix (see Exhibit 7.1). This matrix provides detailed criteria with an objective level of interest. The categories are all encompassing and extensive, and have been scored and weighted. The scores "favorable to unacceptable" and the weighting emphasize the importance of the category according to the steering committee. For instance, an active flood zone rating would be more significant than the proximity of public transportation, or two diverse feeds of power may be weighted more than redundant source of potable water. (However, if you do not have cooling, you do not have power.)

The most logical way to navigate through the often-protracted process of data center site selection or business continuity planning is to inspect the candidate properties, take images of them, interview the relevant utilities, and visit the building department and subcode officials to document zoning and

		Site A			Site B		
		Site Score:	39%	252	Site Score:	51%	328
	Weighting	Description	Rating	Score	Description	Rating	Score
Available White Space	3	To be built; 20,000 data center space available, space in mountain. 12–24 months for delivery	4	12	9,000 sf white space	4	12
Price	2	$45 per sf per month per year	0	0	Pricing next week; est. $876 per ft per year including power	1	2
Existing Total Project Sq Footage	4	none; ROW's established to surface of mountain	4	16	31,500 white space	1	4
Zoning (If rezoning is required what is the impact?)	4	As-of right	1	4	As-of right	4	16
Description	3	All land in mountain; horizontal, 34 feet to ceiling; multistory in mountain	3	9	Multistory; multitenant	0	0
Water and Water Storage Second Source (high-level study of well and aquifers)	5	Surface storage	1	5	As-of right	4	20
Sewer to satisfy data center (and runoff)	4	In place; pumps and pumping required	0	0	As-of right	4	16
Security Setbacks: berming, etc.	4	In mountain, multiple tenants	0	0	Triple fail-safe, in place; multiple users	4	16

EXHIBIT 7.1 WEIGHTED MATRIX *(continued)*

		Site A			Site B		
		Site Score:	39%	252	Site Score:	51%	328
	Weighting	Description	Rating	Score	Description	Rating	Score
Accessible Public Transportation (access for vendors and home office, not daily commutation)	2	None	0	0	None	0	0
Soil Conditions (benefits and drawbacks of solid or rock foundations)	3	Dolomite mountain	1	3	In building	1	3
Human Resource Depth (other companies nearby, college/ universities)	4	TBD	0	0	Atlanta	4	16
Proximity to Current Data Center Operations	5	301 miles	2	10	389 miles	2	10
Sales Tax (local/state)	5	7.23	1	5	0%	4	20
Installation Costs (local labor)	3	TBD	0	0	TBD	0	0
Power Plant/Rough Order of Magnitude Pricing	3	8 miles	1	3	None	4	12
Cost per kWh (peak/off peak)	5	4.9	0	0	Included	4	20
Tariffs (other)	3	TBD	0	0	TBD	0	0
EDC Benefits (local)	4	TBD	0	0	TBD	0	0
State (incentives)	4	TBD	0	0	TBD	0	0
Telco Transmission Costs	5	Century Tel; Lycor, Empire State	0	0	TBD	0	0

Exhibit 7.1 Weighted Matrix *(continued)*

		Site A			Site B		
		Site Score:	39%	252	**Site Score:**	51%	328
	Weighting	**Description**	**Rating**	**Score**	**Description**	**Rating**	**Score**
Power/Electricity: 150 watts/sf (capability/ scalability: 30 megawatts capability from each substation. Day 1 power of 5 MW from each substation)	5	150 watts per sq ft plant in design	2	10	168 watts per sq foot	4	20
Diverse Electrical Feeds from Separate Substations (route distances for each—aerial or terrestrial; note highway, railroad, or other ROWs that create risks)	5	2 substations in place	4	20	2 feeds; 1 substation	3	15
Facilities Fiber and Telecom (3 facilities-based providers, separate ROWs)	5	In place	1	5	TBD	0	0
Longitude/ Latitude		TBD	0	0	TBD	0	0
Generators (Department of Environmental Protection, Environmental Protection Agency)	3	TBD	0	0	6 generators; 2.5 megawatts	4	12
Fuel Storage (potential challenges of service storage or buried)	4	Surface	1	4	In place; 2 days	3	12
Floodplain: 100/500 (portion or percentage of	5	In mountain	4	20	500 year	4	20

EXHIBIT 7.1   WEIGHTED MATRIX *(continued)*

		Site A			Site B		
		Site Score:	39%	252	Site Score:	51%	328
	Weighting	Description	Rating	Score	Description	Rating	Score
acreage in flood zone as well as access roads in flood zone)							
Earthquake	4	In mountain, near fault	2	8	Nonseismic	4	16
Tornado/ Hurricane (highlighting sensitiveness to disruption of OSP services: power poles, power towers, etc.)	4	In mountain	4	16	Some risk	2	8
Wildfires	3	In mountain	4	12	Some risk	2	6
Landslide Possibilities	3	In mountain	4	12	None	4	12
Drought	2	Water pumping may be issue	1	2	Currently	0	0
Snow/Ice (relevance to power lines, fiber optic lines, and road access/ accidents)	4	Roads and power risk	1	4	Low risk	3	12
Lightning Activity	4	In mountain	4	16	Some risk	3	12
Composite Risk (overall)	4	Average	2	8	Moderate	2	8
Distance from Railroad Freight and Passenger (minimum of 3,000 linear feet)	4	In mountain	4	16	TBD	0	0
Regional Declared Disasters (within past 10 years)	3	TBD	0	0	TBD	0	0
Nuclear Power Plant Proximity (minimum of 18	3	In mountain	4	12	TBD	0	0

EXHIBIT 7.1 WEIGHTED MATRIX *(continued)*

		Site A			Site B		
		Site Score:	39%	252	Site Score:	51%	328
	Weighting	Description	Rating	Score	Description	Rating	Score
linear miles/shaded to 50 miles downwind of potential event)							
Highway Proximity (minimum of 3,000 feet 4-lane highway)	4	1 mile to Route 65	1	4	3 miles	1	4
Airport Proximity (minimum of 15 linear miles from FBO or commercial airfield)	4	TBD	0	0	15 miles	1	4
Hazardous Facilities (minimum of 5 linear miles of contaminated soil or water)	4	Other tenants	1	4	TBD	0	0
Natural Gas Lines: transmission and distribution (minimum of 3,000 linear feet from pressurized transmission lines)	4	TBD	0	0	TBD	0	0
Electronic Interference (minimum of 2 linear miles from point to point or panel system)	3	In mountain	4	12	TBD	0	0
Building Department Process Case	2	TBD	0	0	TBD	0	0

EXHIBIT 7.1   WEIGHTED MATRIX   *(continued)*

permitting issues regarding candidate properties. Quite often local subcode officials can and will supersede the building owners' contractors association or building owners' management association guidelines based on recent or relevant experience; or worse, just by making an arbitrary call. These folks are very important to the process. They are generally very intelligent and caring. Sometimes they are misunderstood because users often start the relationship under the pressure of time, zoning, setbacks, and so forth, which require reviews and public notices. Subcode officials generally want and need to enforce law and precedent. Early and candid visits to the building department are strongly suggested to populate as much of the weighted matrix in Exhibit 7.1 to weigh properly. Building department officials are problem solvers, but they are human and have feelings and self-esteem issues as well. How you articulate what you are proposing is crucial. Humility, professionalism, and documentation are the keys to this part of the process.

Next we turn to some scoring criteria on a short list of candidate properties to anticipate entitlement, zoning, and construction issues that have and will continue to impact schedule and budget. I cannot tell you how many times I have seen good teams go down the wrong path for the seemingly right reasons due to poor or slow intelligence regarding some of these criteria. Once they pass a certain point in the process, changing direction can be too painful or embarrassing. These are career-killer decisions.

Although we are living in a digital age that provides good and useful information, there are still parts of the United States that are mired in the paper world, and some legacy municipal or vendor personnel may be digital natives or digital immigrants. Speed and accuracy of good intelligence requires the measure-twice-and-cut-once mentality. Intelligence available only on paper is not necessarily poor; likewise, just because intelligence can pop up on your home computer does not make it accurate. Frankly, some of the best intelligence I have gotten from the field is from people who have personal knowledge of acts of God, human intervention, and the permitting or entitlement process. The next list helps the steering committee weigh, score, and level the candidate properties and municipalities against each other. It also starts a specific dialogue among the committee members inspired by war stories from members on what happened to them in various circumstances.

- As-of right use
- Demolition protocol
- Building coverage to land ratio
- Curb cut protocol
- Permitting costs

- Site plan approval duration
- Site plan approval minimum requirements (for speed)
- Can construction documents be submitted with the site plan in the interest in time?
- Department of Environmental Protection (DEP)/Environmental Protection Agency (EPA) submittal requirements (fuel, water and emissions)
- Land loss to wetlands, rights-of-way (ROWs) easements, other
- Can DEP/EPA submittals go in with the site plan?
- Water detention scenarios and local law
- Sewer to satisfy runoff, cooling tower, and human waste by gravity, pumps, or both
- Geotect study
- Hazardous materials local and regional study
- Local "Superfund" or remediation relevance and history
- Frequency of local, permitting, and state legislative meetings requirements and possible variances or incentives?
- Allowable-buildable envelope "as-of right"
- Duration of variance process
- Parking required
- Fire road distance requirement
- Setback considerations
- Decibel or sound attenuation requirements at perimeter
- Fuel storage consideration (above or below)
- Minimum distance from power transmission lines
- Process of back and forth with site plan, environmental or construction documents (back and forth or end of the line)
- Expediter recommend or not (wrong expeditor can add time)
- Bedrock and aquifer identification
- Temporary certificate of occupancy or certificate of occupancy process and timing

The rest is "special sauce."

Whether in-house or outsourced, there needs to be consensus within the steering committee on the weighting of the categories and solid documentation of properties to score assets if for no other reason than to stimulate the dialogue. (Consensus by intimidation or because "I said so" is not recommended, and discourages the creative thought that the client pays for). This should be done by people in-house or vendors outsourced who actually have done this or do this for a living more that once every five or ten years, not junior vendors playing "check the box" on some 25-page diatribe.

Do not ask a lawyer to do building department subcode due diligence. Do not ask risk management personnel to negotiate utility rates or substation costs. This should not be treated as a school for preferred vendors to "help" brokers to sort out fiber optics or multiplexing at the certificate of occupancy. Do not ask a civil engineer to do ROW or telecommunications network infrastructure. Never send a telecom network engineer to sort out one-time and future utility costs for various tariff footprints. Negative first impressions with critical disciplines from the field or building departments are very hard to undo. Utility network engineers, building subcode officials, fire marshals, and telecom network managers are the heart and soul of our nation's infrastructure.

Sending a weak bench or a "B" team of vendors to gather intelligence from such a critical human infrastructure is a recipe for disaster and done more times than it is not done.

Tantamount to where the asset is placed is the day-to-day human infrastructure to support the asset and the company at the asset during a short-term or prolonged interruption. Strategic employees need to be able and willing to continue work. Special emphasis should be on in-house multitasking individuals.

If the asset is within 26 route kilometers asynchronous encryption distance to a primary asset, it may well be affected by the same act of God or human intervention. This may cause significant congestion in the railways, road, air transportation, telecommunications, but most important, the willingness of the human infrastructure to work (e.g., in some places in New Jersey, the New Jersey Turnpike, Garden State Parkway, Amtrak, and N.J. Transit trains are all within three miles from each other). The farther away users are from the event, the more likely they will be able and willing to recover the operations.

Encryption of data can be vaulted and saved in a timely fashion (in intervals) near the primary data center and then made recoverable remotely by a tertiary site. This can be done at the vaulting or business recovery level, either leveraging existing assets in a company's inventory or acquiring building/new facilities.

The human resource component is often overlooked when selecting primary, secondary, and tertiary sites. The devil is in the details when analyzing a site's OSP improvements, flexibility, and scalability. However, the weighting of the categories is a protracted process. Integrating the human resource component in weighted matrixes for site selection can and will shorten the time of searching and bring more experience and credibility to everyone's efforts. In the data centers, the ratio of cost per square foot to employee is very high; put another way, there are few jobs for in data centers. These jobs are generally well paying, offering 30 to 40% higher-than-average compensation. It is important to have feeder schools or other technology-related companies nearby to get new employees, but the effort is hardly worth the gymnastics that users need to go through to qualify for employee tax credit benefits (often in blighted areas) from local or state governments.

Some of the criteria suggested earlier takes the "winging it" or "gut check" component out of multimarket data center site selection process. While most of the employees of the data centers come from the immediate region, key or senior officers and key multitaskers often are transferred in.

"Corporate governance" (meaning it is your job or else!) is the new fear tactic used by vendors. It is like the 1990s, when we sold "Can you imagine selling fear as a business?" It's been the biggest moneymaker since the Y2K hype. If it is not documented, if there is no process, and if there is no electronic or paper trail telling you how to get from here to there, who is accountable? Who crafted the documents? Fear, fear, fear! Vendors appear out of the blue and articulate what corporate governance is and how noncompliant the user is. The fact is, there is no universal blueprint for corporate governance and there was no silver bullet to Y2K. One size does not fit all. What are the consequences of noncompliance? What are the windows to cure? What are best practices? How can I manage at a low cost? In the United States, governance means following the laws, rules, and guidelines of the relevant industry and the Sarbanes-Oxley Act.

As we can see, much time and thought has been given to what used to be called disaster recovery and is now called business and continuity planning. The terminology associated with the topics changes as frequently as the width of men's ties. In some cases, the ideas associated with the recovery are recirculated with a fresh new phrase to articulate the same principle. For example, what was once called "electronic vaulting" could now be considered "triangulation of data." Vaulting is the periodic sending of data from one site to another. An outstanding solution to capturing, retrieving, and storing data is locating a smaller data center synchronous to the primary facility with data sent real time to a remote site out of the region. This is triangulation.

The ideas of saving time and working as close to real-time encryption of data and having able and working humans "willing to support same" are not new. Events within the last 15 years—the Bishop's Gate bomb in London, Seaport Substation outage, first World Trade Center attack, Chicago Loop flood, California fires, Texas droughts, second World Trade Center attack,

Katrina, and West Coast and East Coast negative cascading of power—have given the uptime critical world some tangible results of the unexpected. The data points are in. Not many companies actually report losses accurately. Some are not able to report these numbers publicly; others are not willing to do so. Although the numbers used in this book are quoted accurately, I believe they are off or underreported by at least 100%.

8

PUBLIC SECTOR LAWS: GUIDANCE AND CONSEQUENCES

The cumulative results of the events of September 11, 2001 have been articulated in two white papers distributed by the Securities and Exchange Commission (SEC) on October 21, 2002, and October 7, 2003, respectively, as well as in rules from the National Association of Securities Dealers (NASD) that followed September 13, 2003 with the Sarbanes-Oxley Act of 2004, the Homeland Security Act of 2002, Secure Cyberspace February 2003, national infrastructure protection plan 2006, the Patriot Act 2002, the National Fire Protection Agency 1600 Standard on Disaster/Emergency Management and Continuity of Programs 2004 edition as a subset of the Patriot Act and Guidelines for Disaster Preparedness, the interim national preparedness goals, Homeland Security, Presidential Directive and, National Preparedness Developed by Homeland Security March 31, 2005, the Federal Financial Institutions Council Business Continuity Planning March 2003.

On March 9, 2004, the U.S. Public Company Accounting Oversight Board (PCAOB) approved Auditing Standard No. 2, *An Audit of Internal Control Over Financial Reporting Performed in Conjunction with an Audit of Financial Statements*. This audit standard establishes the requirements for performing an audit of internal control over financial reporting and provides some important directions on the scope required for auditors.

Auditing Standard No. 2 includes specific requirements for auditors to understand the flow of transactions, including how transactions are initiated, authorized, recorded, processed, and reported. While general in nature, these PCAOB principles provide direction on where SEC registrants should focus their efforts to determine whether specific information technology (IT) controls over transactions are properly designed and operating effectively. It was a start and put IT in the game.

In brief, the Sarbanes-Oxley Act (SOX) is the most sweeping legislation affecting corporate governance, disclosure, and financial reporting. Partially inspired by the "bad guys" at MCI, Enron, and others, this law effectively applies a hammer to the most minimum and basic documentation this country could mandate on the private sector. Specifically, Sections 302 and 404 require chief executive officers and chief financial officers, independent auditors, and appropriate in-house support committee to:

- Certify the accuracy of the financial statements.
- Indicate if there were changes in internal controls.
- Report the controls for financial reporting that have been evaluated within the past 90 days.

Section 404 of SOX became effective June 15, 2004, for all SEC-reporting companies. The deadline for compliance was April 15, 2005. Failure to comply with SOX exposed senior management to possible imprisonment and significant penalties as well as loss of public trust and permanent damage to the company value (brand).

The SEC has approved the NASD rules 3510/3520 as published in the Federal Register on April 10, 2004. These rules have NASD "clearing firms" establish business continuity plans other than issues of rules 3510 and 3520 (October 2004) for:

Tier 1. Companies with $75 million in daily market capitalization.
Tier 2. Market capitalization overnight of $75 million.

In brief, the SEC approved NASD rules and required member companies to:

- Have a brief continuity business plan (BCP).
- Update, plan any significant changes occurring in company or process.
- Update and review the planning, or have a plan, document a plan, and test the plan.

In brief, BCPs address at a minimum:

- Data backup and recovery (hard and electronic)
- Updating and reviewing assessments
- Alternate communication between members of customers and members of employees
- Uptime critical systems
- Real estate or footprint for human recovery

The net result of Section 404 of SOX and SEC and NASD 3510/3520 and 446 was the guidelines put forth in the joint white papers distributed by the Department of Treasury, New York Office of the Controller, and the SEC on April 7, 2003. They put an accelerated push for commonsense solutions to what was then known as disaster recovery and is now called business continuity planning. A silo was created in the corporate architecture. BCP was now a full-time job.

With little more than six months to go before some companies were required to comply with SOX Section 404, a survey found that 36% of the companies had a long way to go. In addition, 30% of respondents in the same survey indicated that compliance would have a significant negative impact on their company's profitability that came from the BCP compliance report. Compliance is expensive, and can be a sinkhole of time and resources if done properly and in anticipation of audits.

I have worked on BCP or DR space for the last 20 years. It is clear that a meeting at a bar or at a hotel following an event is no longer a viable option for a company in the financial services industry. Also, the "buddy system" has been almost entirely taken off the table of considerations. In the buddy system, if a client or customer of another larger or similar client or customer needed space, it would be provided and shared for key personnel or moneymakers to work/trade and so forth. This was not very practical for large migrations or long-term interruptions, but it was certainly low cost. Formal agreements with "dedicated seat" scenarios or "shared seat" models with some or all IT infrastructure in place are expensive if fitted out with appropriate and seamless market data services.

This is now a real business for mission-critical and non-mission-critical users. Philosophically, for many people in and around this industry, it is like overselling the seats of an aircraft. (Airlines count on a certain number of no-shows.) The bet is that not everyone will show up from all the companies subscribed at the same time for the same event. It is a first-come, first-serve basis. All the users have as a "hammer" is a lawsuit or offset of future fees to claw back financially. A dedicated facility or dedicated seat is the most reliable model for mission-critical businesses.

The cost in real dollars to perform a business impact analysis, develop a strategy, and test maintenance is a challenging process that almost always finds its way into the three following these concepts matrix for the strategy to be implemented.

1. Stand-alone is inherently a secure solution and provides integrity of human and technology resources. Generally it is the most expensive solution. Distances from acts of God are a minimum of 26 miles versus 250 miles. Users are often in dedicated, not shared, facilities.

2. Shared infrastructure is a dedicated footprint for the user in an asset of multiple tenants with access to uninterruptible power supply, generator,

cooling, diverse telecommunications, and so forth. Generally the facility has less security and integrity.

3. The business continuity planning (BCP) footprint of shared or dedicated seeds with "hot hands" to support IT's data and telecommunications needs, dedicated space with seats that are less expensive. Shared seats and footprint are less expensive and a greater risk. This solution satisfies new laws at a low cost. It is acceptable at the boardroom level but is not always a real solution and is often viewed as an enhanced insurance policy. Some providers are better than others.

Finding the right human infrastructure to guide users through this process (in-house or outsourced) is critical from a time and money point of view. Recently the work has become a new discipline. No longer is the chief financial officer or risk manager tasked with sorting it out. Business continuity planning is now a discipline.

It is critical for those in charge of BCP to work hand in glove with facilities and the IT user group. Separate silo configurations driven by budget, arrogance, turf, and fear will fail, and the cost to the company will be irreplaceable time, money, and credibility. Humility is the key for users and vendors. We all have something to add and learn.

If we learned anything from the events surrounding Y2K, it was that it is very easy to overspend when shared experience and levels of expertise are in short supply and fear is malignant. Ask any serious executive where headquarters should be and what it should look like, and you will get several intelligent responses. Ask the same senior-level executives where the primary or secondary data centers should be, how far they should be from the primary headquarters, and you will get long silences and a few good questions.

The selection of BCP industry experts or the hiring of an in-house BCP expert needs to be well thought out. These experts will be protecting the most important assets of your company: intellectual capital, time, and money.

The public sector has done a good job of providing guidelines for businesses uniquely impacted by both short-term and prolonged human interventions and acts of God. Self-help and understanding your peers' best practices are the most common and time- and cost-sensitive methods of protecting a company's brand, life, and revenue. Understand the local, state, federal, and association rules and laws but be judicious and prudent about how and where to spend your most valuable resource: time.

9

Government's Role: Summary of National Infrastructure Protection Plan of 2006

It is worth discussing the government's role in the world of business continuity and mission-critical facilities. Some believe the government has participated too much in parameters and protocol for siting and planning. Many believe it has not gone far enough in guiding or mandating levels of redundancy required and minimum distances for business continuity planning (BCP) sites from primary sites.

Two big drivers for recent legislation and visibility for mission-critical facilities siting and infrastructure integrity are the Enron/MCI insider bad behavior and the events of September 11, 2001. The Sarbanes-Oxley (SOX) legislation and subsequent law that was a reaction to bad-guy behavior on Wall Street did identify some facility and information technology (IT) benchmarks that are now landmarks for financial compliance and indirect facilities that support IT kit that confirm that compliance. The falling of the towers inspired partnerships of best practices to identify and solve the challenges of how to keep the free markets operating without government intervention, efficiently and with reasonable liquidity. The challenges identified included but were not limited to IT, human, facilities, outside plant (OSP) telecom, and OSP power.

A summary of the "national strategies" for what to do and how to do it is outlined by the Homeland Securities Doctrine July 2002. It establishes the nation's strategic Homeland Security objectives and outlines the six critical missions and areas necessary to achieve those objectives. The strategy also provides a framework to earn resources over the federal budget directly to the task of securing the homeland. The strategy specifies eight major initiatives to protect the nation's Critical Infrastructure and Key Resources, one of which specifically calls for the development of the National Institute of Physical Protection (NIPP).

The National Strategy for Physical Protection of Critical Infrastructures and Key Assets was established in February 2003. It identifies policy, goals, objectives, and principles for actions needed to "secure the infrastructures and key assets, national security, governance, public health and safety, economy, and public confidence." It also provides a unifying organizational structure for the Critical Infrastructure and Key Resources and protection, and identifies specific initiatives related to the NIPP to drive near-term national production priorities and inform the resource allocation process.

The National Strategy to Secure Cyberspace established in February 2003 sets forth objectives and specific actions to prevent cyberattacks against America's Critical Infrastructure and Key Resources, reduce nationally identified vulnerability to cybertax, minimize damage, and recover time from cyberattacks. The strategy provides vision for server security and serves as the foundation for security for the country's Critical Infrastructure and Key Resources.

The National Strategy to Combat Terrorism was established in February 2003. This strategy provides a comprehensive overview of the terrorist threat and sets specific goals and objectives to combat this threat including measures to:

- Defeat terrorism and their organizations.
- Deny sponsorship support and sanctuary for terrorists.
- Diminish the underlying conditions that terrorist attacks seek to exploit.
- Defend U.S. citizens and an incumbent interest at home and abroad.

The National Society for Maritime Security, established in September 2005, provides the framework to integrate and synchronize the existing department-level strategies and ensure their effective and efficient implementation. It aligns all the federal government's maritime security programs and initiatives into a comprehensive and cohesive national effort involving appropriate federal, state, local, and private entities.

The National Intelligence Strategy of the United States outlines the fundamental values, priorities, and orientation of the intelligence community. As directed by the director of national intelligence, the strategy outlines the specific mission objectives that relate to efforts to predict, penetrate, and preempt threats to national security. To establish this, the efforts of the different enterprises of the intelligence community are integrated through policy doctrine technology and by ensuring that the intelligence efforts are coordinated through the nation's Homeland Security missions. This requires real and significant cooperation between humans of various organizations, egos aside.

The Homeland Security Presidential Directives (HSPD), which are different from the national strategies, come in the form of HSPD 1, which is an organization and operation of the Homeland Security Council established in October 2001.

HSPD 1 establishes the Homeland Security Council and the committing structure for developing, coordinating, and embedding Homeland Security policy among executive departments and agencies. The directive provides a mandate for the Homeland Security Council to ensure the coordination of all Homeland Security–related activities among the executive departments and agencies and promotes the effective development and implementation of all Homeland Security policies. The council is responsible for arbitrating and coordinating any policy issues that may arise among the different partners and agencies under the NIPP.

HSPD 2, which combats terrorism through immigration policies, was established in October 2001. HSPD 2 establishes policies and programs to enhance the federal government's capabilities for preventing aliens who engage in and/or support terrorist activities from entering the United States and for detaining, prosecuting, or deporting any such aliens who are in the country. HSPD 2 also directs the Attorney General to create the foreign terrorist tracking task force to ensure that the maximum enforcement extent permitted by law. Federal agencies coordinate programs to deny entry into the United States of aliens associated with, suspected of being engaged in, or supporting terrorist activity; and to locate, detain, prosecute, and deport any such aliens already present in the United States.

HSPD 3, established in March 2002, is the Homeland Security Advisory system. It mandates the creation of an alert system for disseminating information regarding the risk of terrorist acts to the federal, state, and local authorities as well as the public. It also includes the requirement for coordinating a set of proactive measures for federal, state, and local governments to be implemented depending on the threat conditions such as systems that provide warnings in the form of a set of graduated threat conditions that are elevated at risk or threat increases. For each threat condition, federal departments and agencies are required to implement a corresponding set of protective measures. Remember orange and red notices and alerts?

HSPD 4, established in 2002, is the National Strategy to Combat Weapons of Mass Destruction (WMD). This directive outlines a strategy that includes three principal pillars:

1. Counterproliferation to combat WMD use
2. Strengthen nonproliferation to combat WMD proliferation
3. Consequence management to respond to WMD use

It also outlines four cross-cutting functions to be pursued on the priority basis:

1. Intelligent collection and analysis on WMD delivery systems and related technologies
2. Our need to improve our ability to address evolving threats
3. Bilateral and multilateral cooperation
4. Targeted strategies against hostile nations and terrorists

HSPD 5, the Management of Domestic Incidents, was established in February 2003. It establishes a national approach to domestic management that ensures effective coordination among all levels of government and the private sector. Central to this approach is the National Incident Management System (NIMS), an organization framework for all levels of government, and the National Response Plan (NRP), an operation framework for the national incident response.

In this directive, the president designates the secretary of Homeland Security as the principal federal official for domestic incident management and empowers the secretary to coordinate federal resources for the prevention, preparedness, response, and recovery related to terrorist attacks, major disasters, and other emergencies. The directive assigns specific responsibilities to the Attorney General, secretary of Defense, secretary of State, and assistants to the president for the Homeland Security and national security affairs, and directs the heads of all federal departments and agencies to provide their "full and prompt coordination, resources, and support" as appropriate and consistent with their own responsibilities for protecting national security to the secretary of Homeland Security, Attorney General, secretary of Defense, secretary of State, and the exercise of leadership and responsibilities and missions assigned in HSPD 5.

HSPD 6, an integration use of screening information, was established in September 2003. HSPD 6 consolidates the federal government's approach to terrorist screening by establishing a terrorist screening center. Federal departments and agencies are directed to provide terrorist information to the terrorist threat integration center, which is then required to provide all relevant information intelligence to the terrorist screening center to protect against terrorism. This directive established the national policy to:

1. Develop, integrate, and maintain thorough, accurate, and current information about which individuals are known or are appropriately expected to be or have been engaging in conduct constituting the preparation for, in the aid of, or related to terrorism.

2. Use that information as appropriate and to the full extent permitted by law to support a federal, state, territory or local, tribal form of government, and private sector screening process by diplomatic, military intelligence, law enforcement, immigration, visa, and protective processes.

HSPD 7, established in December 2003, is perhaps the most important directive. HSPD 7 establishes the framework for the federal department and agencies to identify, prioritize, and protect the critical infrastructure and key resources from terrorist attacks, with emphasis on protecting against catastrophic health effects and mass casualties. This directive establishes the national policy for federal departments and agencies to identify and prioritize U.S. Critical Infrastructure (CI) and Key Resources (KR) and to protect them from terrorist attacks. It mandates the creation and implementation of the NIPP and sets forth and protects responsibilities for the Department of Homeland Security, Social Security Administration, and other federal departments and agencies, state, local, tribal, private sector, and other security partners.

HSPD 8, the national preparedness directive, was established in December 2003. HSPD 8 establishes policies to strengthen the preparedness of the United States to prevent, protect, respond to, and recover from threat under actual domestic terrorist attacks, major disasters, and other agencies by requiring national domestic all-hazard preparedness goals. It establishes mechanisms for improved delivery of federal preparedness, assistance to state and local governments, and outlines actions to strengthen the capabilities of federal, state, and local entities. This directive mandates the development of the goal to guide emergency preparedness training, planning, equipment, and exercises and to ensure that all entities involved adhere to the same standards. It calls for an inventory of the federal response capabilities and refines the process by which preparedness grants are administered, distributed, and utilized at the state and local levels.

HSPD 9, the directive regarding the defense of U.S. agriculture and food, was established in January 2004. HSPD 9 establishes an integrated national policy for improving intellectual intelligence operations, emergency response capabilities, information-sharing mechanisms, migration strategies, and sector vulnerabilities assessment to defend the agriculture and food system against terrorist attacks, major disasters, and other emergencies.

HSPD 11, the Comprehensive Terrorist Related Screening Procedures directive, was established in August 2004 and requires the creation of a strategy and implementation plan for the coordinated and comprehensive approach to terrorist screening in order to improve and expand procedures to screen people, cargo, conveyances, and other entities and objects that pose a threat.

HSPD 12, a policy for Common Identification for federal employees and contractors, was established in August 2004. It establishes a mandatory, government-wide standard for securing reliable forms of identification issued by the federal government to its employees and contractors in order to enhance security, increase government efficiency, reduce identity fraud, and protect personal privacy. The resulting mandatory standard was issued by the National Institute of Standards and Technology as the federal information process standard publication.

HSPD 13 is a Maritime Security Policy established in December 2004. It directs the coordination of the U.S. government and maritime security programs and initiatives to achieve a comprehensive and cohesive national effort involving the appropriate federal, state, local, and private entities. The directive also establishes a maritime security policy coordination committee to coordinate interagency maritime security policy efforts.

HSPD 14 is a Domestic Nuclear Detection Organization established in April 2005. HSPD 14 establishes the effect of nuclear and radiological detection capabilities across federal, state, local, and tribal governments in the private sector for a managed, coordinative response. This directive supports and enhances the effective sharing and use of appropriate information generated by the intelligence committee, law enforcement agencies, the counterterrorism committee, and other government agencies, and foreign governments, as well as providing appropriate information to those entities.

Other supporting groups designed to enhance security are "Authorities Relevant to the Monitoring and Protection of Our National Infrastructure and Security of the Homeland" as it relates to Mission Critical Facilities and effectively the American Freedoms or Executive Order 13231, Critical Infrastructure Protection in the Information Age, established in October 2001 and amended February 28, 2003. This executive order provides specific policy direction to ensure the protection of information systems for critical infrastructure including emergency preparedness communications, and the physical assets that support such systems. It is nice to know that provisions the government has in place as a corporate user allocate resources for business continuity and second-site mission-critical facilities. The government recognizes the important role that networked information systems (critical information infrastructure) play in supporting all aspects of our civil society in the economy and the increased degree to which other critical infrastructure sectors have become dependent on such systems. This executive order formally establishes the U.S. policy, recognizes the need to protect against the disruption of the operations of these systems, and ensures that any disruptions that do occur are infrequent, of minimal duration, manageable, and cause the least damage possible. The executive order specifically calls for the implementation of the policy to include "a voluntary public private partnership involving corporate, nongovernment organizations."

The order also reaffirms existing authorities and responsibilities assigned to various executive branch agencies and interagency committees to secure the security and integration of federal information systems generally and national security information systems in particular. This is a unique and special executive order. Communications distributed are private sector and quasi public sector critical organizations. Best practices between such organizations are sometimes partially shared, but not entirely, due to obvious market edge and market penetration concerns. Best practices and documentation (maps) are even more challenging to access for strategically placed data centers due to heightened security in the post–September 11 world. In reality, however, more often than not the vendor is too lazy to provide accurate documentation or too embarrassed to show that mapping has not been updated recently in the expense-cutting world. The first telecommunications people to be fired in the effort to contain operating expenses were mapping people, since no more fiber was going in the ground.

The National Infrastructure Security Council (NIAC) is another authority established on September 29, 2005. It establishes the NIAC as the president's principal advisor and panel on critical infrastructure issues spanning all sectors. The NIAC is composed of not more than 30 members appointed by the president who are selected from private sector academia and state and local government representing senior executive leadership, expertise from the critical infrastructure, and the key resource areas as delineated in HSPD 7. This is important. It is the president's attempt to effectively get the pulse to the people. Those who sit on this board can and do influence public sector initiatives and spending.

The NIAC provides the president, through the secretary of Homeland Security, with advice on the security of critical infrastructure, both physical and cyber, supporting important sections of the economy. It also has the authority to provide advice directly to the heads of other departments who have shared responsibility for critical infrastructure protection, including Homeland Security (HS), the Department of Transportation (DOT), and the Department of Energy (DOE). The NIAC is charged to improve the cooperation and partnership between the public and private sectors in securing critical infrastructure. It advises on policies and strategies that range from risk assessment and management to information sharing to protective strategies and clarification on roles and responsibilities between public and private sectors.

Executive order 12382 is the president's National Security Telecommunications Advisory Committee (NSTAC), amended February 28, 2003. This executive order creates the NSTAC, which provides the president, through the secretary of Homeland Security, information and advice from the perspective of the telecommunications industry with respect to implementation of the national security telecommunications policy. This order establishes best practices among telecommunications since the deregulation of 1996. The last authority worth mentioning at this point is the executive order 12472, which is the assignment of the national security and emergency preparedness telecommunications functions, amended February 28, 2003. This order assigns to the National Security Council emergency procedures telecommunications functions during both wartime and peace. Office of Science, Technology Policy (OSTP), Homeland Security Council, Office of Management and Budget (OMB), another federal agency. The executive orders seek to ensure that the federal government has telecommunication services that will function under all conditions, including emergencies. This executive order established the National Communication System (NCS) with the mission to assist the president on the National Security Council, the Homeland Security Council, and directors of the OSTP and the OMB. The exercise of the telecommunications functions and responsibilities set forth in the executive order, the coordination of planning for the provision of national security/emergency procedures communications for the federal government under all circumstances including crisis and emergency, tack recovery, and reconstitution. This is of unique interest for citizens in New York. Our ability to communicate among ourselves and with the financial markets as well as with the national government is critical. These communications capabilities need to be to military specifications. My proprietary solution for such challenges is the "Air Pipe Mini Man" system, which is a nonterrestrial and terrestrial (patent pending) telecommunications solution that combines Centrex and Internet protocol technologies through free space optics (FSO), and radio-frequency (RF) aerial solutions coupled with self-healing scalable, burstable, and synchronous optical networks (SONET).

SONET metropolitan area networks footprints in rings in urban environments. The business model incorporates equal parts of capital participation among the government, landlords, optronics providers, and telecom operating companies.

Long-distance and short-distance technology had to be considered before migrating to RF and FSO and fiber solution. Satellite technology has been around since October 4, 1957, with the launch of the Soviet Union's Sputnik. The United States had bounced radar signals off the moon since 1948. In 1958, the United States launched Explorer 1, which provided environmental information to. These projects led the way for commercially viable communications applications. The first broadcast from space or satellite came on December 19, 1958, when President Dwight D. Eisenhower broadcast a Christmas greeting.

The mission-critical applications for satellites are not considered commercially viable due to latency from extraordinary travel distances of the five "bands":

1. L band
2. S band
3. C band
4. K band
5. X band (military)

Another reason for the reluctance to consider the satellite system for mission-critical use are the multiple Earth stations (requiring uninterruptable power supply [UPS] support) that double as single points of failure.

The candidate commercially deployed satellite options are:

- **LEOs.** Low Earth orbit—2,000 kilometers from Earth
- **MEOs.** Medium Earth orbit—10,000 kilometers from Earth
- **GEOs.** Geostationary (rotates twice in 24 hours)—35,000 kilometers from Earth

The latency of the data from Earth to the satellite and back to Earth varies with the size of the "packet" (package of encryption). For noncritical applications, this is a viable transmission application. On July 10, 1962, Elvis Presley performed live via AT&T's Telestar 1. On September 30, 1975, Home Box Office offered the Ali–Frazier heavyweight fight, "Thrilla in Manila," live. In 1976, Ted Turner launched his supersized network from Atlanta. Improvements were made in the late 1970s to the National Oceanic Atlantic Association System for weather and INMARSAT (International Maritime Organization of the Satellite Organization), which provided a global positioning system (GPS) to the seas. Currently *USA Today* sends its news by satellite to be printed locally rather than shipping paper around the world just in time.

GEOs are the most reliable and largest bandwidth but the farthest away. LEOs are the closest and fastest, but due to gravitational pull, they last only five to seven years before they come through Earth's atmosphere and disintegrate. (Currently thousands of satellites are orbiting Earth; plenty are junk.) LEOs are the size of a small van, and several can be launched with a single rocket; only two satellites of the GEO size can be launched with a single rocket.

The long and the short of it is that the latency and serviceability of the assets discourage real-time users with .15 to .35 milliseconds or shorter self-healing thresholds by the options of fiber optic–based systems. This does not stop credit card companies and others from using satellites. I believe that the shorter-distance RF and FSO applications are viable.

In one speaking engagement following the attacks of September 11, 2001, Stanley Sporkin, the Securities and Exchange Commission's enforcement director, stated:

> The public corporation is under severe attack because of the many improper revelations of corporate activity. It is not simple to assess the cause of this misconduct since it has taken so many forms. The one-dimensional explanation that such conduct is a way of life is simply not acceptable.

Sporkin was outlining benefits of what was to become the Sarbanes-Oxley Act. Was SOX a wise policy or a political overreaction to the actions of Enron, WorldCom, Tyco, Adelphia, and others? What does it have to do with data centers and business continuity?

> To prevent organizations from defaulting on their obligations and creating a widespread solvency crisis, the Federal Reserve provided over $320,000,000,000 in funding to banks over the period from September 11 to September 14, 2001.[1]

The SEC effectively was saying that the free market system was at risk, and the U.S. government covered all bets for "in-flight," or open, trades. Whether the SOX legislation was an overreaction to the ethical shortcomings of corporate America, a cornerstone for the need to "have a plan, test the plan, and document the plan," as the legislation indicates, or a financial reaction to the $320 billion of at-risk money the United States put up to cover all trades on September 11, industry trends were now forming.

- Where do I place a primary, secondary, or tertiary data center?
- How large should the facility be? What is the growth delta given today's potential and future technology?

- How do I weigh the outside plan consideration of power distribution, air flight paths, gas lines, topology, railway proximity, multitenant, multistory, and so on?
- Do I stay synchronous or go asynchronous for SONET distribution of encrypted data?
- What size human component should support the site?
- What duration of interruption should I plan for?
- What are my peers doing and where?
- Should the U.S. government be a stakeholder in solutions?

To answer some of these questions, there are some inherent discrepancies based on white paper 1, white paper 2, documented acts of God, and commercially deployed IT technology that need to be identified. White paper 1 asked the United States and appropriate associations and companies what measures should be taken to minimize future challenges created by regional and catastrophic events. The second white paper summarized the first white paper's response as a best practice summary from companies, individuals, and associations, each with different levels of experience and outage impact.

According to the association of contingency planners, the minimum for distances in miles from a primary site varies depend on the act of God or human intervention. For instance, for a volcano, it is over 100 miles. For a civilian airport, it is just over 20 miles. So just briefly, steering committees prefer that the primary data center to be a minimum of:

- 20 miles from a civilian airport
- 25 miles from a central office, telecommunications hub for optronics, and IP telephony
- 30 miles from a power grid failure
- 30 miles from a tornado
- 32 miles from a forest fire
- 45 miles from a military installation
- 45 miles from flooding
- 50 miles from a tsunami
- 60 miles from an earthquake
- 63 miles from snow, sleet, and ice
- Over 100 miles from a hurricane

In other words, the path of destruction given various failures or acts of God is based on relevant data.

What does this have to do with a minimum preferred distance in miles from a primary site of event? The thinking is that the event should not cause a catastrophic failure of both environments: the home office and the data center.

For second-site location criteria, the association of contingency planners was asked another question: Is it permissible for the alternate site to be subject to the same threat/risk as the primary site? In other words, can these two be in the same relevant footprint? The answers vary depending on the threat/risk.

Risk	% that Say No
Earthquake	97%
Hurricane	97%
Tsunami	97%
Forest fire	95%
Power grid	95%
Central office	94%
Volcano	94%
Flood	92%
Military installation	81%
Tornado	76%
Snow, sleet, ice	72%

You get the point. Critical assets should not be in the same relevant footprint. So what becomes the challenge?

The challenge becomes SEC white paper 1, which effectively asks what you think we ought to do. In the survey that preceded the white paper, 74 respondents (including me) responded. The second white paper came out months later and said "this is what we think you think." It indicates that second sites should be about 250 miles away from primary sites. What this means is that effectively, throughput data of either technology needs to catch up with the distance, or there will be a failure in SONET of volume and scale in the unlikely event of an interruption. As I said earlier, commercially deployed synchronous technology is plus or minus 40 route miles. If the Euclidean distance suggested in white paper 2 is 250 miles and we can only successfully capture data 40 route miles (or 20 to 30 Euclidean miles), an inherent conflict exists. Companies can vault encryption approximately 180 miles synchronously vendor specific (with some corruption or data latency), but we believe the technology will catch up to the distances and grow synchronous rings. But a challenge exists for companies trying to comply now and that want to protect their valuable assets of brand, human infrastructure, and time.

Also, one size does not fit all. The SEC guidelines for financial service firms effectively divided users into two groups for compliance prior to April 2006:

Tier 1. Two-hour recovery for core clearing and payment users.

Tier 2. Four-hour recovery for firms playing a significant role in financial fabric of the markets (effectively all others).

So if you are Tier 1 and you are clearing, if you are doing core clearing for payment users, effectively clearing for broker-dealers in other companies, the SEC mandates that you need a two-hour recovery time for core clearing. Tier 2 is effectively everybody else. These two tiers make up the SOX mandate to have a plan, document a plan, and test a plan.

This legislation and law effectively gave a framework for those looking for guidance and only guidance for the planning of a second site or primary site given the governmental framework. The National Fire Protection Association (NFPA) 1600 guidelines evolved from the National Association of Securities Dealers (NASD) rules. There really is no framework in NFPA 1600. It does not say N plus 1, N plus 2, how many modules, how much redundancy, how many humans, how big the test lab space should be, what the time of duration planned for is, what type of space, how much fuel storage, or how much water storage. Nor is there is a lot of documentation regarding these details. NFPA 1600 is four pages of copy out of 63 pages referencing nonspecific parameters coupled with a directory of whom to call in your region for support. There is not a lot of specific direction provided. I am not sure there should be, since a one-size solution does not fit all; but if you are looking for a connect-the-dots solution, you won't find it here.

What the NASD and NFPA 1600 did do is open up the doors for business continuity planning at a high level. They effectively helped guide users by explaining:

- A thorough business impact analysis needs to be developed or a profit and loss for a company as well as a facility's IT legal executive and human resources.
- Companies must develop a strategy for satisfying a business impact analysis via options analysis based on the following criteria. A tiered recovery structure that is driven by established recovery time objectives,
- A recovery sequence that is driven from system/application in human interdependencies (untangling the kit).
- Rough order of magnitude (ROM) cost associated with each recovery option.

The SEC coupled with SOX's Sections 302 and 304 effectively created the framework for legitimate corporate governance.

Again, SOX Section 302 indicates that chief executive officers and chief financial officers shall personally certify financial statements and filings as well as affirm that they are responsible for establishing and enforcing controls.

SOX Section 404 requires an annual evaluation of internal controls and procedures for financial reports and their testing/maintenance. This effectively put corporate responsibility on the user.

SOX Section 302 requires a statement:

- Certifying that officers are responsible for establishing and maintaining internal control over financial reporting.
- Certifying that officers who are designing internal controls apply generally accepted accounting principles (GAAP) methods.
- That reports any changes in the internal reporting methods.

This section effectively puts IT in the SOX compliance game. It is where internal controls at a material level can be implemented and managed in documents. Effectively, the SEC became the "beat." It became the new cops. A net result of SOX implementation was that more than 1,300 public companies needed to be tracked:

- 7,500 broker-dealers had to fall into compliance. Of those, many were in Tier 2 or under $75 million of market capitalization.
- 8,500 investment advisors needed to comply.
- 40,000 mutual funds needed to be compliant.

SOX compliance put and associated IT, real estate, and BCP challenges in the game of risk assessment and revenue protection, and that is extraordinary.

SOX and real estate effectively communicated a few results:

- SOX spelled out a law contained in Section 404 requirements that generated more ripples into the IT industry (and associated spending) than any of the legislation or meaningful events since Y2K.
- A significant outcome of Section 404 is that IT can no longer keep the technology lid on its world.
- SOX auditors will be delving deeply into IT infrastructure to test the validity and accruing of internal IT controls. Currently, we are waiting for SOX Two. SOX is not conclusive. I believe a body of a work in progress and will change with the sensitivities of the public to monitoring and catching the bad guys. It will also change with the collective and legislative willingness to add cost to compliance and conduct business in the United States versus other less regulated or

monitored parts of the world. Last, it will change based on current events of businesspeople behaving badly and business interruption via human intervention or acts of God.

SOX also requires that auditors maintain their work for five years:

- This prohibits the destruction of documents.
- There is up to a 20-year prison sentence if SOX is not complied with.
- The reason for such a harsh penalty is that no forensic accounting is possible without data. Documentation is required.
- The role of IT and specialized real estate is critical.

There is a catch regarding SOX in the future. SOX is intentionally vague and broad on what internal controls are required to meet auditing standards. Although GAAP methods are applied, standards are not. It is likely that, in the future, SOX will morph into another, less tangled legislation. However, SOX was a good starting point. It was based on the financial outcry of investors but has drifted into the value and importance of IT, systems managers, integrators, BCP compliance, and disaster recovery auditors. Failure to comply with Sarbanes-Oxley exposes senior management to possible prison time—up to 20 years, with penalties up to $5 million, or both. Addressing and satisfying some of the new legislation inspired by SOX, SEC guidelines, and common sense highlight the importance of what is often referred to as the three Cs:

1. **Communication.** The relevant needs of the user groups and the concentric circles of impact. Those needs have an IT facilities and human infrastructure.
2. **Cooperation.** Implementing the give-and-take of process management with full disclosure of time scope and budget challenges among user groups.
3. **Coordination.** Coordination of the mission statement with scheduled breakpoints in the process of design and development for the outside plant and inside plant improvement civility program.

The data center must be placed where there is the day-to-day human infrastructure to support the company at the asset during a short-term or prolonged interruption. Strategic employees need to be able and willing to continue the business of business.

As discussed earlier, if the asset is within 26 kilometers of synchronous encryption distance to a primary asset, it may well be affected by the same act of God or human intervention. This may cause significant congestion in the railways, transportation, telecommunications, but most important, in the willingness of a human infrastructure to work. The farther away from the event, the more likely the staff is to be able and willing to recover the operations. Those of us who lived in the Northeast mourned, cried, and were moved by the catastrophic bombing in Oklahoma City. However, we went to work. During the events of September 11, 2001, people in Boston, Philadelphia, and Washington were less likely to go to work because everybody knew someone who was impacted by the catastrophic event.

One of the more popular solutions to the challenges put forth by the seamless continuation of operations for a company is a bunker scenario.

Triangulation is being employed more and more for the preservation and storage of both critical and noncritical data. The synchronous relevance of data has been discussed as well as the importance of the route miles and speed-of-light threshold that must be recognized and respected. The asynchronous and remote topology assumes that remote data storage and manipulation and BCP operations can and will be effective in parts of the world that are less expensive by 30 to 50% and just as effective for nonmirrored applications (see Exhibit 9.1).

What is a bunker and why a bunker? Second-site selection for the standalone asset or bunker scenario has become more exacting, effectively capturing in-flight data synchronously or relevant to primary accounting. We will discuss sites within sites and the value of milliseconds in Chapter 16.

The unsettled part of the process is that it has a level of interest in direct relationship to current events and particularly media covered same as acts of God are largely responsible for the extended or prolonged outages.

Guidelines for this bunker scenario are not to be interrupted is generally:

- Single story, high ceiling, heavy floor load (two-story building is acceptable).
- Walls and roof built to withstand minimum winds of 150 to 250 miles per hour with debris category 3 to 4.
- Diverse feeds of power and telecommunications are buried into asset.
- One mile from highway. First ring of evacuation by first-responder emergency medical service (EMS), fire, or police is 1,500 feet for spill containment, fire, or hazardous materials.
- 15 miles from commercial airports of fixed based operations (FBOs). Distance where instrument flight ratings turn to manual flight ratings where the pilot effectively takes back the controls for take-offs and landings. This is the riskiest part of air flight. Landing is effectively an organized crash.

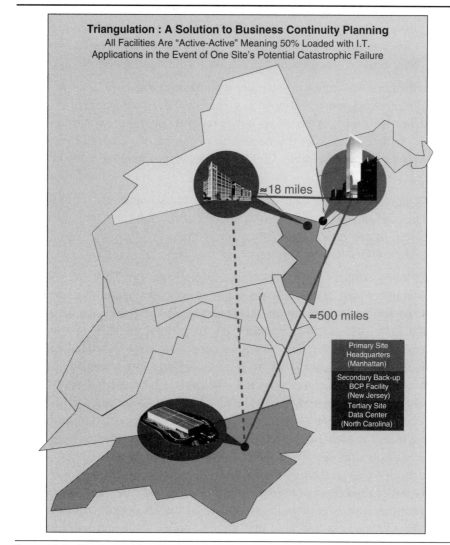

EXHIBIT 9.1   TOPOLOGY MAP: TRIANGULATION

- 50 miles from nuclear facility. Kill zone is 18 miles downwind of an event, where potassium iodine pills are issued by the government to retard contamination and effects of exposure. The Nuclear Regulatory Committee states that 50 miles is the kill zone for agriculture and livestock.

- 20 miles from urban or dirty bomb scenarios. That is a conservative distance for wind drift for nuclear particles or germ warfare. (By the way, this rules out most assets synchronous to New York City.)
- Near remote, passable transportation for human support.

For financial institutions, securities companies, and banks, what to do, how to protect accounts, and how to secure new accounts requires the right human infrastructure, in house or outsourced, to guide a user through this process and is critical from a time and money point of view. It is very easy to overspend in this discipline. Commonsense suggestions for newcomers to this area are:

- Understand the fundamentals of the business impact analysis (BIA).
- In brief, understand the pros and cons of the four recovery scenarios.
- Be familiar with a short list of acronyms.
- Align yourself with experience.

Like many parts of business continuity planning and BIA, the devil is in the details, which means "do the math." Metric evaluation of engineered system performance is becoming commonplace. Not only should systems be evaluated to determine availability, but they should be designed initially with availability in mind. The increased collection of historical failure data is allowing mathematical models to more accurately reflect engineered system functions. Point estimates, such as mean time between failure (MTBF) and mean time between repair (MTBR), are being augmented with more sophisticated distribution estimates to develop system-level failure profiles.

Say a user's goal is get to five 9s or six 9s reliability. That equates to 35 seconds of downtime per year. What if the system is to last 6 or 60 years? How does that change the metrics? Solutions to this problem are derived from the mission or mission system requirements and include the monetary cost of the downtime. This is done in the BIA. The BIA analyzes how much money is lost by the moment and how that metric applies to capital improvement dollars and upper expense expectations. A team champion, an organizer, or a facilities head or IT manager may evaluate each subsystem by the effect of the outage on mission successes. For instance, why would you put a two-N generator plant in a facility with a single telecommunications fiber optic feed? In other words, there needs to be consistency and continuity in systems integrity from power distribution, to cooling, to IT distribution, to redundancy at the rack. As discussed earlier, I suggest setting, as a team, benchmarks or a framework for expectations early on and working toward them as a team.

The failure of any firm that plays a significant role in the financial markets to perform critical services could present a systemic risk and therefore a risk to the U.S. economy. Such firms include printing companies, employment agencies, IT outsourcing, and others. Many, if not most, of the 15 to 20 major banks and the 5 to 10 major securities firms and possibly others play at least one significant role in at least one critical market. This means that effectively all components—human, IT, facilities, real estate, financial, and intellectual capital—need to be on the same page in terms of level of redundancy and time and effort associated with designing and implementing meaningful BCPs.

Let me return to why we go through the time and effort to orchestrate, coordinate, and implement plans anticipating a short- or long-term interruption of power of fiber optic distribution, two critical assets of critical data.

Exhibit 9.2 reveals in an easy-to-read format the source and duration of the unplanned outage. Collectively we determine the reliability of a circuit by 9s by breaking down the minutes lost per year and then by average. We then make judgments regarding the source of the interruption. For instance, if the

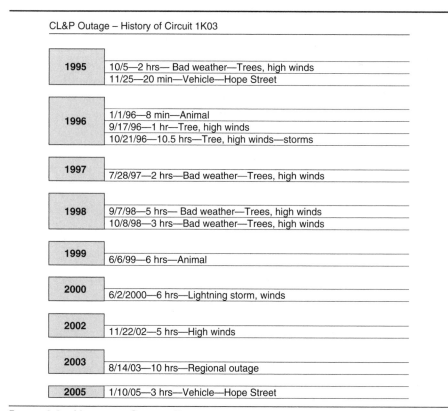

CL&P Outage – History of Circuit 1K03

| 1995 | 10/5—2 hrs— Bad weather—Trees, high winds |
| | 11/25—20 min—Vehicle—Hope Street |

1996	1/1/96—8 min—Animal
	9/17/96—1 hr—Tree, high winds
	10/21/96—10.5 hrs—Tree, high winds—storms

| 1997 | |
| | 7/28/97—2 hrs—Bad weather—Trees, high winds |

| 1998 | 9/7/98—5 hrs— Bad weather—Trees, high winds |
| | 10/8/98—3 hrs—Bad weather—Trees, high winds |

| 1999 | |
| | 6/6/99—6 hrs—Animal |

| 2000 | |
| | 6/2/2000—6 hrs—Lightning storm, winds |

| 2002 | |
| | 11/22/02—5 hrs—High winds |

| 2003 | |
| | 8/14/03—10 hrs—Regional outage |

| 2005 | 1/10/05—3 hrs—Vehicle—Hope Street |

EXHIBIT 9.2   HISTORY OF OUTAGES TEMPLATE

circuit is mounted on a timber pole and we see "drunk driver" as a source with frequency, we can make some conclusions about the road conditions, pole placements, and part of region. Often we see rodent or fallen branches, and we can make assumptions about maintenance or tree trimming. As our national infrastructure gets older and repair and replacement get more important to the utilities, tenants or users need to make some broad assumptions of the outside plant infrastructure in conjunction with the useful life of any potential mission-critical asset. Plenty of the nation's circuits and substations are meeting or surpassing their useful life. As we find ourselves in the world of "not in my backyard," we take the history of interruptions and consider the infrastructure repair, replacement, and growth possibilities. Many substations are now landlocked with no growth possible. Many areas will be reluctant to have new high-voltage lines or towers near or close to newly populated areas.

As Exhibit 9.3 shows, the causes of unplanned downtime are 7% uncertain, 8% environmental factors (natural disaster), 17% network transmission failure, 18% human error, 23% hardware system failure, and 27% software system failure. The 18% human error can also have an impact on system software failure, so that data point could be coupled elsewhere. The interesting data points here are the environmentals, or the natural disasters; they account for only 8% of the outages. However, these natural outages are of significant duration. Software, hardware, or human issues generally are resolved and rectified within an hour. Natural factors, however, often continue 6 to 12 hours.

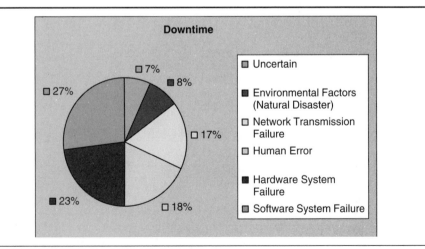

EXHIBIT 9.3 TIME DURATION OF INTERRUPTION

Causes of unplanned downtime over 12 hours for data points, source contingency plan, and research, 4% of 12-hour outages is other, 7% hardware, 9% earthquake, 13% fire and bombing, 16% flood and burst pipe, 20% storm damage, and 31% power related. Data points for storm damage and power related are often combined, but effectively 50%, 20%, and then 31%. Effectively 50% of prolonged outages are power and storm related; that is why we spend so much time evaluating the OSP issues of acts of God and man-made challenges. Over 35% of a data center spend is on unique improvements for unintended interruptions; often these run into the multimillion-dollar range. That is why we spend so much time with utilities, rights-of-way, tree trimming, and maintenance and operation of substations. The well-documented negative cascading issues of the West Coast and in the Northeast have brought real dollar consequences not only to the financial institutions but to all user groups.

Homeland Security Presidential Directive 8, approved in 2003, transformed how the federal government proposes to strengthen the nation's preparedness to protect, prevent, respond, and recover from terrorist attacks, major disasters, and other emergencies, and how the government proposes to invest resources in order to achieve the greatest return on investment for the nation's homeland security. To date, the collective efforts of the local, state, and federal governments are worth mentioning, if for no other reason than to show the private sector how much and how long to prepare for unknown consequences, given our capital spend and human infrastructure in the free society.

HSPD 7, the interim national preparedness goal, establishes the national vision and sets measurable readiness targets to strengthen the nation's preparedness. It should be utilized in conjunction with two planning tools: national planning scenarios and target capabilities lists. HSPD 7 is not a microlevel plan to specify how users should to do their work or execute their missions. This document as well as the Homeland Security document, the national infrastructure protection plan, and the secure cyberspace plan really have no parameters regarding primary data center site selection, construction, implementation, or operation.

In 2007, the government's focus was to broaden and address the critical risk-based priorities within its newly defined 36 capabilities or levels of preparedness. States and urban areas revised their programs anticipating crisis or interruption. The states and cities then competed against each other for new funds to satisfy or fulfill requested capabilities. The result was a "mismanagement" of funds. The squeaky wheel does not always get the oil. The challenge of distributing funds was obvious. Rural parts of the United States were likely underfunded and had the most antiquated communications and emergency or first-responder vehicles/equipment and were in most need of training. However, these rural cities and states are also the least likely to be hit by human intervention or acts of God, and disasters there might not play as meaningful a negative role in the U.S. economy as disasters in urban areas. Politics had something to do with where the money went in some cases. Homeland Security submitted fully "updated" preparedness strategies pursuant to the final goal in order to receive federal preparedness assistance. In other words, they had to "have a plan," "document a plan," and "test a plan." This is consistent with SOX's goals for business continuity. These funds are likely to be reduced in many cases.

Remember, the national strategy for the Homeland Security issued in July 2002 stated that the nation must develop "interconnected and complementary homeland security systems that are reinforcing rather than duplicative, and that ensure essential requirements are met." The national strategy provided a framework to align the resources of the federal budget directly to the talk of securing the homeland. That is about as broad as you can make it. The aim of HSPD 8 was:

> to establish policies to strengthen the preparedness of the United States to prevent and respond to threatened or actual domestic terrorist attacks, major disasters, and other emergencies by requiring a national domestic all hazards preparedness goal establishing mechanisms for improved delivery of federal preparedness assistance to state and local governments, and outlining the actions to strengthen the preparedness capabilities to the federal, state, and local entities.

HSPD 8 is the national strategy for homeland security. HSPD 5, 7, and 8 are organizational charts with an implied command chain. There are national initiatives and a national incident management system, but it is not clear how we talk to each other or communicate. There is a national response plan, but how is it implemented? The national infrastructure protection plan has no details. The nation's nuclear power facilities, dams, and other critical infrastructure are protected by little more than a few fences in place; nothing more meaningful to discourage willful acts of human intervention. Realistically, strengthening the protection of all these facilities would be prohibitively expensive.

So what are the results from all the policy directives? A new document, "A Common Approach to National Incident Management, Prevention, Protection, Response, Recovery, and Preparedness." These phrases all sound clever and catchy; however, are we truly safer now? The fact is we have porous borders, our security is not much better, and if we lull ourselves into a sense of false security that our transportation, critical infrastructure, power, pipelines, and urban environments are any safer today than they were on September 10, 2001, it would be truly misleading.

Many of these government-established initiatives call for "engag[ing] the federal, state, local, and tribal entities, their private and nongovernmental partners, and the general public to achieve their sustained, risk-based target levels of capability to prevent, protect against, respond to, and recover from major events in order to minimize the impact on lives, property, and the economy." When was the last time that you went to an ocean or a lake and were asked what were you taking out of the car? When was the last time you went on or near a substation and someone was protecting the infrastructure? To protect a free society, the trickle-down cost would be extraordinary. The reality is a best effort is all we can really do for some regions of the country and infrastructure but plenty of time, money, and facilities should be spent private and public on others.

HSPD 8 states that the national preparedness goals will establish measurable readiness targets that appropriately balance the potential threat and magnitude of terrorist attacks, major disasters, and other emergencies with the resources required to prevent, respond to, and recover from them. This directive was crafted well before the events of Hurricane Katrina. The risk-based target levels of capability will meet that requirement. Effectively, what Homeland Security officials have developed are national planning scenarios that highlight a scope of magnitude and complexity of plausible catastrophic terrorist attacks and major disasters. They developed 15 scenarios that include, but are not limited to, chemical, biological, radiological, nuclear explosive, food, agricultural, and cyber terrorism. A host of natural disasters are included, as well as a pandemic influenza. From the scenarios, the officials have developed tasks, a universal task list (UTL), and provided a menu of tasks from all the resources that may be performed should major events occur. Effectively, they tell you what to do. It is a road map. After they selected only the tasks that apply to their assigned roles and responsibility, prevention, protection, recovery, and response. The intent of the UTL is to guide the design. That is effectively the cornerstone of most of the government documents I have uncovered. Finally the capabilities-based planning and target readiness: Its goal is to have the capabilities. The targeted capabilities list (TCL) provides guidance on specific capabilities and levels of capability that the federal, local, state, and tribal entities will be expected to develop and maintain. There are 36 capabilities summaries. They include, but are not limited to, description outcome, annex, associated critical tasks, measures, capability elements, link capabilities, and event conditions references. They are tailored to two levels of government based on assigned roles and responsibility and tailored to tiers, groups, or jurisdictions based on risk factors. Again, these are guides and guidelines.

The UTL in itself is a bit overwhelming. Merely articulating, documenting, and updating the 36 capabilities would be costly. Think of the time, intellectual capital, and resources it will take for every local, state, and federal government agency to fulfill or satisfy this list of capabilities:

- Animal health emergency support
- Citizen protection, evacuation, and or place protection
- Critical infrastructure protection
- Critical resource logistics and distribution
- Economic and community recovery
- Emergency operations, center management
- Emergency public information and warning
- Environmental health and vector control
- Explosive device response operations
- Fatality management
- Firefighters' operations/support
- Food and agriculture safety and defense
- Information collection and threat recognition
- Information sharing and collaboration
- Intelligence, fusion, and analysis
- Inter-optical communications
- Isolation and quarantine
- Mass care (sheltering, feeding, and related services)
- Mass prophylaxis
- Medical supplies management and distribution
- Medical surge
- On-site incident management
- Planning
- Public health, epidemiological investigation, and laboratory testing
- Public safety and security response
- Restoration of lifelines
- Risk analysis
- Search and rescue
- Structural damage and assessment and mitigation
- Terrorism investigation and intervention
- Triage and pre-hospital treatment
- Volunteer management and donations

- Weapons of mass destruction/hazardous materials response and decontamination
- Worker health and safety

Each capability in the TCL is documented in template format and includes a statement of outcome resulting from the performance of one or more critical tasks to a specific performance standard that may vary for specific operating conditions. For example, a 6-minute response time is called for in clear weather versus a 30-minute response time in a blizzard. A capability may be delivered in an emergency with any combination of elements that achieves the required outcome—namely, properly planned, organized, equipped, trained, and exercised personnel.

The elements of the capability effectively are broken down into six components. Remember, someone needs to put this together, organize it, fund it, document it, and update it.

1. **Personnel.** People who are paid and volunteer staff who meet relevant qualifications, certification standards necessary to perform assigned missions and tasks.

2. **Planning.** Collection and analysis of intelligence and information in the development of policies, plans, procedures, mutual aid agreements, strategies, and other publications to comply with relevant laws, regulations, and guidance necessary to perform assigned missions and tasks.

3. **Organization and leadership.** Individual teams and overall organizational structure and leadership to achieve success levels in the structure that comply with relevant laws, regulations, and guidance necessary to perform assigned missions and tasks.

4. **Equipment and systems.** Major items of equipment, supplies, facilities, and systems that comply with relevant standards necessary to perform assigned missions and tasks.

5. **Training.** Content and methods of delivery that comply with relevant training standards necessary to perform assigned missions and tasks.

6. **Exercises, evaluations, and corrective actions.** Exercises, self-assessments, peer assessments, outside review, compliance monitoring, actual major events that provide opportunities to demonstrate, evaluate, and approve the combined capability of interoperability of the other elements to perform assigned missions and tasks to standards necessary to achieve successful outcomes.

The Department of Homeland Security alleges that their personnel work with federal, state, local, tribal, and private nongovernmental subject matter experts to update the TCL for reissuance. The updated TCL will define levels of capability or success that will enable a nation to minimize the impact on lives, property, and economy for all scenarios.

In the interim national imperatives goal, or HSPD 8, local and state government summarizes the actions that need to be assessed annually with a report card, which they have not been doing very well on. They note that we live in a world transformed by the attacks on September 11, 2001. The 9/11 commission wrote that "a rededication to the preparedness is perhaps the best way to honor the memories of those we lost that day." I believe we are woefully behind in our preparedness and implementation efforts to date. Now the funds are at risk due to misappropriations or misuse, public apathy, and the $10 billion-a-month tab we are running in the Middle East.

If we are looking for meaningful guidance on disaster emergency management and BCP, the government suggests we should look at NFPA 1600 (discussed earlier). The NFPA standards council was established to meet the disaster management committee's needs in January 1991. The committee was given the responsibility for developing documents relating to preparedness for response to and recovery from disasters coming from natural, human, or technological events. The first cut of that committee focused on NFPA 1600 and "recommended practice for disaster management." NFPA 1600 was presented to the NFPA membership at the 1995 annual meeting. That effort produced the 1995 edition of NFPA 1600. The 2000 edition committee incorporated the total program approach "for the disaster management, emergency management, and business continuity programs in its revision of the document from a recommended practice to a standard." The 2004 edition contains updated terminology that has been editorially reformatted to follow the NFPA manual style. The committee added significant information sources to annexes B, C, D, and E. As mentioned, NFPA 1600 itself is only five pages long. The rest of the document is made up of resources, annexes, where to call, and a host of organizations to be contacted in establishing or implementing a disaster recovery program. That, in and of itself, is a little suspicious.

The aim of NFPA 1600 is to standardize and establish a common set of criteria for disaster management, emergency management, and business continuity planning for the private and public sectors. The standards are strategically vague, as are most of the laws, guidelines, decision trees, and best practices.

The private sector has taken the lead and developed standard operating procedures for levels of integrity, pricing, and service-level agreements. According to the Gartner report of October 2007, "Customers reviewing collocation contracts should expect to see at least a 20% price increase in pricing, maybe as much as triple that of three years ago." I disagree with many of their data points, but as a rough order of magnitude they are on point. The Gardner Group consults. They do not build or buy services in a meaningful way. They report.

The Uptime Institute publishes construction costs by tier and kilowatt. It does not build these facilities or take space in them. They are around data points, but they are not "the" data points. In their defense, many of the data points that mission-critical users are looking for often come with qualifiers of day 1 improvements versus future improvements, partially populated cabinet power needs versus fully populated cabinet need, and so on. Users want simple, crisp answers to complex questions. Such answers are hard to come by in mission-critical or business continuity facilities. It is like asking a project manager how much it will cost or how long it will take to build something; unless you buy or trade a piece of long lead equipment, how can you say with credibility what the data points are? They become a group of data points that are cut and pasted from recent bodies of work governed by arrogance and false intelligence. This is typical of garbage in and garbage out.

In summary, NFPA guidelines, public sector required reading, and private sector white papers and "hot topic" copy are often misleading. Often they are crafted by people with no expertise and those who are easily swayed by the opinions of the last person they spoke with.

A standard or vision should provide those with the responsibility for disaster and emergency management and BCPs the criteria to assess current programs or to develop and maintain a program to mitigate, prepare for, respond to, and recover from disasters and emergencies. Vendors who purport to tell you how to do it better, faster, cheaper are common. The standard should guide users to the legitimate questions and concerns.

The standard should apply to both public and private programs. Although the programs may have little in common, tolerances (or lack thereof) for downtime should be similar. Again, beware of vendors who do everything for everybody. Would you hire a sound attenuation expert to handle your structural load issues? Then do not hire an engineer for outside plant telecom, an incentives group for acts of God, or a permitting or accounting company for inside plant design criteria or outside plant topology. Use a little common sense. If the vendor cannot or has not implemented or executed, it should not advise. This is a "process," not a "school."

It is worth mentioning that NFPA 1600 for 1991, 1995, 2000, and 2004 does not approve, inspect, certify, verify, or provide warranties for any installations, procedures, or materials. Nor does it approve or evaluate the testing of laboratories and inside plant infrastructure improvements. Rather, NFPA gives guidelines and is valued for that role. For construction, the local jurisdictions or the local NFPA guidelines and standards are applicable. If you are looking for specific details on how to make something scalable, flexible, and burstable in a cost-efficient manner, NFPA 1600 is probably not the document to use, but it is not a bad starting place.

As we develop our criteria with users on various outside planned consider-ations of acts of God and man-made considerations are tantamount inclusive of railroad tracks, highways, air fields, gas lines, and the ominous nuclear power plant. A case study is the Indian Point Nuclear Power Plant located in Buchanan, New York. Like all nuclear power plants, it has the poten-tial for catastrophic failure. The consequences for such a catastrophic failure are immediate as well as far-reaching. We have 103 nuclear facilities in the United States with more in the design and planning stages; they present unique concerns. If you consider that only 4 ounces of dynamite qualifies as a weapon of mass destruction and a thimbleful of uranium can power an equivalent of 150 barrels of oil, you can see the sensitivity of the larger concerns as well as the dirty bomb (suitcase) scenarios for this man-made substance if fixed or mobile.

Exhibit 9.4 provides visual guidance on the likely and catastrophic rings of damage and potential death given a nuclear failure and leak.

The basis of our opinion is the current radiological emergency prepared-ness plan of New York State, which governs the Indian Point facility, and the Nuclear Regulatory Commission (NRC). The Indian Point Radiologi-cal Emergency Preparedness Plan is certified annually by the governor of New York, four county executives, and the Federal Emergency Management Agency. This is relevant for businesses and citizens who want to know who is responsible for this nuclear power plant.

The focus of the NRC's plan is to evacuate a 10-mile radius surrounding a nuclear facility. We believe the distance of 10 miles surrounding the facility is related to:

- The mathematically, remarkably, and unlikely chance of an event (human or equipment).
- The fact that the average uptime of a nuclear facility in the United States is well over five 9s of reliability.
- In the event of seepage of nuclear waste, it will likely be detected and contained (due to improved detection) swiftly. West-to-east winds will carry such particles of waste one to two knots on average over a short distance (one to five miles).

In 1981, the Indian Point Nuclear Power Facility had the highest population within 10, 30, and 50 miles of any nuclear power plant in the nation. At that time, its population at 50 miles was more than double any other plant

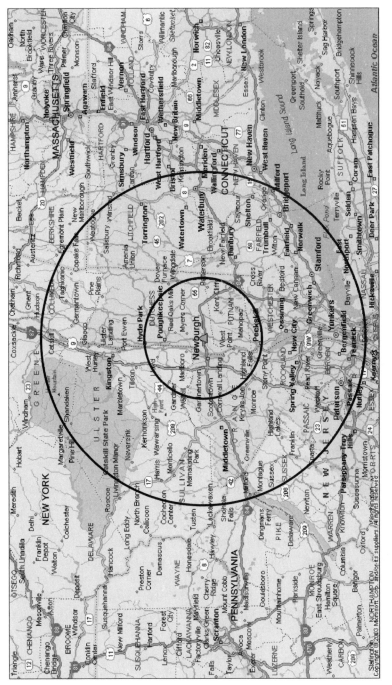

EXHIBIT 9.4 Nuclear Power Plant and Kill Zone Map

site population. The vigilant planning, suggested distances, monitoring, and protection reflect that population density.

Safety and operation of nuclear facilities have received unique attention and safety consideration in the shadow of September 11, 2001. A July 2002 report titled "Making the Nation Safer, the Rule of Science and Technology in Countering Terrorism" by the National Research Council states that it is probably not feasible to attack nuclear power plants from the ground or air using U.S. assets.

If that statement is accurate, the chances of a catastrophic failure at Indian Point or another nuclear facility causing a shutdown or meltdown are even more unlikely due to increased spending on terrestrial/airborne security and new Federal Aviation Association procedures. A no-fly zone of 1,500 feet altitude and seven miles at the perimeter surrounds all U.S. nuclear facilities. A no-boat zone is marked by a series of buoys. Local fixed base operations monitor and report on air traffic, probably 24 hours a day, 7 days a week.

Based on law and pending legislation, industry experts, and common sense, critical operations near nuclear facilities should be located at the indicated distances:

- Data center or uptime critical facility: Outside the 10-mile radius (per the Department of Environmental Protection and the governance of New York).
- Peak "injury zones": Within a 17.5-mile radius from site (per NRC). This was noted in a 1982 study that postulated it would be worse with calculable results from accidents in U.S. reactors. (This is called the "kill zone.")
- Distribution of potassium iodine tablets within a 20-mile radius of nuclear power plants. (This is common practice today.)
- Peak ingestion zone: Up to 50-mile radius (livestock and crops a consideration-evacuation zone). A 1980 House of Representatives sub-committee stated that "increasing the evacuation distance from 10 to 25 miles could substantially reduce the peak consequences."
- "Ingestion zone" radius of 50 miles: "an area within which people could be at risk if radioactive materials come to rest on crops, pastures, gardens, lakes, rivers; over 11,000 dairy cows exist in New York State's counties within 53 miles radius of Indian Point" as of January 1, 2002.

The NRC study of 1982 describes the potential disaster scenarios. The report says that "the chances of catastrophic disaster are incalculably small. The results presented in this report do not represent nuclear power risk." The report concludes: "Such a doomsday scenario might happen once if a reactor ran for 100,000 years."

An overview of the Indian Point Nuclear Power Plant operating status follows.

- Constructed first reactor in 1962.
- Reactor number one went dark in 1974 (Con Ed decided not to invest and suggest improvements and required fixes.)
- Reactors two and three still run, producing approximately 1,950 megawatts of power on 240 acres midway between Manhattan and Poughkeepsie.
- Entergy buys the facility on September 6, 2001.
- Several improvements, said Neil Shecchan of the NRC.
- Steel-reinforced dome over reactors were designed to withstand earthquakes, tornadoes, and winds over 260 miles and drastic changes in atmospheric pressure.
- December 2005: The Nuclear Energy Institute claims the domes are strong enough to withstand a hit from a fully fueled 767 aircraft.
- A study illustrated the extraordinary skill required by potential pilots to hit the reactor with smaller aircraft used on the World Trade Center and Pentagon.
- The NRC calls Indian Point the most heavily defended plant in the country.
- Private security on-site.
- State police on-site.
- National Guardsmen on-site.
- Multiple physical barriers on-site.
- Entergy spent over $3 million after September 11, 2001, to improve security and employ more officers, redeploy them in defensive positions, and erect new physical barriers.

Given this information, occupancy in Fishkill, Ulcer, and Kingston, New York, has slight or minimal risk due to the location due north of nuclear facility and that "downwind."

NOTE

1. Government Accountability Office Report Committee on Financial Services, House of Representatives, potential terrorist attacks. Additional actions needed to be better prepared for critical financial market participants, February 2003.

10

TIER 4: BASIS OF DESIGN

This chapter provides a shorthand checklist for resilient redundancy for mission-critical facilities with survivability in mind. Because there have been many mission-critical seminars and white papers, consultants have become familiar with phrases that articulate what a design is and is not. *This is not perfect and is still subjective in some areas.* However, we are collectively better off now in grouping and recognizing a design and its relative integrity, cost, and duration to design, build, and maintain. In the early stages of site selection, we spend most of our time articulating the differences and values of the various improvements that make up the various tier levels. Then we spend time understanding the differences between Tiers 2 and 3 and the capital expenditure and operations expenditure to support them and discussing what peers are doing. The improvements associated with Tiers 3 and 4 are relegated to mission-critical facilities only or to users who can demonstrate, via the business impact analysis, that they can lose enough money by the moment to support such an investment of capital and human resources. Concurrent maintainability is the theme for Tiers 3 and 4 in anticipation of required maintenance and failure of some components of the electrical and mechanical systems. Purists do not embrace the use of Tier 3 plus or Tier 4 minus solutions; they believe the requirement either is or is not Tier 3 or Tier 4. If a business impact analysis has been done and the user can identify an appropriate level of redundancy based on potential and unlikely losses during an unplanned outage, then the data center or outsourced vendor's data center should line up with acceptable levels of risk. An advertising agency's data center or recovery center will likely have fewer belts and braces than a financial institution will have.

Keep in mind that architectural components are not part of Uptime Institute's tiering system, which industry experts often refer to; neither are acts of

God or man-made challenges. Their tiering focus is on mechanical, electrical, and plumbing issues and their concurrent maintainability. My guidelines and suggested parameters follow.

Acts of God

- Out of 100-year flood zone by over 1,500 feet and 15 feet of elevation.
- Out of systemically sensitive zones above 14% of acceleration as per the U.S. Geological Society's October 2002 report (40 to 60 miles).
- Out of the range of F2 class tornadoes and above. (Most of the United States can burst up to 95 miles per hour with debris.)
- Matrix of tornadoes:

Class	Width	Length	Area
2	100 meters	6 miles	0.4 miles
3	200 meters	12 miles	1.5 miles
4	350 meters	24 miles	5.1 miles
5	600 meters	36 miles	14 miles

- Out of high-risk tornado zones.
- Out of or 40 to 50 miles away from landslide/mudslide regions.
- Out of or 40 to 50 miles away from volcanic regions.
- Out of or 20 to 30 miles away from tsunami/tidal wave regions.
- Low to moderate lightning protection.
- Low to moderate snow/ice accumulation.
- Low to moderate high winds (75 miles and below).
- Low to moderate forest fire (60 to 80 miles away).

Man-Made Potential Challenges

- Highway: First responder to ring of evacuation: 1,500 feet; second ring: 3,000 feet (fire, hazardous materials [hazmat], explosion, etc.).
- Railroad, freight and passenger: First responder ring of evacuation: 1,500 feet (fire, hazmat, explosion, etc.).
- Commercial airport or fixed base operation: Minimum of 15 to 20 miles instrument flight rating to visual flight rating approximate distance from tower.
- Nuclear power plant: 18-mile kill zone, 25 to 50 miles various evacuation levels.
- Hydroelectric power plant: 15 miles hazmat contamination and flooding.
- Know BLEVES (boil, liquid, evaporating, vapor, explosion)/storage of explosives).

- Cell tower/radio frequency tower: Minimum of 3 miles.
- Waste stations: 3,000 feet (hazmats, evacuation).
- Landfills, dumps: 3,000 feet primary explosion; 3 to 5 miles evacuation (wind related).
- Germ/biological event: 30 to 40 miles evacuation; minimum of 20 to 60 miles minimum evacuation (wind related).
- Weapons of mass destruction: 4 ounces of explosive substance, 1,500 feet to 60 miles.

In all these scenarios, it is critical to consider two likelihoods:

1. The outside plant infrastructure—power, fiber optics, water, transportation—cannot impact the primary facility by event, impacting a user's secondary or business continuity planning facility because they are within 3 to 20 miles of each other.
2. If the event is so catastrophic on the critical infrastructure personnel or outside plant vendors, not just able to perform, but more important willing to work.

Most mission-critical documentation does not focus on architectural design criteria for facilities because one size does not fit all. The Uptime Institute does not emphasize or go into the detail regarding the architectural structural components of greenfield data centers. The language relates primarily to mechanical, electrical, and plumbing issues and level of redundancy or concurrent maintainability. Building codes are more vigilant than the 2006 International Building Code (IBC) in most areas due to their intended use. The next sections are often used as guidelines or baselines:

Design load other than self-weight should be:

- Flooring: 150 pounds (lathing, design, and pattern unique).
- Hanging load: 50 pounds.
- Roof (concrete suggested): 60 pounds.
- Wind: Lift considerations must be identified for roof and equipment on roof. This often comes down to the size and number of mechanical fittings attaching kit to roof and dunnage. No equipment on the roof is preferred.

Geotypical and footings. The IBC maximum is ~HF-inch width and ~TQF-inch differential over 10 feet. We suggest a unique sensitivity and time to be spent on clays, expansive soils, water, and rock configurations. The superhighway of conduit below the earth for power and fiber will create heat and earth movement. Creeping water tables will impact the low earth fuel and water storage as well as impact the below-conduit placement and integrity.

Perimeter perimeter/wind speed considerations. The Fugita Scale is used for measuring the 2,500-year interval. Any consideration should be given to the local fixed base operations or airport wind records for history of sustained wind bursts.

Seismic criteria. IBC 2006 (essential facilities, building classification for seismic design group 3).

Foundations. IBC 2006. Typical footings and columns to be set below highway of power conduit, very important.

Columns. As few as reasonable to suit 13,000 to 20,000 square feet for a pod or module of wide space. Concrete roof will create challenges.

Roof. Concrete.

Perimeter. Tilt up or reinforce concrete masonry unit to withstand sustained winds of 150 to 250 miles an hour. Give special consideration to equipment exposed to the elements on roof and outside. Expect the perimeter to be 10 to 15 inches thick (lathed).

National Electric Code parameters for high-density (18- to 14-inch lathed) environmentals with Tier 4 components (and concurrent maintainability):

- One or two utility transmissions or primary feeds on site.
- Two sources of potable water (utility or stored or pumped).
- Minimum of two telecom facilities feeders in and out of site.
- Emergency power supply two (N + 1): three days.
- Uninterruptable power supply two (N + 1): 15 minutes.
- Cooling, 2 N.
- Cooling, on floor, N + 4.
- Dual-feed cabinets.
- Dual source of cooling tower and refrigerants.
- Water storage/cooling: three days.
- High-density cooling and humidification controls for modules, batteries, and switchgear for uninterruptible power supply.

Lightning protection/grounding:

- Equipment to be UL (Underwriters Laboratories) rated (rods or bulbs).
- Welded connectors preferred to mechanical connections.
- National Electric Code (NEC) and Institute of Electrical and Electronics Engineers (IEEE) criteria and standards to be used.
- Welded strainer system recommended to master ground bar.

- Transvoltage surge suppressors or transvoltage surge suppression are strongly recommended.
- No chemical ground fields recommended.

Monitoring. Human monitoring on-site is strongly recommended. A "smart" building effectively communicates with itself. Visual, audible, or strobe alarms are installed and required to prevent catastrophic events from happening or smaller events from escalating.

Power monitoring. On-site and remote for primary and breaker size distribution:

- Quality: dranetz or similar—circuit transformer (CT).
- Interruption.
- Duration.
- Source.

Network operating control center (NOCC) to monitor power and cooling:

- Mechanical monitoring on-site and remote for primary (cooling tower, direct absorption, and distribution.
- Temp and temp in, outflow.
- Flow rate.
- Humidification.
- Leak protection.
- Air flow/cubic feet per minute.
- Outside temperature: ambient.
- Inside temperature: conditioned.

Security. A minimum of triple fail-safe system should be employed with these criteria:

- Human: visual and physical presence.
- Closed circuit television, visual and recorded remote monitoring.
- Proximity: electronic control access supplements key access.
- Berming: 3 feet horizontal for every 1 foot vertical on each side.
- Department of Defense: "Bollards" are anchored, minimum of 3 feet deep, 18 to 16 inches wide, and 3.5 to 4.5 feet apart.
- Biometrics or retinal, palm- or fingerprint: required for critical areas.
- Minimum of one armed guard on all three shifts; minimum of two guards for every shift.
- Security operating control center (SOCC) to manage network infrastructure.

Office area. Approximately 10% of white space is designed to support wide space, exclusive of NOCC or SOCC.

Storage. 20 to 30% of white space; stores information technology (IT) equipment and large parts from environmentals.

Lab. 3% of white space where IT kit is provisioned and handled prior to deployment of white space.

Expansion. Maximum of 100% of day 1 needs, anticipating acceleration of enterprise, mainframe, and storage requirements based on recent growth, Moore's Law, anamolic growth of acquisitions, consolidations, and so forth.

Environmentals. Based on Tier 4 redundancy and concurrent maintainability, is 1.5 to 2 times the white space, depending on the cooling method.

Conference (war room), pantry, bathrooms. Designed with business continuity planning and prolonged outages in mind.

Telecom:

- Minimum of two points of entry, a minimum of 150 feet apart from each other. Right-of-way for multiple facilities based fiber providers not to be shared with power or plumbing conduits.
- Telecom to aggregate in (MDF), mainframe distribution, main distribution room, and decentralized to intermediate distribution frames for diversity and redundancy. Both rooms are protected by uninterruptible power supply or computer-grade power and cooling.
- Telecom to be prescreened or vetted for meaningful bandwidth upstream of facility and as resilient and burstable at all points on-site.
- Multiplexing in place for large data centers should be dense wavelength division multiplexing (DWDM) at OC-192 with over 40 Lambdas of commercially deployed capacity. The Internet Protocol capability should be able to scale to 40 to 60 gigabytes to terabits.

11

Unique Challenges of Cooling

The historic growth that data centers are undergoing began with a pent-up demand for processing and storage that grew out of the economic rebound of 2002 to 2004.

Following the overdesigned, overvendored solution of Y2K and the overreaction of the overselling and overfiring of 2002 and 2003, the U.S. economy found itself on a steady pace of growth across the board. Financial companies, insurance companies, pharmaceuticals, real estate, retail, and most service industries experienced growth with accelerated loss largely due to two things:

1. Most companies were not directly impacted by the events of September 11, 2001. They used the events and the atmosphere (postbubble) to lay off 10 to 20% of staff and cut other nonessential operating expenses because of retreating price/earnings ratios on publicly traded companies. One way to avoid human resource issues with a mass layoff or reduction in force in the face of such a trememdous event was to blame it on the bad guys. Traditionally, at any given time, the lower 10% of a company's workforce could be cut. Cash was king (again). Companies were not paying vendors or for noncritical cash flow items (information technology [IT] included). Contracts or agreements were being signed, but cash flow from assignments were prenegotiated for 12 to 18 months out following the execution and deliverables.

   The point here is that the economy had slowed to a stop, legacy kit of Y2K and the bubble was not antiquated and legacy. The human infrastructure of most IT organizations was cannibalized, because the real talent leaves first. Those who stayed were the B team, who had neither the vision nor the budget to make a difference. Nevertheless, they were in a position to employ new technology and more powerful

IT software/hardware to create efficiencies. The IT solutions provided would make us more efficient and therefore more profitable.

2. The other reason for the recent accelerated velocity of growth is that upon reviewing the ability of existing data centers to accept the new kit coming to market, we saw real changes.

The IT groups were busy losing credibility with the world (coupled with the long technology of Wall Streets bulls...remember Mary Meeker?) while the chief information officer was held accountable to the chief financial officer, once again for why we need this and why we have to migrate to that. The facilities or envelope to accept the hardware and software was no longer adequate.

Suddenly data center environmentals became less than required; they were not able to satisfy the rapidly growing power and cooling needs. IT capacity was growing three times faster every 18 months, and power efficiencies were being reduced by only half over the same period. This will chart positive absorption of power well beyond the Environmental Protection Agency's 1.5% of overall power utilization if not challenged or fundamentally changed.

The typical 12- to 18-inch raised floor to satisfy the typical 8 foot 6 inch to 9 foot data center space had congested underfloor voids filled with cabling dams, power conduits, and fixed cooling (plumbing conduits) that were effectively monolithic from a move management point of view.

Like the old kit, the new kit was designed generally to work better/faster/ cheaper. The more powerful chips do more things; they can multitask with adjacencies and store and retrieve encryption faster and more accurately. The end goal of these efficiencies is to increase productivity among all industries and to reduce operating expenses: for humans, legacy kit, and software licenses (and taxes).

The new interesting but not so surprising news was that the new kit was exceeding the design criteria for legacy data centers. The reality often hits home only once every 15 years as users migrate out of the legacy assets with exception of smaller (spoke and wheel) data centers and the users topology. The new metrics or costs for the data center are becoming alarmingly high by Y2K standards. Tier 4 data centers are moving from $2,200 per square foot to $2,850 per square foot to satisfy the cooling and high-density footprints. I am not a fan of in-cabinet cooling. The equipment currently commercially deployed does not have the commercial operating hours to determine effectiveness. Freon is not an ecological option, and combinations of gas and water should be limited to the mainframe to reduce route feet of risk. The safety net of employing additional computer room air-conditioning (CRAC) or computer room air-handling (CRAH) units in the data center defeats the arguments about saving space and saving money.

The conversation has to fundamentally change to power to application and not power to devise metric. User groups need to share processing kit and virtualize as much as reasonable. The kilowatt to application in direct current (DC) terms will change the conversation and total cost of ownership (TCO) dramatically. Sharing human assets would help infighting and reduce duplication of spend, salary bonus, maintenance, and so forth. Just opening a door will not offset new heating challenges. Although water has been in the data center for some time in the mainframe, unless forced into adjacencies of heat loads, I am more comfortable with spreading loads and higher ceiling or plenums, virtualizing or spreading processing remotely, and measuring applications rather than servers or blades. Loading the cabinets, sucking the hot air, and blowing the cool air is a Stone Age approach to a simple challenge. The question is how to reduce heat (the waste product of energy) in design and implementation. Remember, you are paying for that 65 to 75% of waste called heat at every point power is touched, manipulated, transformed, or distributed. Can we collapse 15 to 20 blades or processing power into one Z or equivalent? Yes. Will it take less footprint, power, and cooling? Yes. Does it have risk? Yes. But it is worthy of discussion and implementation.

Effectively the data center had:

- Piping that was too small.
- A ceiling that was too low to let heat out.
- Underfloor cable dams.
- Upgrade improvements, very risky in live environments.
- Power that was fairly easy to upgrade.

Assuming there is space available to accept the additional uninterruptible power supply (UPS) batteries, circuits can be brought to the floor; however, the challenges to cool the wide space present real issues. Coupled with geographic challenges of rising outside temperatures, regional droughts, and fewer wells, cooling in the United States was getting interesting.

On the power side of things (right-sizing of the facility was really testing our collective gray matter), the sticker shock of new data centers, the fluid in fuel dynamic atmosphere of the power and the chip collectively created an inability to make legacy data centers work and challenged our right-sizing question. Most data center managers think their facilities can and should be managed better. Most facilities managers do not know when or what is showing up far enough in advance to provision with other than just-in-time solutions.

Unique cooling challenges and associated origins can be traced back to the mainframe. It was a defining moment. With traditional cooling methods, we could not get the heating away from the chips or discs fast enough without the equipment overheating.

Because of air limitations of how much cooling can affect a heating element, cooling via water or gas had to be introduced to the equipment to supplement the heat extraction from the immediate area. Air carries less heat than gas or liquids.

As chips have gotten smaller and more complex with more functionality, they throw off more heat. Air cannot carry away that much heat or force enough cool air over the chip or heat-dissipating devices at the needed velocity. The air will be cool enough but at 125 miles per hour, it will blow past the heat source; at the right space it will be appropriate; beyond that space the air will be too warm to be effective.

For the more ecologically conscious, the gaseous cooling element freon or water should be as limited as "reasonable." We have become somewhat (and rightfully so) hydrophobic; we have a healthy fear of water or gas in the cabinet and data center in general. We are solving the wrong problems. The high-density challenges and solutions are based on the wrong math.

In the data center world of cooling challenges, attacking the area of waste in distribution is a unique area of interest. The conversion of power in the server is the greatest source of heat and waste. The conversion of alternating current (AC) power to direct current (DC) accounts for 25% of the "billable" loss and 25% of the heat dissipation. The challenge is not if freon is better than water, or if 6-foot pitches are better than 8-foot pitches in aisle spacing. This is a story of efficiency. This is not a circuitous diatribe about spot cooling, perforated tile placement and efficiencies, and calling that a solution. Those "solutions" do not address the problem but merely respond dysfunctionally to it.

Space, money, and brain trust will be best used in focusing on the distribution inefficiencies and how they impact the utilization and TCO rather than putting critical data at risk by creating bigger ice cubes and fans to cool warmer hot spots.

Getting at the waste and inefficiencies is an industry or business killer. By that I mean a DC plant solution will not eliminate the need or use of AC UPS plants for computer-grade power, but it will seriously cut into the multibillion-dollar market share for some of these reasons:

- Without as much heat at the source, there is less need for unique cooling (another multibillion-dollar industry).
- Emergency power supply needs are static.

- UPS needs space and money. It is 20 to 27% of the day 1 spend, 30 to 34% of the annual maintenance costs, and it can be reduced or eliminated.
- Cooling to satisfy components, unique cooling components, and the associated real estate to house cooling components can be reduced significantly.

To virtualize a "Z" series via Linux or the like would create minimal power and cooling challenges in a single or mirrored footprint with IT manipulation and storage benefits remotely without reinventing the heating and cooling challenges footprint by footprint. These are two solutions away from how to spot cool, blend loads, and so forth that would not stop the power/heating and cooling quagmire, but it would slow it down.

If you consider that there will be seven to ten IT upgrades or refreshes over a life of a 15- to 20-year fixed environmental of power and cooling, and the velocity of power and cooling far exceeds Moore's Law, how do we right-size such an environment that changes every 18 months to 3 years? We do not. We make bets. The bet is we will satisfy 5 to 7 years of forecastable future based on what we know. We establish some large building blocks of sanity and build on them. We cannot pretend that we know the velocity of growth based on history.

The good news is that some of the limitations of science are now being commercially deployed. The production chip is as about as:

- Small as practical.
- Fast to produce as possible.
- Cost relevant as possible.
- Able to work on as possible.

The speed of light, functionality, and heat anticipation is as close to the edge as possible today. Virtualization models will peak in the next two to four years. Then we are back to blocking and tackling solutions. The metric of success needs to change fundamentally. (Remember when collocation solution providers started pricing by the kilowatt or amp instead of square foot and nobody got it? We are getting it now!) The challenges of enterprise production and adjacencies will continue to morph, but greater opportunities and inefficiencies, production, and cost savings exist in storage.

Given the last three years of collective success in enterprise and mainframe and storage productivity, new opportunities exist to be a "rock star" in the IT world. Developing or reconfiguring for TCO inner-chip models to expand applications is a priority; the emphasis should be on getting human and software expenses under control. The problem is not just an inherent facilities and IT turf war but a new breed of "us and them" inside IT. Sending batch work offshore to taskmasters has new and unwelcome operating expense creep and quality control issues.

The efficiency or utility expense creep of power to and cooling for the mission-critical environmental infrastructure contributes to the operating side of operating expense creep. Operating expenses represent approximately 25% of the annual TCO; cooling represents 25 to 50% of that number. Thus, cooling costs can be over $200 million for 20 years for a large data center. A 10, 15, or 25% reduction in power demand or cooling requirements could impress shareholders or allow management latitude in improving profitability.

Efficiency solutions are being driven by:

- Getting hot air out.
- Getting cool air closer.
- Getting cool air not to blow past hot spots, but cool enough that air will be effective when it reaches the hot-spot destination.
- Perforated tile size and placement.
- Distance to cooling elements (hot aisle or cool aisle).
- Floor void too small (too much friction).
- Floor void too deep (fans cannot create enough pressure).
- Ceiling height too low; heat cannot get out swiftly.
- Ceiling height too high; too many cubic feet to keep ambient with proper humidification.
- Power technologies: AC, DC, remote power panels, power distribution units, fans above or below the cabinet.
- Cooling in the cabinet: How fast will the kit "fail"?
- Environmental concerns or Leadership in Energy Environmental Design (LEED) issues.
- Manufacturer's agenda.
- Vendor's agenda.
- Cogeneration fundamentally needs to sync utility power with cogeneration plant power. All or nothing...figure it out, guys...you both win.

In energy, not only is cooling chasing the unsuccessful third rail of power in this dog-eat-dog world of efficiency solutions, but the government is appropriately issuing a challenge: Sort out the ecofriendly "F" gases covered in the Kyoto Protocol (which the United States has not signed).

Environmental guidelines of right now and signed into law in the United Kingdom on July 4, 2007; it is the responsibility of the data center operator to store or limit the leakage, maintenance, and removal of gaseous hazardous materials. By 2009, a registered or certified engineer must have this responsibility; financial penalties have been established. Many data centers continue using gas systems in CRAC units and others, although their use is rarely without consequence. Interrupting the existing insanity may bring about new solutions that would increase, not decrease, carbon dioxide emissions. Right now we are at a self-help point on the cooling solutions road. I am not sure that it is the government's place to show the way here, but appropriate penalties for inefficient systems and regular inspections at the subcode level will force U.S. operators to limit losses for the growing heat load, high-density paradigm that we are in. If a system loses 20 to 30% efficiency in an environment growing in power and cooling needs, the waste to cool systems has concentric circles of risk, waste, and financial loss.

I am an advocate of free cooling where appropriate and thermal storage as a primary or backup system for mission-critical facilities. Freezing a supersize ice cube and blowing it into the heated environment is not efficient. The more complex we make our solutions, the more linear feet of solutions we put in the "risk" pile. More distance, more risk! What I learned working in the World Trade Center was that distance created risk and inefficiencies. At the time we built the world's tallest UPS plant on the 107th floor. It was littered with challenges. The first thing I realized was the riser loss: the condition of current coming up multiple "bus bars" from the subbasement substation. I learned that what you bought from the utility was not what you got. You lost something in transmission; that was travel loss. Coupled with that loss was the risk that other users could and would tap into the bar, creating new points of maintenance and failure. Every time that power took a 90-degree turn or was stepped up or stepped down, risk was added. The breaker's timing, transformers, and maintenance became my electronic lifeblood.

Similarly with cooling. If you are a "CRAC" head or "CRAH" fan (pun definitely intended), or moving gas or water to the cabinet; every 90-degree turn you make creates friction or risk. Every foot of distribution adds a metric to your risk. Before you pick a way to cool the real or imagined heat loads being barked at you by IT or facilities, realize that failing at this mission is a career killer. In the design development or basis of design phase, ask yourself which system has fewer 90-degree turns and fewer points of failure. The second question is the TCO. Because we view the data or encryption as generally valuable to a user's success, making sure we stay up is paramount; containing costs may be tantamount but often is a pass-along or cost-of-doing-business black hole.

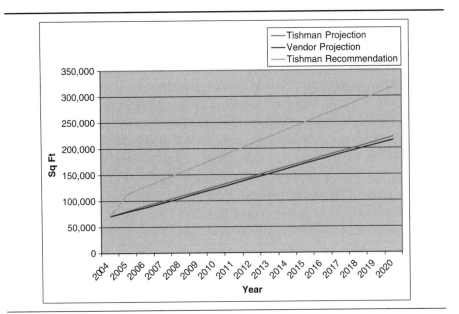

EXHIBIT 11.1 TOTAL SPACE PROJECTION

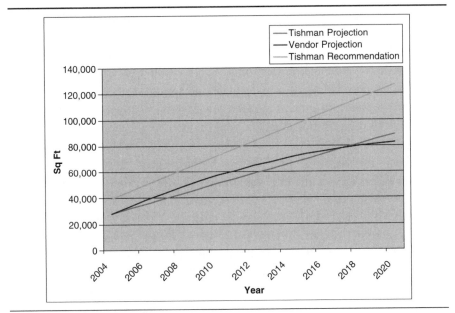

EXHIBIT 11.2 WHITE SPACE PROJECTION

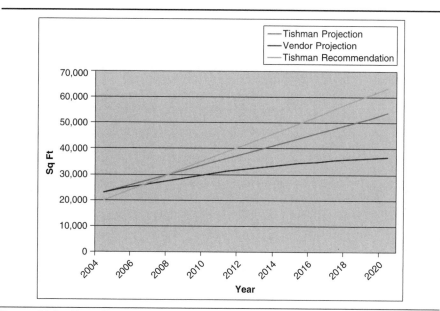

EXHIBIT 11.3 OFFICE/ANCILLARY SPACE PROJECTION

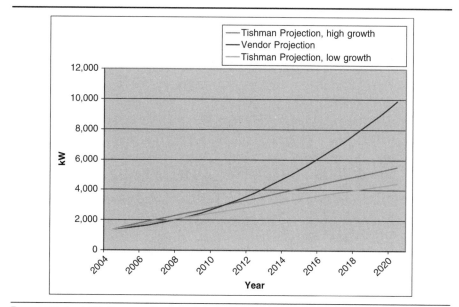

EXHIBIT 11.4 UPS GROWTH PROJECTION

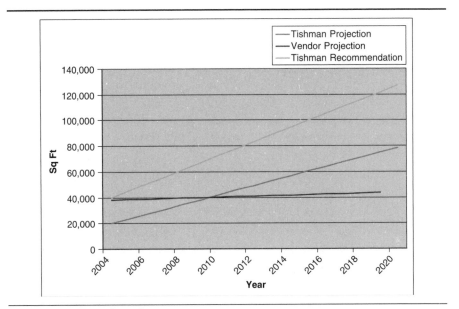

EXHIBIT 11.5 PLANT SPACE PROJECTION

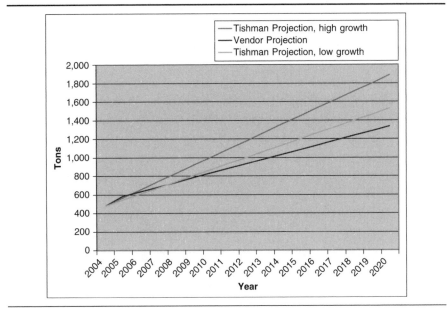

EXHIBIT 11.6 COOLING LOAD PROJECTION

We often look at a user's power usage (see Exhibit 11.4) and velocity of change to determine the right-sizing of a new data center white space (see Exhibit 11.2) for total space (see Exhibit 11.1) or a mission-critical facility. This is often more than an exercise in printing out load histories and sizing of infrastructure equipment. Data mining efforts or the velocity and consistency of taking old equipment out of the data center is relevant to loads and real estate needs. The utilization of new kit is relevant. Can we use more capacity of the existing kit before we add a new piece of kit of cabinet? We consider anomolic growth or likelihoods of upcoming data center consolidations or company acquisitions that will impact power needs (see Exhibit 11.4), cooling (see Exhibit 11.6), IT, infrastructure to house environmentals (see Exhibit 11.5), and real estate needs. The reality is that we can effectively plan only three to five years out with confidence. The rest is good guesswork, taking into consideration the company's vision, relevant history, equipment changes and challenges, budget, and schedule. We make these three- to five-year models work in 15- to 20-year useful life envelopes of the data center and the real estate (with outside plant improvements) that they sit on. The human space (see Exhibit 11.3) and storage becomes the hedge of flexible variable to help with unforeseen environmental needs (see Exhibit 11.4)

12

UNIQUE CHALLENGES OF POWER

The early and perhaps most important consideration in outside plant power leveling, weighing, and ultimate selection is the operator. Choice or selection of the utility was less interesting or compelling before utility regulation. Regulation effectively divided the assets into generating companies and wire services.

The generating companies effectively create power and sell it. Their profits are driven by reduction in operating expenses, which are divided into human salaries and facilities costs. The fossil, nuclear, and hydroelectric power that the generating companies buy is marked up and taxed, but not by excessive margins. Generating companies are weighed and scored on their uptime availability and cost, which is driven by the commoditized source and relative demand.

If the source is in limited supply, the price will go up. Coal, for instance, is an abundant supply, but not very popular for ecological reasons. Fifty permits for new power plants were recently rejected! China currently uses more coal for generation than any other country and contributes more to the carbon dioxide (CO_2) emissions for largely the same reason. China builds a coal generation plant every two days! In the United States, natural gas reserves are in abundant supply but not mined. Coal is cheaper than gas. This will change. Less expensive regions of hydroelectric or nuclear generation should be \$0.4 to \$0.6 cents per kilowatt-hour (kWh) cheaper; coal or gas will be \$0.22 to \$0.25 per kWh (the one exception is western New York State).

The recent and collective consensus is that coal- and gas-sourced power-generating plants are overheating the Earth. Another nagging reality is that many nuclear facilities, nationally and internationally, will be decommissioned over the next 10 to 20 years. We are now looking for nontraditional methods of energy creation for mission-critical and non-mission-critical usage that are Earth-friendly and do not create more energy "well to wheel" than existing methods. In other words, some energy solutions create more waste, cost, and energy to make than to use. With a shrinking supply and an increased demand (usage is projected to go up by 50% by 2031 and by 100% by 2050), we can take several baby steps to meet the challenge to find the solution swiftly, or have the courage to take larger steps on other technologies to provide self-help in power supply and power conservation in mission-critical facilities.

The commercially deployed technologies available are:

- **Biomass.** There are many sources of biomass, but the most common use corn or soybeans to create ethanol. Blended with 15% unleaded gasoline, ethanol is commercially viable for cars, and stations are springing up. Biomass is not practical for mission-critical usage. It supplies fuel for cars and trucks and will deplete agricultural resources and raise their prices.
- **Geothermal.** Heat from the Earth is harnessed to drive generators and accounts for about 15 billion kWh (equal to 25 million barrels of fuel oil or 6 million tons of coal annually). It is appropriate for mission-critical uses due to its 98% of availability reliability, similar to our existing systems. It is, however, more cost effective and reliable than wind or solar technologies. More will be done to harness this energy
- **Wind.** Wind energy is created with the movement of large blades turning generators. The challenge with wind is the high cost of installation, accidental killing of birds, and low financial return. Low-velocity wind cannot push the blades. This is not a useful solution for mission-critical needs.
- **Solar.** One of the more commercially deployed and viable non-mission-critical sources of energy, solar power has a growth rate in the double digits. International production has improved to create and manufacture solar photovoltaic (solar PV) cells and panels to turn sunlight directly into electricity. Solar power is great for homes and non-mission-critical uses. It does and will take the strain off existing and traditional generating companies. Solar PV sales have grown 600% since 2000 and 41% since 2006.
- **Water.** Water can and does run continuously for 24-hour periods with fairly consistent velocity. Except for infrequent droughts, it is the most reliable alternative method of generating power and accounts for 7% of power generation in the United States and 75% of the alternative power generation. The water flow through dams pushes massive turbines to

create power. Other than disturbing some fish populations, this is an ecofriendly alternative with very low hazardous emissions.

- **Gas/Coal.** Gas and coal are the predominant sources of power nationally and internationally. We burn coal, shale, and gas to create steam or boiling water to move turbines or generators and create energy. These sources are the most damaging to the atmosphere, but they are the least expensive sources of energy. They account for about half of the source of CO_2 emissions globally. China is now the number-one CO_2 emissions producer; it surpassed the United States in 2007.

- **Nuclear.** Unlike energy production from fossil fuels, nuclear energy is created from the energy stored in an atom's nucleus, which is composed of protons and neutrons. The energy creation is done through a process called fission. In fission, a uranium atom's nucleus is shot by an outside neutron, which splits it apart and creates a chain reaction of uranium neutrons hitting and splitting other neutrons. Energy is created when the heat released from the splitting of neutrons is captured; steam is generated from water surrounding tubes. The steam turns blades of large turbines and creates electricity. The steam is cooled and stored then converted back to water for reuse.

Of the 103 nuclear plants in the United States, 24 are located in regions of drought in the southeastern United States and all but 2 of those are located strategically on a lake or river for easy access to cooling. Do not kid yourself; coal- and gas-fired generating plants require water as well, just not as much. Some of the conduits that feed a nuclear site are 18 feet in diameter and can run a mile to deliver water from the deep part of a body of water to the site. The risk is that the plants will not be able to access water for cooling and will be forced to shut down. This will not cause a power shutdown but will likely increase the cost of power. This is simple supply-and-demand modeling. In Alabama in 2006, the Huntsville nuclear site shut down briefly. In Europe in 2006, during a drought in which thousands of people died, several nuclear plants had to shut down for about a week in Germany, France, and Spain. The volume of water required by a nuclear plant is extraordinary—in the millions of gallons per day—and it is not a candidate for surface storage. Repiping or engineering water pipes to deeper areas away from sediment and fish is expensive and time consuming. The water access is a gotcha with nuclear planning and implementation. It is resolvable, however, and *not* a showstopper.

Close to 80% of the 441 nuclear reactors operating around the globe are more than 15 years old. The life expectancy can be 30 to 45 years with regular maintenance. However, many of the nuclear plants in the United States are coming dangerously close to decommissioning time. Nuclear power is a low-cost and appropriate means of power creation with some real, but minimal, environmental concerns. No new plants have been started in 30 years in the United States, but the world is now viewing nuclear power in a favorable light. Besides those in the United States, there are 337 reactors, with 28 under construction, 62 planned, and 162 proposed worldwide.

The site closest to completion in the United States is the Tennessee Valley Authority (TVA) restart of Watts Bar, set to open in 2013, and two others are to come on line in Texas in 2014. The United States has the most nuclear facilities in the world. Nuclear power currently contributes to about 20% of the global power grid. Most of these facilities were built in the 1970s and 1980s. Their 30-year licenses have been extended to 60 years with suggested maintenance in most cases. Demand for power is outpacing supply, and energy conservation efforts are outpacing energy creation efforts. The market effects of supply and demand will price utility rates prohibitively, put higher loads on an aging and complex just-in-time network of the power grid, and will increase risk and lower reliability in most regions of the country. Only six sites have been shut down but all will likely face obsolescence between 2020 and 2030. China is planning 15 to 30 nuclear facilities by 2020, and Russia plans 42 sites by 2030. We are not alone in the power paradigm! However, the Green Party in Germany has committed to shutting down all of that country's 17 sites by 2021 for ecological reasons. If nuclear energy is to hold its market share and keep up with high demand and CO_2-conscious states and municipalities, we need to build nuclear plants now.

Although leveling, components of outside plant (OSP) power consideration are:

- Taxes on usage.
- Reservation fees (often for mission-critical facilities as well as second feeder).
- Capital cost to build.
- Cost deliveries of primary and transmission distribution becoming de minimis.
- Negative cascading protection (engineering).
- Monitoring of network operating control centers (NOCC) are large alarms: disruptions required, human infrastructure/service.
- History of outage data, including source in durations of outages (drunken drivers, rodents, wind, debris, ice storms).
- Equipment failure (transformer failures).

- Distance and size of substations or transmission lines to asset ($200,000 to $1 million per mile to distribute power; $5 million to $8 million to build a substation).
- The inside plant (ISP) power, right-sizing for the enterprise mainframe, storage, and mechanical components of the data center can be as complex as we want to make them. The fundamentals for what we do are remarkably simple and governed by four-function math. We can complicate the issues and cloud them with a "parade of horribles" as well as apply fears and concerns of the fluid and dynamic information technology (IT) world.
- Right-sizing the power needed, even if modular, for 15 to 20 years in the IT footprints can be challenging, but the math is simple. This is the target-rich environment for cost savings. The energy loss from transmission lines from substation to the cabinet is 30 to 40%, and greater by some estimates. Like telecommunications, every time the current or throughput reads, is manipulated by, or touches another piece of equipment, it loses efficiency. Think about it: Power from a cable to a switch gear is then transformed into smaller pieces of power, then transformed into still smaller pieces, then rectified from alternating current (AC) to direct current (DC) to AC, then switched to the remote power panel or power distribution units and then to the power strip at the cabinet.

We cannot talk about power without the corresponding input of cooling and cooling power to operate it. As power users, we are spending between $6 billion to $8 billion per year on power consumption. The cost to power server or enterprise-based devices even in low-cost footprints of $0.4 to $0.6 per kWh is greater than the cost for the device itself in two to three years. That bears repeating: The cost to power/cool the device is more than the price of the device in the short term. Something seems very wrong about that to me.

If we do not figure out how to utilize the waste product of power (heat) or reduce the creation of the waste product, we will be in big trouble collectively.

Chip makers and vendors are paying special interest to the problem. The "Green Grid" is made up of big-brand power users: IBM, AMD, HP, Microsoft, AMC, and others. Their goal is to create efficiencies and standards. The situation is analogous to what happened in the telecom world: They have had to move from Centrex or DMS, 5 E switches to IP or "soft switches" and cannibalize successful business lines to get green. Then we will have to wait three to five years for commercially deployed solutions other than those discussed in this book.

13

GOING GREEN

The green data center is somewhat of an oxymoron. It is currently taking first place for white paper content and seminars, eclipsing the blade server, high density, hot aisle, cold aisle, and urgent and mandatory meetings. Today, the low energy electron diffraction (LEED) topics of economic and good corporate and ecological interest are growing in visibility to a point where the economic challenges and short-term inefficiencies are worthwhile and being implemented.

The challenges are fairly obvious. Currently deployed equipment and static solutions for a data center demand increase the inefficiencies of power from the transmission line or substation to the cabinet. The 65 to 75% of waste is generally in the form of heat—effectively the exhaust of the manipulation of electrical current. Then comes the inefficient cooling requirements to satisfy the inefficient power and to stock all the mission-critical gear to service same.

LEED solutions are found in a minority of the footprint in the office and storage components. Painting the roof white and putting in bike racks are easy to do. Waterless urinals, new commodes, radio-frequency sinks, and "scrubbers" on mufflers are a bit more expensive but much more costly to retrofit if the municipality chooses to mandate lower levels on emissions. The waste product of the scrubber or high-penetration filtration system needs to be owned and maintained, but it is the right thing to do as a good corporate citizen and financially it is cheaper than a complete retrofit.

There are not many ecofriendly solutions to the traditional challenges of the data centers. Generally they come with an added risk component of reliability, expense, cosmetics, functionality, and maintenance. Having said that, you might think that I am on an "off course" for design and implementation of mission-critical facilities. I am not if we recognize the fact that we have

grown as a population by 400% in 100 years and that according to the
United Nations, we will double that population by 2050. Now assume that
our resources are finite. The environment, not just carbon dioxide (CO_2)
emissions, is as important as any national priority and with the same urgency.

Today, solutions, criteria, and time frames for emissions controls and credits for recycled materials should be as important as landing the man on the
moon was to President Kennedy in 1962 and as winning the cold war was to
President Reagan in the early 1980s. In both examples we effectively outspent
the solution by a mile but not the goals and reaped the benefits.

The world looks to the West for technology creation and enhancements
as well as for the new financial mouse traps to keep the service economies
rolling. The United States often looks to California and Denver as the leading thought providers for implementation of ecofriendly solutions for old
problems.

The cold reality is that a majority of our challenges revolve around oil,
coal, and fossil fuels. Solutions to today's and tomorrow's challenges are
new to commercial deployment but rock solid in man-hours at testing. It
is expected that the first three to five years of commercial deployment will
be expensive and not perfect and likely "short" maintainability options. We
need intelligence and experienced personnel; but this is a path we need to go
down, kicking and screaming if need be.

Back to the data center. Regarding cooling solutions, thermal storage
should be employed for a percentage of the heat produced during operations
to complement or supplement peak and off-peak use.

Batch runs of data that can push the chip utilization from 30 to 70% and
associated heat produced by noncritical or time-sensitive batch runs should
be run off hours, when the power grid (if utilized) is under less demand and
power is less costly.

Generally and cosmetically, we have gotten away from the data center
as the showcase it was in the dot-com days. I remember building a data
center once with "black lights" in the white space for dramatic impact; the
architect thought it would be "cool." Another data center user installed a
motion detector that opened to a 180-degree view of the white space used
for a conference room.

Today we spend our dollars on infrastructure. We should and will be more
selective regarding the few pieces of furniture, floor covering, chairs, and so
forth that are recycled and not of great visual importance.

Chapter 17 presents more on ecosolutions. At this point, and for a high
level of understanding of what the U.S. green building (or ecofriendly) believe

are the main drivers or categories for environmentally sound design and construction of a facility are the LEED categories:

- Sustainable sites
- Water efficiency
- Waste and atmosphere
- Materials and resources
- Indoor environmental quality
- Innovation and design process

The categories of LEED success and associated benefits are:

- Certified: 26 to 32 points
- Silver: 33 to 38 points
- Gold: 39 to 51 points
- Platinum: 52 to 69 points

The results of design and implementation for data centers to be LEED compliant are listed in a yes/no format and inspected by certified personnel. In the mission-critical world, there are not many environmentally friendly improvements possible. Due to the uncommon or unique usage of the facility with fewer humans and the ratio of humans to square foot and the commercially deployed mission-critical gear to support information technology (IT) equipment within the white-space envelope, ecofriendly improvements and processes are difficult to achieve.

Having said that, it is possible and realistic to achieve gold and perhaps high status for mission-critical environments. As discussed in other parts of the book, some uncommon improvements and designs may be required. Some may appear expensive or seem to be inefficient spending in the short term but may be long-term winners financially and in line with most new corporate governance criteria and mandates (in other words, they are environmentally forward thinking). I look forward to data center–specific revisions to the checklist that follows.

The checklist covers most of the improvement criteria. Solutions to these challenges have displaced the overdiscussed blade server, high-density cooling seminars, and teleconferences that have been beaten to death for the last three years.

Sustainable Sites

Construction Activity: Pollution Prevention—Prerequisite
Credits 1.0: Site Selection
Credits 2.0: Development Density and Community Connectivity
Credits 3.0: Brownfield Redevelopment

Credits 4.1: Alternative Transportation—Public Transportation Access

Credits 4.2: Alternative Transportation—Bike Storage/Racks and Changing Room

Credits 4.3: Alternative Transportation—Low-Emitting and Fuel-Efficient Vehicles

Credits 4.4: Alternative Transportation—Parking Capacity

Credits 5.1: Site Development—Protect and Restore Habitat

Credits 5.2: Site Development—Maximize Open Space

Credits 6.1: Storm Water Design—Quantity Design

Credits 6.2: Storm Water Design—Quality Design

Credits 7.1: Heat Island Effect—Nonroof

Credits 7.2: Heat Island Effect—Roof

Credits 8.0: Light Pollution Reduction

Water Efficiency

Credits 1.1: Water-Efficient Landscaping—Reduce 50%

Credits 1.2: Water-Efficient Landscaping—No Potable Use/No Irrigation

Credits 2.0: Innovative Wastewater Technologies

Credits 3.1: Water Use Reduction—20% Reduction

Credits 3.1: Water Use Reduction—30% Reduction

Energy Efficiency

Fundamental Commissioning of the Building Energy Systems—Prerequisite

Minimum Energy Performance—Prerequisite

Fundamental Refrigerant Management—Prerequisite

Credits 1.0: Optimize Energy Performance

Credits 2.0: On-Site Renewable Energy

Credits 3.0: Enhanced Commissioning

Credits 4.0: Enhanced Refrigerant Management

Credits 5.0: Measurement and Verification

Credits 6.0: Green Power

Materials and Resources

Storage and Collection of Recyclables: Prerequisite

Credits 1.1: Building Reuse—Maintain 75% of Existing Walls, Floors, and Roof

Credits 1.2: Building Reuse—Maintain 100% of Existing Walls, Floors, and Roof

Credits 1.3: Building Reuse—50% of Interior Nonstructural Elements

Credits 2.1: Construction Waste Management—Divert 50% from Disposal

Credits 2.2: Construction Waste Management—Divert 75% from Disposal

Credits 3.1: Materials Reuse—5%

Credits 3.2: Materials Reuse—10%
Credits 4.1: Recycle Content—10% (postconsumer plus half preconsumer)
Credits 4.2: Recycle Content—20% (postconsumer plus half preconsumer)
Credits 5.1: Regional Materials—10% Extracted, Processed, and Made Regionally
Credits 5.2: Regional Materials—20% Extracted, Processed, and Made Regionally
Credits 6.0: Rapidly Renewable Materials
Credits 7.0: Certified Wood

Indoor Environmental Quality
Environmental Tobacco Smoke Control—Prerequisite
Credits 1.0: Outdoor Air Delivery Monitoring
Credits 2.0: Increased Ventilation
Credits 3.1: Construction IAC Management Plan during Construction
Credits 3.2: Construction IAC Management Plan before Occupancy
Credits 4.1: Low-Emitting Materials—Paints and Coatings
Credits 4.2: Low-Emitting Materials—Carpet Systems
Credits 4.3: Low-Emitting Materials—Composite Wood and Antifiber Materials
Credits 5.0: Indoor Chemical and Pollution Sources Control
Credits 6.1: Controllability of Systems—Lighting
Credits 6.2: Controllability of Systems—Thermal Comfort
Credits 7.1: Thermal Comfort—Design
Credits 7.2: Thermal Comfort—Verification
Credits 8.1: Daylight and Views—75% of Space
Credits 8.2: Daylight and Views—90% of Space

Innovation and Design Process
Credits 1.1: Innovation in Design—Specific Title
Credits 1.2: Innovation in Design—Specific Title
Credits 1.3: Innovation in Design—Specific Title
Credits 1.4: Innovation in Design—Specific Title
Credits 2.0: LEED-Accredited Professional

Totals _____.

As you can see, some criteria are easier to achieve than others. Putting in bike racks and painting a roof white are a bit easier to get done than providing 90% daylight for a data center!

Companies able and willing to develop and distribute power more efficiently back to the grid should receive credits for doing so. Surface aggregation of precipitation and treatment of well water from aquifers should be weighted uniquely. We are headed in the right direction in changing the way we think about the design, construction, sustainability, and maintainability of these facilities, but it is like turning a ship. It takes careful and strategic navigation as well as miles.

The culture is changing to accommodate common sense and strategic changes to enhance asset utilization, existing facilities, waste, and renewable sources of energy. It is important to note that many of the design and implementation decision makers grew up when smoking was allowed on airplanes and corporate trash was turned over to the lowest bidder.

New leaders or innovative vendors and users need to meet the obvious challenges and opportunities.

14

NEW METHODS OF EFFECTIVE SITE SELECTION: NEGOTIATION AND EXECUTION

The new methods for forward-thinking users and consultants to use to navigate the process of site selection are established as a basis of design for the cabinet and mainframe storage components of end users. We encourage users to separate the "vital" or critical and noncritical, or synchronous versus asynchronous with adjacencies to establish that systems can be separated for financial and logistical reasons. We can quantify day 1 and future needs.

We then establish the velocity of growth in existing white space while validating and incorporating:

- Data mining efforts
- Growth within 12 to 18 months
- Anamolyic growth of accelerating acquisitions or decelerating consolidations or sold user groups
- Useful life of environmentals of the business life cycle (exit strategy)

In greenfield and often with augmentation scenarios, we incorporate primary considerations of primary blast, secondary damage, and evacuation models based on a host of unlikely but possible scenarios. We apply relevant and regional intelligence and consider the likelihood of catastrophic events happening, apply the budget and scheduled mitigation to help steering committees make a go/no go decision regarding the issue.

We establish these models for all acts of God and relevant "man-made disasters" to comply with corporate governance. Exhibit 14.1 shows a nuclear power facility in the Northeast, and Exhibit 14.2 shows the kill zone and agricultural rings around the Indian Point nuclear facility.

Security/Human Intervention
Building Evacuation Distances from Explosion

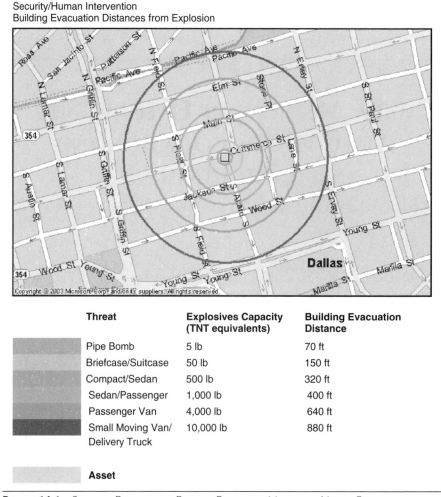

Threat	Explosives Capacity (TNT equivalents)	Building Evacuation Distance
Pipe Bomb	5 lb	70 ft
Briefcase/Suitcase	50 lb	150 ft
Compact/Sedan	500 lb	320 ft
Sedan/Passenger	1,000 lb	400 ft
Passenger Van	4,000 lb	640 ft
Small Moving Van/ Delivery Truck	10,000 lb	880 ft

Asset

EXHIBIT 14.1   SECURITY BREACH AND RING OF RELEVANCE MAP OF AN URBAN ENVIRONMENT

We take images from the field conditions to help the steering committee weight and score the situation and apply some common sense to the "parade of horribles."

Exhibit 14.3 shows the typical bomb blast rings for highway with rings of relevance for first responders to evacuate potential catastrophe. The first responders can establish whether no evacuation or significant evacuation is necessary. When the emergency medical service (EMS), fire officials, or police knock on the door to evacuate, the situation is not negotiable. They are trying to preserve life, and you do what they say. Some passionate tenants

Security/Human Intervention
Outdoor Evacuation Distances from Explosion

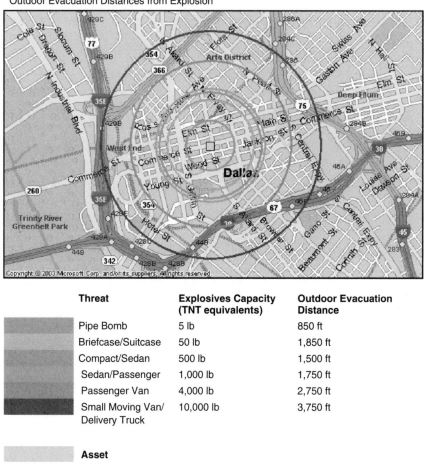

Threat	Explosives Capacity (TNT equivalents)	Outdoor Evacuation Distance
Pipe Bomb	5 lb	850 ft
Briefcase/Suitcase	50 lb	1,850 ft
Compact/Sedan	500 lb	1,500 ft
Sedan/Passenger	1,000 lb	1,750 ft
Passenger Van	4,000 lb	2,750 ft
Small Moving Van/ Delivery Truck	10,000 lb	3,750 ft

Asset

EXHIBIT 14.2   EVACUATION RING

or operators say they will refuse to accede to the demands of first responders and will have better things to do during the event rather than submitting to a forced evacuation.

In New Jersey, for instance, hazardous materials (hazmat) contamination for contaminated land is a real issue. Finding land or buildings away from contamination or Superfund sites can be a challenge. Large power distribution sites are often located near former manufacturing facilities. New Jersey is one of the leading contaminated states in the country; it also has more pharmaceutical company headquarters than any other state. What a coincidence.

Security/Human Intervention
Building Evacuation Distances from Explosion

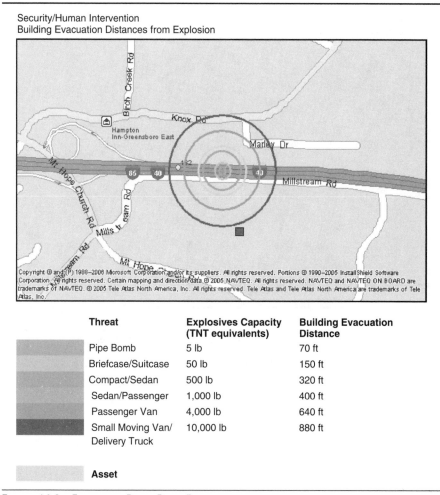

Threat	Explosives Capacity (TNT equivalents)	Building Evacuation Distance
Pipe Bomb	5 lb	70 ft
Briefcase/Suitcase	50 lb	150 ft
Compact/Sedan	500 lb	320 ft
Sedan/Passenger	1,000 lb	400 ft
Passenger Van	4,000 lb	640 ft
Small Moving Van/ Delivery Truck	10,000 lb	880 ft

Asset

EXHIBIT 14.3 EXAMPLE OF BOMB BLAST RINGS

Every year New Jersey retires a minimum of 13 wells due to contamination of leaching hazmats. This fact puts more pressure on surface storage of potable water for consumption and cooling.

We continue to keep the keen eye on commercial airfields and fixed base operations (FBOs) when we site data centers. As mentioned, landings are basically organized crashes. Statistically, take-offs and landings are the highest-risk times. Ground or "movement" events are less likely and less likely to cause evacuation. Since the airline crash of 2002 in New York City on the heels of September 11, 2001, terrorist attacks, there has been a heightened sense of awareness of the same. In 2007, jet fuel and its distribution lines were discovered to be strategic targets at Kennedy, LaGuardia, and Newark airports.

Because FBOs serve smaller aircraft with fewer flights and carry less fuel, they present less risk. However, most of these pilots have fewer hours of flight time than commercial pilots. Most FBOs do not have a tower (there are only five in the state of New Jersey), and runways are generally shorter with challenging approaches or residential no-fly zones that require swift banking after take-offs and outer approaches even at night.

Waste stations or landfills have ongoing explosion potential with open flames and frequent gas combustion causing hazmats to drift into the one direction. The recommended distance for siting data centers is 1,500 to 3,000 linear feet from waste stations and dumps.

The blasting at mines and quarries can interrupt the radio-frequency (RF) and optronic signals to sensitive information technology equipment. A suggested safe distance to site a data center is two to four miles from mines and quarries.

Limiting or mitigating risks during the site selection process is the job of state, local, or corporate governance. It relates back to the business impact analysis (BIA) for a company's ability and willingness to take risk and the associated time, money, and human effort the company is willing to spend to mitigate that risk.

The greatest asset for the steering committee of the BIA and the site selection committee is knowledge and intellectual capital relevant to candidate regions as well as infrastructure, real estate, and the total cost of ownership (TCO) specifically.

This does not mean that commercial real estate brokers are best suited to do the work; far from it. The big early drivers for data center siting are accessibility to power and telecommunications, which are not the core competencies of brokers.

Most meaningful power and fiber can be found on the perimeter or above the cities of 250,000 people. Users' best interests are served if consultants contact utility, transmission utility, and the location's economic development committee (EDC) early in the siting process. Power is a commodity and a large part of the total budget. Hiring a favorite or an incumbent real estate vendor to understand the language and goals is a waste of time and effort. Vendors doing branch work. Advance lease renewals, leases, purchases, or buybacks for space acquisitions are not likely the best suited for data centers.

People from EDCs and the state have been remarkably helpful and knowl-edgeable about this type of requirement. They have great visuals and docu-mentation to support the process. Their technology and "fingertip" knowledge have made them more useful than brokers in most cases. Many EDC and state employees are overworked and undercompensated. An incentive model needs to be created to recognize outstanding performance. Bigger deals or greater revenue should be recognized as contributing to the tax and community base and rewarded accordingly.

Finally, it all really comes down to the TCO model, where we incorporate the one-time and future cost associated with sites for consideration.

Like the matrix of scoring the acts of God and man-made considerations, the fact that an asset may score poorly does not take it off the list. These are guides. There are always some intangibles, client preferences, and relevant war stories that kill sites or make them. The goal of the BIA is to understand the unlikely financial and human challenges of working through unplanned outages. How much time, effort, and money will be allocated to satisfy the same and how to implement. There is no one-size-fits-all scenario nor should there be. Recent laws and guidelines are helpful, but more should and likely will be crafted.

We strongly recommend negotiating with a minimum of two utilities and states in competition with each other. Most states cannot make any out-of-program concessions without documented interest and competition.

State/local and utility expenses (with/without taxes) are two of the largest operating expenses in the TCO. The utility can contribute to users' needs by way of:

- Transformers or primary taps at the source
- Make-before-break transmission improvements
- Looped configurations for redundancy
- Substation improvements
- Cost per kilowatt-hour
- Caps on escalations
- Spot buying of power
- Reservation of unused capacity of power and improvements
- Rights-of-way: easements, one time and future acquisition and cost
- Unique tree trimming schedules
- Spare parts at the regional service area
- Spare parts at the site
- Time-sensitive and contractual response times
- Network operating control center monitoring unique to the asset

Committees of local and state representatives can be flexible on:

- Local sales tax on equipment
- Local and state sales tax on "sticks and bricks" (materials for improvements)
- State and local tax for utilities and telecommunications

Without going into too many specifics, I can say with confidence that if the documents and BOD are accurate from site to site and if the revised documentation is current and written, the process is solid. Note: Selective memory is pervasive in the on-the-record/off-the-record world of negotiations and prenegotiations. This is all "buyer beware" in the disclaimer world.

My experience is that over 50% of the time, owners' information and brokers' collateral are patently untrue and often directly misleading. The utility information needs a few layers of filtering to get the right "one-time" and future costs. In their defense, the utilities have been tortured by "half-baked" real estate with world-beating whiz-bang requirements that require the double back with a full twisting gainer... not. Often they are papered to death by accounting firms (experts, believe it or not) to sort out power transmission, reliability, and so forth. Vendors often want immediate answers to complex answers. They are in a hurry to check the box or fill in the Excel cell for an important and expensive component. Good information is worth waiting for. This process cannot start too soon.

As discussed earlier, the real estate component is a small part of the strategic migration of a data center. The buy, sell, or lease dynamic is rather simple. The only meaningful component is the over- or underinformed landlord who will price the asset consistent with the frothiness or low activity as well as relevance of nearby meaningful power and fiber.

A strategic plan considering the power, fiber optics, water, and local/state incentives is required to support a traditional real estate decision.

15

CYBERTERRORISM

According to relevant and confidential sources, the U.S. economy loses over $6.5 billion annually as a result of what can be called cyberterrorism. Cyberterrorism is defined as intrusive efforts by those hacking into unwanted Web sites, stealing credit card information, and infiltrating financial institutions, retail organizations, and personal accounts.

Cybercrime or software bombs have caused problems for public and private networks for years. Information technology (IT) staff has been playing catch-up to cybercriminals in the high-stakes game of manipulating and preserving data. One of the first major cyberterrorism events occurred in 1988 at a securities trading company in Texas. Approximately 170,000 payroll records were deleted from the database months after the perpetrator had left the company; the aim was to time a "bomb" to go off later and not cause the cyberthief to be considered a suspect.

If you consider that 70% of outages are human and 21% are human error (spontaneous), only 9% of outages are management or process related. Thus cybercrime, or human intervention (the politically correct term), is a meaningful part of IT or plant interruptions.

Consider the 2002 "Logic Bomb" that was planted in the UBS Paine Webber data system by a disgruntled employee. This bomb was made up of approximately 50 to 70 lines of computer code that U.S. prosecutors claim took down about 2,000 servers. Approximately 8,000 brokers were left without access to intelligence and were unable to perform their duties. This act allegedly stemmed from an employee who had expected to receive approximately $15,000 at year-end. The business impact associated with the event well exceeded that amount.

Companies can take steps to defuse bombs, but more often than not they are hidden in plain sight. One proactive measure companies have taken is to make sure that employees or programmers who write the code do not test the code or that the company has protocols in place to work around this challenge. Other cybercriminals are learning ways to penetrate or break into Internet Protocol (IP) or Voice-Over-Internet Protocol (VOIP). One owner of a small VOIP telephone company was arrested in 2006 for breaking into protocol and rerouting calls to another network, profiting by over $1 million. He would use another company's facilities and bill for the time. This is sort of like charging rent for an apartment that you do not own.

In the foreseeable future, low lights for cybercrime are:

- In 2002, 180,000 cyberattacks occurred in the United States. The number of cyberattacks has doubled since then.
- Businesses will experience 32 cyber break-ins or more in one week on average.
- One vendor interviewed was attacked over 400 times in one day.
- According to the existing velocity of cyberterrorism, events will double each year, based on Moore's Law.

Regardless of industry, 92% of all companies experience cyberattacks. (Financial institutions, credit card, and retail companies experience a higher percentage of attacks.)

There are a number of direct and indirect cost implications of cyberterrorism:

- There is an obvious loss of sales during disruptions to monitor and capture the event.
- There is a loss of staff time, network delays, and loss of access to network to monitor, track, and arrest violators who breach firewalls and break the law.
- There is an obvious increase in insurance costs due to litigation. This is due to the trickle-down effect of all crime, including automobile, fire, and theft.
- There is a loss of intellectual property. (Criminals breach, copy, and distribute best practices, proprietary protocols, firewalls, and nonintrusive events.)

The cost of cyberterrorism often is not listed on the company's profit and loss spreadsheet and never shows up in the total cost of ownership. It often finds itself in the theft pile and therefore is dealt with at a board or steering committee level; more cameras or guards are hired instead of firewall protection and IT surveillance.

These costs are both uncommon and staggering:

- The cost of forensics and recovery. The costs of staying ahead of the cyberterrorists and to adhere to best practices and catch them accelerate with Moore's Law.
- The loss of critical, nonretrievable information. Once it is gone, it is gone.

There are numerous indirect costs of cyberterrorism:

- The most obvious and hurtful long-term indirect cost of cyberterrorism or espionage is the loss of confidence and credibility in the finance industry. Once a security system is breached, the confidence of investors in or users of in the brand or institution can and does go down significantly. Recent examples of such a breach of trust are the AOL crash of the late 1990s and the Research in Motion crash of 2006.
- The public image of victim organizations is tarnished. The public trusts certain brands for their integrity, scalability, burstability, and security to protect private information.
- Customer loyalty among financial institutions is at an all-time low. We have learned that markets are no longer a place but rather a price. Private investors are migrating to low-cost securities and banking companies, trusting that their information is secure. They have *less* trust in the intellectual property and branding of larger institutions and *more* trust in their own ability to do research and due diligence to secure their finances for the future.
- The announcement that the Social Security numbers of the Veterans Administration's customers and clients were revealed led to a loss of trust in the government and the computer industry. Once this confidence and security wall is breached, the public faith in the country's greatest brand, the United States of America, is tarnished significantly.

Who are the cyberterrorists? Who is taking the time and effort to breach our firewalls and to compromise our integrity?

- 90% of all breaches or events are caused by amateur hackers—cyber joy-riders. According to the IBM Global Securities arm located in Yorktown Heights, New York:
- 9.9% are corporate spies whose full-time job is to make their way into their peers' best practices for their own company's benefit.
- 1% is world-class cybercriminals, the best and brightest of the bad guys who cause catastrophic damage, destruction, and compromise of security via worms and viruses.

The U.S. government carries out attacks to test its own defenses. Like any proactive preventive maintenance group, it tests firewalls to determine how good our defenses are and how destructive the bad guys can be. The Defense Information Security Agency spearheads these efforts. It found that 88% of the 3,000 defense computer systems it attacked were "easily penetrable":

- 96% of the attacks on these systems were not detected. (That means the bad guys entered, captured data, and exited without being detected.)
- 4% were detected (or left a cybertrail).
- 5% were reported or investigated. That leaves 83% of attacks or events without consequences.

The Federal Bureau of Investigation estimates that U.S. businesses lose $138 million every year due to hackers. The Central Intelligence Agency estimates over the past three years, government systems have been illegally entered 250,000 times. Approximately $2 billion per year is lost on VISA or euro-pay systems that are compromised. (This is one reason why fees and premiums are rising.)

According to the Government Accountability Office, "due to more and more sustainable attacks in the ether, the U.S. Government agencies may not be able to respond effectively to such attacks." What does this have to do with business continuity practices and a business impact analysis? Plenty! We often think of acts of God, human intervention, and human error as the source of a system becoming compromised, inoperable, and causing remote systems to come into play. Cyberterrorism and the proactive events of criminals can and will be part of the interruptions of various industries, including the public sector, in the near future.

In 1998, Richard Clarke, the first special advisor to the president on the security infrastructure, created the counterterrorism group reporting to the National Security Advisor, Condoleezza Rice, and the newly appointed director of Homeland Security, Tom Ridge. This may be considered the origins of identifying the need for surveillance and protection of facilities and software vulnerabilities for the public and private sectors. After reading a cover story in the *Waters* magazine featuring Howard Lutnick in the late 1990s, it was clear to me that two things defined his future and mine:

1. Cantor Fitzgerald was a technology company. Contrary to financial publications and reporting, this company, its day-to-day activities, its corporate spend (like other financial companies), and its maintenance were technology driven. Market data had to be faster, with better visuals, more weapons. The kit on the desktop was becoming commoditized and needed a value-added upgrade, or changes to keep it

relevant to users' needs. Technology would be a desktop differentiator for this company. At this time, Cantor Fitzgerald's IT spend was new and extraordinary. The "one-time" and recurring costs were eclipsing the salaries, rent, and travel and entertainment, to mention a few.

2. Howard Lutnick was driven to get between the "wall and the wallpaper" for margins, fees, and profitability. To me this meant that he would have to be more willing to make a few, faster nickels than a slow dime.

Because I am a niche player and an anomaly to many with whom I work, I have to prove myself account by account. I can, and do, work effectively outside the box not because I have familiarized myself with a few handy acronyms but because I have been blessed and fortunate enough to have done multidisciplinary work from the C suite through to execution (as a vendor) for extraordinary people like Doug Gardner and Charlie Waters at Cantor Fitzgerald.

This book would likely not have been written without the influence of Doug and Charlie. It is worth taking a moment (even in the cyberterrorism chapter) to explain why that is so. Indulge me here... many of us fall in love with the memories of those in death more than life. In a dysfunctional way, it is far more romantic. It can make our time on earth more purposeful when "doing it" for someone else—or "in memory of."

The events of September 11, 2001, brought out the very best and worst in all of us. I include myself in that theory. Most of us have a person or situation that we can say was a defining moment in our careers, a boss's kind words following a massive screw-up, getting fired, good luck, bad luck, or other. Doug and Charlie were mine. I had made 17 cold calls to Doug when he finally took my call at 6:45 AM in October 1996 and said to come up. Doug and Charlie made me a better person.

- He would not take my call after 7:30 AM and made me realize that not only did people wake up at 7:30, but were already at their desks!
- Doug worked out (before it was fashionable) before he went to work. That meant he had to get up at 5:00 AM or so.
- He told me that if the work did not get done before 10:00 AM, it was never getting done that day.
- Only wimps went out for lunch.
- Like basketball, this was a team sport. I had to recognize that I had to trust other people to do their job or delegate if I was to be truly effective.
- He taught me to laugh at myself and not to take myself too seriously.
- He taught me to laugh at meetings.

- He taught me to prepare to answer all his questions and ask "ourselves" tougher questions.
- He taught me that it was OK to say "I don't know."
- He taught me to read my own documents carefully before it was to be "Doug Proofed."
- He trusted me to lead or follow on four continents and seven countries on his behalf... describing me to a vendor as "his conscience in the field." I became his "hot hands."
- He led by example. He was my age, and I could not get enough of being around him.
- Loyalty was most important, and doing what was "right" is better than doing what was "best" in the long run. Tell the hard truth always!

Charlie was better than I was at my job. He often got to the point and the salient facts well before I did. I often followed him and executed on his behalf. He was driven by a job well done, excellence and self-esteem, and love of his wife, Barbara, and their son and twin daughters.

This discussion is self-indulgent and a bit personal, but professionally, the eight-year business relationship that I had with Cantor Fitzgerald started with a $25,000 Disaster Recovery Study (in the paper world of financial services) and grew into several assignments worldwide, including their business continuity facility in the United States and United Kingdom, which had an impact on their ability to resume business after the World Trade Towers fell.

16

NEED FOR SPEED

How far from a primary facility should a secondary or business continuity planning facility be? This question has been touched on by previously documented sources of legislation, SEC white papers 1 and 2, and the indelibly etched images of catastrophic events of the past 15 years. It is an ongoing question we revisited based on the applications considered in the environment and the most recent technology to multiplex voice, data, and video.

We have identified the relevant distances of likely acts of God and consequences of evaluation, explosion, or impact on man-made improvements or intervention.

However, the brain trust to get or keep an edge over the competition is based on the unwavering and static fundamentals of the physics of the speed of light. The speed of light is relevant for a signal to self-heal on a synchronous optical network (SONET) with .25 to .35 milliseconds (millionths of a second) on the SONET ring. This is the driver for the distance to save data from one site to another.

If the distance is too far and a second of inscription is lost at 10 gigabytes or OC-192 dense wavelength division multiplexing (DWDM) (or equivalent), that means that data equivalent to nine three-hour movies will be lost or latent. That is a lot of single-line copy if it were trades!

Uninterrupted, Euclidean (point-to-point) speed of light is 186.3 miles per millisecond. A single photon traveling point to point from Los Angeles to New York would make it in 15 milliseconds one way. That is not a practical model since the signal of encryption would require regeneration of energy and power to gather itself and send a signal every 50 to 100 miles to keep encryption accurate. This is also done with submersible cables under the ocean. The power regeneration model from coast to coast does not take into account route miles versus Euclidean miles. As a rule of thumb, add 30 to 50% to the Euclidean distance to determine the route distance from the point-to-point distance.

Latency, which is the key to successful encryption and for placing or executing an order faster than the other guy, is significantly impacted by the latency created by how many devices a signal will touch or be manipulated in the process of transmissions migrating from fiber or Ethernet to InfiniBand.

InfiniBand is a high-speed input/output technology that speeds up the transfer of data-intensive files across enterprise servers/storage devices in networks. What this means to the exchanges and security firms and banks competing for trades and clients' managed assets is that they are competing to shave fractions of seconds off transmission lines to pinpoint share prices.

Electronic trading has reduced overall trading volatility. For example, track a stock you own and look for a 2 to 7% swing up or down in a given day, then layer over the exchanges and see the trend. Any meaningful swings that exist are being reduced but still precipitated by the herd mentality of buy or sell simultaneously; now the tiny price fluctuations tend to smooth out large moves.

From a profitability point of view, the anonymous electronic trade is transparent because any buyer and seller will be put together on a who-got-there-first model. For instance, a Linux server can trade up to 200 million shares a day. Size matters less, speed matters more! There are no group awards for second through tenth place in trading. If you do not execute to clients' expectations, you lose clients: Darwin's law of trading execution in the new world.

For nonsecurities or financial institutions, recent media-rich content requires a "fatter pipe" and faster encryption. The need for speed is agnostic and applies to all businesses. Ad agencies, service companies, architectural companies, real estate companies, and entertainment companies use video, animation, and drawings as well as digital media as differentiators to secure and keep customers and clients.

For securities companies, placing buy/sell equipment as close as physically possible to the exchange market-making device and splitting or beating a competitor by millionths of a second makes sense. One company that built a facility for 10 billion trades a day years ago was barely making 3 billion trades a day recently. (Time to reinvent itself!) The company realized it was long on real estate, which is not its core business, and had a shirking human infrastructure to support the shrinking trading volume.

Like so many other financial institutions, some data center facilities decided that the cost to build and operate such facilities should be left to others. They could take $100 to $300 million and turn it into $1 billion over three to five years rather than pour it into a nonperforming asset for an overzealous insurance policy. For some companies, the pendulum has swung too far to the risk side of reducing expenses.

One magazine touted a facility in New Jersey as one of the most important data centers in the world. I looked at the facility in 1996–1997 for alternative uses due to three years of 100% vacancy, including a ramped parking facility for buses to travel to New York.

The facility had almost paper-thin floor loads, car parking underneath the asset (bad for car bomb scenarios), less than 100 yards to the mouth of a tunnel to New York City, and was likely to be evacuated after an unfortunate event; also, there were windows on all sides, including the view of the rail system 75 to 100 yards away. The building was 1.7 miles Euclidean miles away from lower Manhattan...too close by some experts' opinions.

This company and others have hired other firms to provide security and infrastructure to make the inside plant and the economy work in an asset that scores a 2 out of 10 in location and a 0 out of 10 by operating in the busiest section of the transportation area for the wrong reasons. If this company failed, it would cripple the nation's economy temporarily. Since there were only guidelines and suggestions without the white papers and the Sarbanes-Oxley Act (SOX), bylaws, the Securities and Exchange Commission (SEC), this company/tenant complied like others to guidelines; by common sense it is questionable. Unfortunately, prior to major terrorism events including September 11, 2001, business continuity was a part-time job often in the risk management silo.

With all the laws and loosely crafted language by the SEC, National Association of Securities Dealers, Patriot Act, and SOX...is it all good? You be the judge.

If you remember anything from this book, please remember these two points: Markets are a price and not a place, and we no longer need to be anywhere specifically to execute. Greensboro, North Carolina, or Columbia, South Carolina, could easily become the new financial hub of transactional packets. Several states now have superior and more reliable power, fiber optics, tax infrastructure, and labor than the five to seven synchronous sites we pore over that are in close proximity to Manhattan.

Critical and asynchronous applications footprints or locations out of region are becoming more compelling from the point of view of total cost of ownership. The major deterrent to remote mirroring or business continuity planning relevance has been the latency of the packets, the cost of the long haul, and the last-mile transmission telecommunications cost. The reliability of remote central offices and hubs has been improved over the past 10 years to satisfy Internet Protocol and Centrex traffic as well as the residential triple play of voice, video, and data. Remote high-speed processing is possible for reliable and consistent data transmission.

Remote data centers in the United States are becoming more common for larger requirements. The "cornfield" scenario is making more and more sense. Remote power-tapping of transmission lines has become relatively simple. The telecom piece for remote data center siting has been less attractive. The cornfield concept will always have a Regional Bell Operating Company or AT&T solution. We as taxpayers built and paid for the remote and the urban infrastructure. Although the remote locations do not always have the necessary processing ability, often they are upgradable for multiplexing in modules or cards in a fairly fast and inexpensive way. The remote competitive local exchange carriers often have leased lines or have no "facilities" to support the network. Many times a utility has a telecom arm that shares rights-of-way. In the past, smaller "mom-and-pop" providers may have been too risky for a data center or for mission-critical facilities. I would say that, in general, the remote telecom outside power network has never been in better shape. The networks are almost always nonlinear and synchronous (self-healing). It is critical to vet the infrastructure and associated optronics to limit the single points of failure and bottlenecking of information technology (IT) transmission. The offshoring of data centers in environmentally friendly parts of the world where "free cooling" is an option make the importance of IT transmission that much more important. Twelve years after deregulation, a host of new submersible cables connecting the planet have made redundant and reliable telecommunications possible in remote parts of the United States and the world at nonprohibitive price points.

17

FUTURE OF DATA CENTER EFFICIENCIES—THINK OUTSIDE THE GRID

The costs of mission-critical facilities have never been as "target rich" for savings as they are now. After reviewing the power and cooling challenges facing the industry, I have come to realize that the best way to sort out the appropriate site or location is to recognize that there is no silver bullet to challenges and that one size or tier does *not* fit all.

I encourage the reader to think outside the box in resolving data center challenges. As smart vendors and users, we often act as lemmings to put industry bandages on super-sized issues or challenges.

In the world of multibillion-dollar total cost of ownership (TCO) modeling, wouldn't it be prudent to aggressively go after the larger components in a meaningful way? By that I mean locating a facility in a tax-friendly environment. Zero percent or nearly zero percent sales tax over 15 to 20 years can be a $30 million to $70 million savings. Compound that with a market or high utility rate for a 20- to 60-megawatt load and you can realize a $60 million to $100 million overpayment in power. With just those two components of the TCO, a user could overpay by up to $170 million to $200 million right at the start.

The thinking outside the box should come from the C suite; in other words, from the top down. Top managers should lay down the challenge to separate critical from noncritical applications to determine the distance between a primary footprint and a secondary or storage footprint. Everything does not need to be 40 route kilometers from the primary center. This is an expensive and ignorant one-size solution for people who are too lazy to sort out critical applications from noncritical ones.

Consultants must vet and build data centers in cool parts of the world or places where there are cool and plentiful aquifers to supply free cooling or geothermal solutions. Why are there not more data centers in Iceland or Greenland and other points north (or cooler)? By choosing such locations, the choice of multiple fiber optics providers will be reduced, but we are dealing with that issue now in remote parts of the United States, Europe, and Asia. If we can reduce power consumption for cooling by thermal storage or free cooling even before turning to other reductions generated by direct current (DC) plant design and implementation, a utility bill can and will come down by 25 to 30%. The longer telecommunications costs and the transmission cost will continue to come down. Big picture they will go up but not meaningfully. Internet Protocol (IP) packet costs will likely be taxed, but both the Centrex and IP costs will continue to go down. In the short term they will be viewed as a rounding error in the super-sized savings or siting the mission-critical facilities in strategic-nontraditional regions of the world with inherent environmental and tax benefits.

Multiplexing at the long-haul and submersible level is making great strides in the quality, scalability, burstability, and self-heading arenas. Fewer cables in remote and cold parts of the world causes greater dependence on few providers, but again, we face that now in remote parts of the United States. When virtualization, not synchronous and storage requirements, are fulfilled in remote and cold parts of the world, the first movers will be recognized as leading thought providers, and secondary movers will rush to the market. No one wants to be the first adopter of such forward-thinking ideas. There is often a fine line between insanity and intelligence.

Expect remote siting for data centers in nontraditional and cold parts of the world. Expect more virtualization. Expect more beta installations of DC plants in users' data centers and larger real-time deployments of DC plants. Expect more cogeneration (cogen) and microcogeneration for mission-critical facilities. Expect more local and state sales tax, personal property, and real estate tax incentive legislation to attract mission-critical users. Why?

We now know:

- Today's data centers require more power per square foot or similar power over greater square footage that we cannot cool satisfactorily.
- Over 80% of existing data centers will run out of white space by 2011 or 2012. As we know, it takes two to three years to build a data center.
- Our national power grid is sagging. It is 40 to 50 years old in most rural regions with recent histories of negative cascading and brownouts.

- No new nuclear facilities have been permitted and operating in the United States in over 20 years, and it takes 13 to 15 years to build a nuclear power plant. (It takes three to five years just to design and get the necessary approvals.) Three are under construction
- Dirty fossil generation is out of favor due to carbon dioxide (CO_2) emissions pollution in the world. Coal is largely the dirtiest fossil fuel. In China, a new coal plant is built every two days. China contributes the greatest CO_2 emissions to the world. It has 16 of the 20 largest cities in the world. If it can create a city the size of New York City every three years, you can see how China needs power.
- Hydroelectric power is regional and does not provide enough capacity to have a national impact. Also, the rotary turbine discharge in the plants create hazardous materials emissions.
- Clean fossil fuel (natural gas), which is abundant in the United States, is a weak lobby in Washington. During the mid-1940s, gas "war lines" were buried without any geotechnical studies. They have a history of breaking due to erosion and shifts in the earth that impact the 36- to 48-inch pipes. The leaking gas emits no odor, which makes breaks very difficult to detect.
- Over the past 100 years the Earth's population has grown 400%.
- Bio- or sustainable supplies are not as visible or reliable for mission-critical facilities. Until biofuels are a reliable source, we will continue to rely on fossil, geothermal, hydroelectric, or nuclear sources to keep mission-critical facilities running. Our job is to mitigate gross inefficiencies in the existing networks.

This leads us to two viable alternatives that I believe are the future of mission-critical facilities. Since people hate change, we will have to take baby steps to incorporate these concepts into data center designs to enhance reliability, increase efficiency, and reduce the total cost of ownership by 30 to 70%.

The first requirement is an open mind. Think back to how many bad real estate, equipment, or information technology (IT) decisions that you are aware of in your own company due to politics, timing, preferred vendors, lack of courage, half-baked bad ideas, change of law or legislation, expiration of benefits, and so forth. As a vendor, I have been late to the decision party and part of the implementation party, which often means cleaning up a broker's bad suggestions. Just because a user is big and profitable does not make it "real estate" smart. Multiple offices across the country do not make a vendor effective; they just make the vendor big. Vendors cannot out-national the locals or out-local the nationals in real estate market intelligence (especially in specialized niche intelligence). Because of the Internet and other electronic resources, over a weekend users can do a national search for dirty or buildings in every U.S. city, including plenty of Tier 2 or Tier 3 cities. The real estate search has become demystified, but siting data centers still is tricky.

The two ideas to flourish over the next five to seven years are:

1. Cogeneration or microcogeneration for data centers, mixed-use data centers, business continuity planning (BCP), and mission-critical office parks
2. Direct current (DC) power plants for data centers (not just telecommunications equipment)

Cogen, also known as combined heat and power, is the production of two kinds of energy: traditionally, electricity and heat from a single source of fuel. Cogen often replaces or complements the traditional method of supply and separately burns natural gas in a boiler to produce heat or steam; it is very nice for assets with static power draws and the need for ambient heat. This is the simple capture of the heat and making the environment ambient (like free cooling during the winter).

Integrated cooling and heating incorporates cooling. It is also called tri-generation: heating, cooling, and electricity. The heat from the engine jacket from the natural gas burn is captured in the exhaust and sent to the cooling absorber. It is a time-tested method. Although it is not the preferred method for data centers, it is a practical concept. The resulting chilled water is sent to process computer room air conditioning, computer room air handler units, and so forth.

The existing utility distribution method of energy is inconvenient for big users. Land or assets are generally within one to three miles from most candidate assets. This distance is remarkably inefficient and wastes up two-thirds of the energy fuel. Users pay for the losses; up to 75% of billings per year are for wasted energy. Over 20 years, a large user could spend about $120 million for wasted but purchased power.

Today cogen is no longer a supersized noncritical application solution for state or federal loads with an office components or hospitals but properly designed, a real solution for five-to six-9s reliability. The principles of cogen have long been known and widely used. Thomas Edison built the first cogeneration plant in 1891; private and public facilities have been capturing heat from energy burn and using it for heat or cooling for years.

Why is cogen a compelling solution for the business continuity or data center business today?

- **Energy savings.** Exclusive of IT spending going forward transmission taxes, real estate taxes and new facilities and new kit-associated software fees; the electric bill, when in less expensive cost or tariff regions will be the first or second highest recurring operating expense for stand-alone data centers. In this cogen model, there is actually a significant payback to the capital cost combined with more efficient energy utilization, tax credits, excess energy sales sold back to the grid get discounts reducing the TCO.

- **High resiliency.** By generating power and heat cooling with redundancy in the plant (N + 1, N + 2, 3N) and by using the power grid as a stand-alone emergency power supply backup sized to take full load, dual-sourced generators in the plant achieving six to seven 9s of reliability are realistic.
- **Cleaner air.** Being a good corporate citizen these days means being more environmentally concise. Generating power, heating, and cooling on-site reduces the dependency on inefficient power plants and will reduce the pollution and dependency on the generating power plants. Remember, data centers account for almost 2% of our total national power consumption at increased velocity of consumption. As mentioned, the U.S. population grew at 400% over the past 100 years; it is expected to double by 2050.
- **Fast.** Scalable systems can be and are built in modules and can be installed as fast, if not faster, than utility substations. Long lead transformers for better equipment at the substation are growing monthly, less desired transformers are being specified for speed similar to when we were buying generators from Europe during the go-go dot-com days; the equipment is not Underwriters Laboratories rated.
- **Good for the kids.** Reducing waste limits our dependency on coal, foreign and domestic oil, and nuclear resources. Gas is cleaner and abundant.

Some of the recent cogeneration activity has come from old data points by the public sector on the efficiencies and payback of the system. The model seems too good to be true. In addition, generous tax credits together with emission reductions mandated by the Kyoto Protocol have stimulated investment, both public and private, in cogen.

The U.S. Department of Energy has established a "goal" of doubling the amount of electricity produced by cogeneration from 9 to 18% by 2010—that's tomorrow! The European Commission has established a similar target. In Switzerland (what some consider the economic epicenter of the world), cogen accounts for 77% of the electricity produced. In Denmark, it accounts for 40%.

If hospitals can use cogen to deliver, service, and protect lives, cogeneration can certainly service and protect our data centers. I cannot tell you how many generators and UPS (uninterruptible power supply) plants did not work during the Seaport Substation outage in lower Manhattan due to no fuel, no generators, or poorly maintained equipment. Sometimes the generators worked; at other times, someone did not turn the cooling system on and the data centers' generators baked and crashed. Also, during times of need or catastrophic events, fuel trucks are not life-saving devices and cannot always pass through inclement weather conditions. If proper fuel storage is not on-site and is not sized for prolonged outages, it cannot be counted on.

Cogen is a time- and cost-sensitive alternative to fossil fuel. If a traditional power station uses 100% fossil fuel, approximately 75% of the energy is a poor business model (or waste). It is here and has been here! Under a cogen model, users will pay 100% of input fuel (which is higher than the cost of low-cost utility power). However, after capturing approximately 50% of useful heat for cooling and heating, 35% would go toward electricity out and 17% rather than 75% is energy lost or "waste" other relevant energy generating sources wasting of time and expense. Other power alternatives that perhaps are not appropriate for mission-critical facilities are wind, wave, solar, geothermal (heat gases escaping from earth), and waste (heat gases captured from molecular breakdown and explosion of solids).

In the event of no or low wind or no or low waves, our storage capabilities are awesome but have reasonable limits. For extended periods of outage coupled with a low source of wind or wave, the consequences are too high. The same risk applies for capturing geothermal and waste energy. What if it stops? I do not know why it stops, but if the Earth stops spitting gas out of the waste dump... then what?

Granted, a single point of failure for cogeneration is the source of gas, but that can be designed around risk and mitigated. The plant can transfer back to the utility grid or burn stored fossil fuel to create energy. Nothing is 100%.

Here is a list of the top 10 reasons cogen has not expanded as actively as common sense dictates in mission-critical or other applications:

1. There are ambiguous regulatory barriers; companies need to learn how to play the game.
2. The interconnection process with incumbent utility can be protracted.
3. Criteria for emission requirements protracted are not friendly.
4. Financing vehicles are difficult.
5. There are too few industry leaders and too many fringe players.
6. There is a lack of market focus not gas versus price of the pump.

7. Market players need to reinvent themselves to be sensitive to mission-critical needs and live above five-9s reliability.
8. There has been a mixed message to market: Cogen is not a standby alternative.
9. There has been a historic lack of environmental concerns (although that is changing swiftly).
10. Cogen is viewed as an engineering solution, not an energy solution with significant environmental benefits.

Cogeneration is a process of creating energy and power by burning a clean fossil fuel. So far we are familiar with generating companies. Our cost to spot-buy gas is similar to other bulk buyers. Cogen operators will not have the defense or offensive buying diversity of nuclear and hydropower. As a pure economic play, cogen would be a short-term loser. However, what California learned and what Texas is learning now is that the cost of gas is going up (coal is out of favor) and driving the cost per kilowatt-hour up from \$0.05 to \$0.06 to \$0.13 to \$0.15. For 30- to 60-megawatt users, the difference can mean over \$100 million or more in the TCO. Cogen makes sense when you capture the heat, create steam, and either use the steam to heat human or ambient components or create cooling from the steam (absorbers). The payback is seven to ten years to a zero-sum gain. But more important: We live in the mandatory load-shedding world. Although today not enough services, municipalities, or banks are able and willing to shed load, shedding will become mandatory.

Cogeneration will be off the grid that is susceptible to shedding. The cogen model can and likely will sell excess power back to the grid and will tap into overabundant natural U.S. resources of gas. Cogen can be a 3 N (turbine, generator, and utility network) scenario while capturing heat via absorbers for cooling by using a silica-based gel to evaporate water. We cannot and will not conserve our way out of the overdemand-and-undersupply paradigm that we are in. Biomass and geothermal solutions are appropriate alternatives of energy supply for non-mission-critical applications, but natural gas is most appropriate for mission-critical uses because:

- It is reliable.
- It is commercially viable, with years of data available.
- It is impervious to international fuel crises.
- It offers LEED- (low-energy-electron-diffraction) rich opportunities.
- It pays for itself, which no other system does, in three to six years, depending on the relative price of gas.

DC power plants are the second power option. If we manipulate the power from generation to transmission and then to distribution as few times as possible, we utilize the current produced to its greatest efficiency. DC power requires less equipment, cost, installation, maintenance, and it is more reliable and is commercially deployable in 2.5-megawatt components. DC power can even supply computer room air-conditioning units (CRAC) units! The coefficient of saving from design, installation, real estate, maintenance, and operating (utility bills) is extraordinary. First movers in this space will reap the rewards.

Again, the inefficiencies of stepping down or transforming at the utility from a higher alternating current (AC) voltage to a lower AC distribution voltage, to rectify from AC to DC back to AC again in the UPS (uninterruptible power supplies to apply battery backup storage into the system), then transform a second time in the PDUs (power distribution units) from 480 VAC to 120/208 VAC, then finally to rectify in the server power supply from AC to DC, convert from higher voltage DC to a lower voltage DC then convert finally to a less than 1 VDC to feed server operations is very inefficient. To make matters worse, most data centers utilize a dual-feed (2N) distribution network that is designed to operate at less than one-half of the rated design per side (so that either side can take over the load if the opposite side were to fail). These dual-ended servers are typically installed in a 42U cabinet to 30U servers running at less than 50% capacity by design, which is a low distribution efficiency of approximately 55 to 70%. Thus we are adrift in inefficiencies and waste. Non-IT related usage accounts for 60 to 70% of the power utilization. If cooling accounts for 60% of demand power usage, that leaves 50% approximately for inefficiencies.

One way to reduce the capital expense of the traditional AC-UPS plant—which accounts for 33 to 37% of the critical plant spending and 10 to 20% of the environmental real estate for Tiers 3 and 4—is in the design and implementation of the power plant.

DC current is very simple in nature and is by definition direct and more constant than alternating current. DC plants have had many years of commercial success and are known for their high reliability in telecom installations with 5E, soft switched, and DMS gear. The utilization of DC power means fewer pieces of critical gear, fewer single points of failure potential (that is why we use diesel generators; they have only seven moving meaningful parts). Cooling for the DC plant is far less demanding than for the AC-UPS plant; it requires less current, which means less cost. There are fewer maintenance agreements, which means less cost, and fewer pieces of mission-critical gear, which means less risk!

However, there are voltage drop concerns with DC, which makes DC very difficult to utilize in data center high-density environments. However, if the distribution voltages of these systems can be increased to the UL (Underwriters Laboratories) limits of 575 VDC, these issues are overcome. As seen in the manufacturers' Validus DC design, data centers can be designed to be up to 40% more efficient than legacy AC UPS–based systems when higher-voltage AC is utilized. The Validus system is designed to make higher-voltage DC directly from the utility (i.e., 15 kilovolts to 575 VDC at the utility pad with the PQM or mission-critical-grade rectifier). The system then feeds a DC main tie main switchboard, where it can be paralleled with other rectifiers and to energy-storage sources. Then the system feeds to a central point of loading converters or power converter units, which convert the 575 VDC to usable, safe, and reliable 48 VDC. This voltage is touch safe and is used by all telecommunications companies; many computer-intense companies use it today in data centers. This system can also be naturally utilized in a 2N scenario where each server is fed twice for redundancy considerations. It is also notable that below 50 volts, these systems are concurrently maintainable as described by Occupational Safety and Health Administration regulations. Most notable is the fact that in this configuration, very high densities can achieved safely.

Data centers are actually already abundantly DC. All of the electronic processors, storage systems, and routing equipment is internally DC. If we could scale DC much like AC is today at higher voltages and rid the system of the many transformations rectifications and inversions, we could in fact feed these systems what they naturally function on: DC. This concept of "hybrid" power utilizes scalable AC design with the inherent benefits of DC. Some of these DC benefits include:

- The use of up to 15% less copper to distribute the same amount of power.
- The ability to bring together the two sources without using expensive and automatic static transfer switches (which bring two sources together so that if one fails the other picks up the load).
- The ability of the system to directly tie renewable energy or storage devices, like photocells, batteries, windmills, fuel cells, and flywheels, onto the distribution system almost anywhere, which makes these systems both efficient and easy to use.

DC is also very beneficial for cooling systems, especially DC electronically controlled plenum fans and DC lighting, such as light-emitting diodes.

It is also noteworthy to mention that mainframes and large storage arrays can and will be powered by high-voltage DC or 575 VDC, as their internals are already DC.

This use of scalable DC brings efficiency, reliability, simplicity, maintainability, constructability, and modularity to the data space. It is in fact the building block for today's green distribution system and eventually will be used in buildings, cities, and utilities. It is used extensively today in light rail, nuclear, military manufacturing, telecommunications, and data centers.

In an end-to-end comparison of 2N DC and AC architectures, an argument can be made that in a five-year TCO scenario that includes installation, operation, and maintenance at a rate of $.10 per kilowatt hour, a DC data center could cost the owner as much as one-half less than the AC data center.

A short-term challenge is to unify the voltage distribution to 380 volts. Server, mainframe, and storage companies do not want to provide multiple voltage selections; doing so drives up the cost of kit on a concept that needs as few barriers to market as possible. The financial and TCO model is sound.

The psychological challenge of turning the ship of the data center designer and operator is huge. Beta and partial installations are realistic short-term goals. Complete conversions to DC plants will take a few more hours (years) of successful field operation on a large scale for big kit. AC UPS manufacturers and associated controls, batteries, and kit providers are the effective lobbyists of the UPS industry. In telecom terms, the DC plant is like the soft switch is to the 5E Centrex switch to commercially deploy an IP solution to business and residence would cannibalize the large margin Centrex legacy system. What the Regional Bell Operating Companies and the long-distance carriers realized was that if they did not cannibalize their revenue base, the competitive local exchange carriers or business local exchange carriers would.

If current AC UPS providers do not take the lead in large DC deployments, telecom or military plant providers will take their market share. DC power plants make too much sense on too many levels to be ignored.

By replacing the typical AC UPS plant with DC power, users are realizing both greater reliability and efficiency. Similar to the keep-it-simple school of design, DC distribution has fewer manipulations by definition and has less expense and space requirements overall.

The mean time between failures (MTBF) for AC power supplies is approximately 100,000 hours. Heat is the main corrosive agent for power supplies. Swings of 20 to 30 degrees Fahrenheit in ambient temperature can reduce useful life by 50%. The MTBF for similar DC power supplies is approximately 250,000 hours—over 100% better than the AC kit.

The main difference in the old technology is that instead of converting the AC power "in the server," the power is converted at the cabinet level, taking a few "Us" with redundant feeds.

These energy losses have been reported on the traditional UPS:

- Power from transmission line to client transformer: 2 to 4%
- Power through UPS, AC to DC to AC: 25%
- Power through PDU or RPP: 2 to 4%
- Power through server, AC to DC: 18 to 23%

That is approximately 50% efficiency on computer-grade or "billable" power.

This list does not recognize upstream inefficiencies of power conversion at the utility or waste for cooling at the chiller, DC, air-handling units, CRAC, or pumps. As you can see, this is a target-rich environment for savings, and DC plants have a place.

The benefits of the remote cogen, DC power, and primary/mirrored or virtual data center processing for open, mainframe, or midware applications located in cooler points geographically in the north are evident. In the multibillion-dollar TCO modeling process, we need to consider uncommon solutions to ongoing, chronic, and expensive one-time and future spending for business continuity and IT solutions to satisfy our daily needs, corporate governance, and legal compliance. The key in this area will be to get IT to work for us again rather than us working for IT.

The answer is not adding a module or generator. The answer is not N + 2 or N + 3. Not all data centers should be outside Manhattan's door! We can save a great deal of money by considering alternative methods of power, cooling, and purchasing these extraordinarily expensive assets. Nontraditional views and an open mind are required.

GLOSSARY

Many of the definitions in this glossary are derived from language from federal laws, acts, and included in national plans including the Homeland Security Act of 2002, the USA Patriot Act of 2001, the national instant management system, and the national response plan, as well as common phrases and jargon from the mission-critical world.

I have often been accused of having my own hybrid language, one I call a cross between hip-hop and engineering. Friends, clients, and customers often smile and shake their heads when I go off on my techno-babble diatribes. The world of mission-critical infrastructure—that is, "rocketship real estate"—has its unique language relevant to real estate acquisitions, outside plan considerations, inside plan considerations, maintenance management, and service-level agreements. You need to use a certain amount of patience to understand the language. Do not push back. Be brave, and embrace some of the language.

All hazards　An approach for prevention, protection, preparedness, response, and recovery that addresses a full range of threats and hazards including domestic terrorist attacks, natural and man-made disasters, accidental disruptions, and other emergencies.

Assets　Contracts, facilities, property, and electronic and nonelectronic records and documents. Unobligated or unexpected balances of appropriations in funds or resources.

Backup generators　A methodology for creating or storing backup files. The youngest or most recent file is referred to as the son, the prior file is called the father, and the file of two generations older is the grandfather. This backup methodology is frequently used to refer to master files or financial applications.

Business continuity　The ability of an organization to continue to function before, during, and after a disaster.

Business impact analysis (BIA)　The process of identifying the potential impact of uncontrolled, nonspecific events in an institution's business process.

Control systems　Computer-based systems used within many infrastructures and industries to monitor and control sensitive processes and physical functions. These systems typically collect measurements and operational data from the field; process and display the information; and relay control commands to local or remote equipment or human/machine interfaces (operations). Examples of types of control systems include SCADA systems, process control systems, and digital control systems.

Critical infrastructure　Asset systems and networks, whether physical or virtual so vital to the United States that the incapacity or destruction of such assets, systems, or networks would have debilitating impact on security, national economy, economic security, public health or safety, or any combination of those.

Critical financial markets Financial markets whose operations are critical to the U.S. economy, including markets for Federal Reserve funds, foreign exchange, commercial paper, and government, corporate, and mortgage-backed securities.

Critical task Those prevention, protection, response, and recovery tasks that require coordination among the appropriate combination of federal, state, local, tribal, private sector, or nongovernmental entities during major events in order to minimize the impacts on lives, property, and economy.

Cybersecurity The prevention of damage due to unauthorized use or exploitation of, and, if needed, the restoration of, electronic information and communication systems, and information contained therein to ensure confidentiality, integrity, and availability. It includes the protection and restoration, when needed, of information networks and wireless satellite public safety answering points, 911, 411, communication systems, and control systems.

Data synchronization The comparison and reconsolidation of interdependent data files at the same time so they can contain the same information.

Dependency The one-directional reliance of an asset system network or a collection thereof within or across such sectors or input, interaction, or other requirements from other sources to function properly.

Disaster recovery plan A plan that describes the process to recover from major unplanned interruptions.

Emergency plan The steps to be followed during and immediately after an emergency such as fire, tornado, bomb threat, and so on.

Emergency An occasion or incidence for which in determination of the present federal assistance is needed to supplement state and local efforts and capabilities to save lives, and to protect property and public health and safety to lessen or avert the threat of catastrophe in any part of the United States.

Emergency response provider Includes federal, state, local, tribal agencies, public safety, law enforcement, emergency response, emergency medical including hospital emergency facilities, that relate to personnel agencies and authorities (see section 2.6, Homeland Security Act 2002).

Encryption The conversion of information to code or cipher.

EPS (emergency power systems) A generator-only method of creating and storing power.

FEMA Acronym for Federal Emergency Management Agency.

First responder A local and nongovernmental police, fire, and emergency person, who in the early stages of an incident is responsible for the protection and preservation of life, property, evidence, and the environment, including emergency response providers as defined in section 2 of the Homeland Security Act of 2002, as well as the emergency management, public health, clinical care, public works, and other skilled support personnel. Jurisdiction: a range or sphere of authority public agencies have jurisdiction on and incident related to their legal responsibilities and authority. Jurisdictional authority at an incident can be "geographical."

Gap analysis Comparison that identifies the difference between actual and desired outcomes.

GETS (Government Emergency Telecommunications Services) A government card program. GETS cards provide emergency access and priority processing for voice communication services in emergency situations.

Government Coordinating Council (GCC) The government counterpart to the Federal Communication Commission (FCC) for each sector established to enable interagency coordination. The GCC is comprised of representatives across various levels of governments (federal, state, local, tribal) as appropriate to the security and operational landscape of each infrastructure.

HVAC Acronym for heating, ventilation, and air conditioning.

Infrastructure The framework of interdependent networks and systems comprised in identifiable industries, institutions (including people and procedures), and distribution of capabilities that provide the reliable flow of products and services essential to the defense and economic security of the United States. The smooth functioning of government at all levels and society as a whole. Consistent with the definition of the Homeland Security Act, infrastructure includes physical, cyber, and/or human.

Interdependency The multi- or bidirectional reliance of an asset system, network, or collection thereof within a cross sector or input interaction or other requirement from other resources in order to function properly.

Key resources Publicly or privately controlled resources essential to the minimal operations to the economy and government.

Local government A county, municipality, city, town, local public authorities, school district, special district, interstate district, council of governments, regardless of whether the council of government is incorporated as not for profit under state law. It is a regional or interstate government entity. It can be tribal or a rural community.

Major disaster A natural catastrophe (including any hurricane, tornado, storm, high water, wind-driven water, tidal wave, tsunami, earthquake, volcanic eruption, landslide, mudslide, snowstorm, or drought, regardless of cause of any fire, flood or explosion.

Measures May include zoning and building codes, floodplain buyouts, and analysis of hazard-related data to determine whether it is safe to build or locate temporary facilities in a region. Mitigation can include efforts to educate governments, businesses, or the public on measures they can take to reduce the injury.

Media Physical objects, stored data such as paper, hard disc drives, tapes, and compact discs (CDs).

Mirroring A process that duplicates data to another location over a computer network in real time or close to real time.

Mitigation Activities designed to reduce or eliminate risk to persons or property or to lessen the actual or potential effects or consequences of an incident. Mitigation measures may be implemented prior to, during, or after an incident. They often are developed in accordance with the lessons learned from prior events. Mitigation involves ongoing actions to reduce exposure to, probability of, or potential loss from hazards.

Network   The group of assets or systems that share information or interact with each other in order to provide infrastructure services within or across sectors. Preparedness, the range of deliberate critical tasks and activities necessary to build, sustain, improve, and implement operational capability to prevent, protect against, respond to, and recover from domestic incidents.

PBX   Acronym for private branch exchange.

Preparedness   A continuous process involving efforts at all levels of government and between government and the private sector and nongovernmental organizations to identify threats, determine vulnerabilities, and identify required activities and resources to mitigate risk.

Prevention   Actions taken to avoid an incident or to intervene to stop an incident from occurring. Prevention involves actions taken to protect lives and property. It involves applying intelligence and other information to a range of activities that may include some countermeasures, such as deterrence operations, heightened inspections, improved surveillance, security operations, and investigations to determine the full nature and source of that threat.

Prioritization   The process of using risk assessment results to identify where risk reduction mitigation efforts are most needed and subsequently to determine which protective actions should be instituted in order to have the greatest effects.

Protection   Actions to mitigate the overall risk to critical infrastructure and key resources (CI/KR) assets, systems, networks, or their interconnecting links resulting from exposure, injury, destruction, incapacitation, or exploitation. Protection includes actions to deter the threat, mitigate vulnerabilities, or minimize consequences associated with a terrorist attack or other incident. Protection can include a wide range of activities, such as critical facilities, building resiliency and redundancy, incorporating hazard resistance into initial facility design, initiating activity or passive countermeasures, installing security systems, promoting workforce security, or implementing cybersecurity measures among various others.

Public and private sector entities   Often quote risk management frameworks in their business continuity plans. Public is assumed to be governmental, quasi-governmental entities at federal,state and local levels. Private entities are corporate or individual.

Recovery   The development, coordination, and execution of service and site restoration plans for impacted communities, and reconstitution of government operations and services through individual private sector, nongovernmental, and public assistance programs that identify needs and resources, provide housing and promotional restoration, invest in long-term care of affected persons, implement additional measures for community restoration, and incorporate mitigation measures and techniques as feasible.

Recovery point objectives (RPOs)   The amount of data that can be lost without severely impacting the recovery of operations.

Recovery site   An alternative location for processing information (and possibly conducting business in an emergency). Usually divided between hot sites, which are fully config-ured centers with compatible computer equipment, and cold sites, which are operational computer centers without the computer equipment.

Recovery time objectives (RTOs)   A period of time that a process can be inoperable.

Resiliency   The capacity of an asset, system, or network to maintain its function during, or to recover from, a terrorist attack or other incident.

Response   Activities that address the short-term direct effects of an impact or incident, including immediate actions to save lives, protect property, and meet basic human needs. Response also includes the execution of emergency operation plans and migration activities designed to limit the loss of life, personal injury, property damage, or other unfavorable outcomes. As indicated by the situation response activities, response includes applying intelligence or other information to lessen the effects of the consequences of the incident.

Risk   A measure of potential harm that encompasses threat, vulnerability, or consequence. Risk is the expected magnitude of loss due to a terrorist attack, national disaster, or other incident.

Risk management framework   A planning methodology that outlines the process for setting security goals; identifying assets, systems, networks, and functions; assessing risk; prioritization and implemention of protective programs; measuring performance; and taking corrective actions.

Routing   The process of moving information from its source to its destination.

SAS 70   An audit report of a servicing organization prepared in accordance with guidance provided by the American Institute of Certified Public Accountants Statement on Auditing Standards Number 70.

Sector   A logical collection of assets, systems, or networks that provides common function to the economy, government, or society. HSPD 7 defines 17 critical infrastructure key resource sectors.

Sector Coordinating Council (SCC)   A private-sector counterpart of the Government Coordinating Council (GCC). These self-organized, self-run, and self-maintained organizations are representative of a spectrum of key stakeholders within the sector. SCC's service governs principal point of entry into each sector for developing and coordinating a wide range of coordinating intelligence (CI) and core services and issues.

Sector partnership model   The framework used to promote mutual interest across sector planning, coordination, collaboration, and information sharing.

Sector-specific agency   Federal departments and agencies identified in HSPD 7 as responsible for a critical infrastructure and key resource protection activity as specified in the critical infrastructure and key resource sectors.

Server   A computer or other device that manages a network service. An example of print server device that manages network printing.

Source program   A program written in programming language (such as C, Pascal). A compiler translates the source code into machine language.

System development life cycle (SDLC) A written strategy or plan for the development and modification of computer systems, including initial approvals, development documentation, testing plans, results and approvals, and documentation of subsequent modifications.

T1 line A specific type of telephone line for digital communication only.

Terrorism Any activity that (1) involves an act that is dangerous to human life or is potentially destructive of critical infrastructure or key resources, and a violation of criminal laws in the United States or of any state or subdivision of the United States, and (2) appears to be intended to intimidate or coerce the civilian population, influence the policy of a government by intimidation or coercion, or affect the conduct of a government by mass destruction, assassination, or kidnapping.

Threat The intention and capability of an adversary to undertake actions that would be detrimental to the critical infrastructure and key resources.

Tier Groupings of jurisdictions that account for regional differences in expected capability levels among entities based on assessments of total population, population density, critical infrastructure, and other significant factors.

UPS (uninterruptible power supply) Typically a collection of batteries and power rectifiers that provide electrical power for a limited period of time.

Vaulting A process that periodically writes backup information over a computer network directly into a recovery site.

Vulnerability A weakness in the design, implementation, or cooperation of an asset, system, or network that can be exploited by an adversary or destroyed by a natural hazard or technological failure.

Weapons of mass destruction Any explosive, incendiary, or poisonous gas; bomb; grenade; rocket having propellant charge of more than four ounces; missile having an explosive or incendiary charge or more than one-quarter ounce; or mines. They are also any weapons that are designated or intended to cause death or serious bodily injury through the release, decimation, or impact of toxic poison chemicals or their precursors. These include any weapons involving a disease organism, or any weapon that is designated to release radiation or radioactivity at a level that is dangerous to human life.

INDEX

A

Accounting standards, 115
Acts of God
  and data center siting, 10, 21, 40
  distances, 99, 111, 134
  examples of natural disasters, 6, 7
  frequency and severity of, 76
  government guidelines, 100
  matrix, 22–38, 168
  and media reporting, 11
  outages, 116, 121
  as threat for data centers, 9, 76
  Tier 4 guidelines, 134
Agriculture and livestock, 15, 21, 105,
  106, 117, 124
"Air Pipe Mini Man" system, 108
Airfields, 13, 21, 51, 86, 111, 116,
  134, 136, 166, 167
Alternating current (AC), 142, 144,
  155, 188–191
Anger range, 10, 11, 73, 83
Architectural design criteria, 135, 136
Asynchronous encryption, 94, 111,
  116, 163, 179
Auditing Standards, 97
Auditors and audits, 115
Authorities Relevant to the Monitoring
  and Protection of Our National
  Infrastructure and Security of the
  Homeland, 106

B

Banks, 118, 119, 173, 178, 187
Bathrooms, 42, 48, 138
Blackouts. *See* Power outages
Blade servers, 59, 61, 71, 141, 157,
  159

Blasting activities, 167
Boil, liquid, evaporating, vapor,
  explosion/storage of explosives
  (BLEVES), 134
Bridges and tunnels, 12, 53, 76, 83,
  179
Brief continuity business plan, 84, 98
Brownouts, 182
Buddy system, 99
Budgets, 10, 47, 68, 92, 100, 115,
  149, 163, 167
Building codes, 135
Building departments, 92–94
Bunker scenario, 85, 116–118
Business contingency plan (BCP),
  47–49
Business continuity planning (BCP),
  99, 100, 113, 184
Business impact analysis (BIA), 9, 21,
  47, 99, 113, 118, 119, 167, 168

C

California, 6, 9, 39, 58, 95, 158, 187
Cantor Fitzgerald, 174–176
Carbon dioxide (CO_2) emissions, 55,
  145, 151, 153, 154,
  158, 183
Cell towers, 135
Centrex, 108, 155, 179, 182, 190
Chief executive officers (CEOs), 98,
  114
Chief financial officers (CFOs), 98,
  100, 114
China, 65, 151, 153, 154, 183
Circuit reliability, 76–78
Coal, 15, 151–153, 158, 183,
  185, 187

Cogeneration and microcogeneration, 13, 68, 75, 76, 144, 182, 184–187, 191
Collocation-caged environments
    collocation contracts, 126
    and costs of cooling, 143
    described, 8
Columns, 136
Common Identification for federal employees and contractors (HSPD 12), 106
Communication, 106–109, 115, 122. *See also* Telecommunications
Comprehensive Terrorist Related Screening Procedures (HSPD 11), 106
Computer room air-conditioning (CRAC), 140, 141, 145, 188, 191
Computer room air-handling (CRAH), 141, 145
Concurrent maintenance, 62
Conference room (war room), 48, 49, 138, 158
Construction costs, 92, 127
Consultants, 21, 65, 69, 100, 133, 163, 167, 182
Cooling systems, 4–6, 58, 59, 61–64, 69, 71, 137, 139–149, 155, 157, 158, 182, 190
Cooperation, communication and coordination, 115
Cornfield siting, 180
Corporate governance, 58, 59, 95, 163, 167
Costs, 140, 144. *See also* Total cost of ownership (TCO)
    cogeneration, 187
    construction, 127
    of cyberterrorism, 171–173
    direct current power plants, 188–190
    environmentals, 68
    negotiation, 168
    operating expenses, 65

power, 73, 75, 151, 155, 187
    reducing, 182
    technology, 68
    tiering, 62, 65, 66
Criminal liability, 84, 98, 115
Critical Infrastructure (CI) and Key Resources (KR) (HSPD 7), 102, 105, 107, 121
Critical Infrastructure Protection in the Information Age (October 2001, amended February 2003), 106, 107, 121
Cyberterrorism, 102, 171–176

D

Damages, consequential, 85
Data centers
    background, 2–7
    centralized approach, 57–68
    collocation-caged, 8
    costs, 140
    going green issues, 157–162
    greenfield, 7, 76, 135, 163
    growth, 57, 69–72
    life cycle, 69
    and natural disasters, generally, 6, 7
    offshoring, 180
    outages, 85. *See also* Power outages
    primary data center location, 83, 87–91, 111–113, 177, 181
    remote siting, 180, 182
    second-site location, 112, 113, 116, 177, 181
    shared infrastructure, 8
    site inspection, 86, 92
    site selection matrix, 16–19, 87–91, 168
    site selection negotiation and execution, 163–169
    siting, 9, 10, 20, 83–96, 115, 184
    siting risk map, 21, 39
    speed, 177–180
    spoke-and-wheel, 58
    stand-alone, 7, 85, 99, 116, 185

sustainable sites, 159, 160
and thinking outside the box,
181–191
Decision making, 183, 184
Dense wavelength division
multiplexing (DWDM), 138, 177
Design load, 135
Direct current (DC), 76, 141, 142,
144, 155, 182, 184, 188–191
Dirty bombs, 86, 118, 128
Disaster recovery, 58, 95, 99, 115,
126. *See also* Business continuity
planning (BCP)
Domestic Nuclear Detection
Organization (HSPD 14), 106
Drought, 9, 14, 95, 141, 152, 153
Due diligence, 94, 173

E

Earthquakes, 6, 9, 15, 39, 41, 111,
112, 121, 131, 136
Economic development committees
(EDCs), 167, 168
Economic growth, 139, 140
Electronic trading, 178
Electronic vaulting, 95
Employees, willingness to work, 85,
94, 95, 115, 116, 135
Encryption, 61, 68, 83, 94–95, 109,
111, 112, 115, 140, 145,
177, 178
Energy sources, 152, 153, 187
Energy use. *See* Power consumption
Environmental issues, 144, 145, 157,
158, 185, 187
Environmental Protection Agency
(EPA), 54, 67, 73, 75, 76, 93, 140
Expansion needs, 76, 138

F

Fear tactics, 10, 95, 100
Federal Emergency Management
Agency (FEMA), 128

Federal Financial Institutions Council
Business Continuity Planning
(March 2003), 97
Federal funds, distribution of, 121, 122
Financial service firms, 113, 118, 119,
139, 172, 178
Fire, 121, 134, 172. *See also* Wildfires
Fire sprinklers, 42, 68
Firewalls, 172–174
First responders, 12, 42, 43, 116, 122,
134, 164, 165
Fixed base operations (FBOs), 9, 130,
134, 136, 166, 167
Floods and floodplains, 6, 7, 11, 12,
42, 43, 45, 46, 51–56, 85, 86, 95,
111, 112, 121, 134
Florida, 9, 14, 39, 55
Footings, 135, 136
Fossil fuels, 78, 153, 158, 183, 186,
187
Foundations, 135, 136
France, 153
Free cooling, 75, 76, 145, 180, 182,
184
Free space optics (FSO), 108–110
Freon, 140, 142
Fujita scale, 45, 136

G

Gardner, Doug, 175, 176
Gas cooling systems, 140, 142, 144,
145
Gas lines, 10, 13, 41, 42, 46, 111, 128,
183. *See also* Natural gas
Generally accepted accounting
principles (GAAP), 59, 114, 115
Generation service, 78
Georgia, 14, 39
Germ/biological events, 118, 135
Germany, 153, 154
Governance. *See* Corporate
governance
Government
and cyberterrorism, 173, 174

Government (*contd.*)
  power usage, 75
Green data center issues, 157–162
Green Grid, 155
Greenfield, 7, 76, 135, 163
Guidelines for Disaster Preparedness,
  97
Gut check, 10, 95

H

Hardware. *See* Mainframes; Servers
Hazardous materials (hazmat)
  contamination, 12, 134, 135,
  165–167
Health Insurance Portability and
  Accountability Act (HIPAA), 59
Heat waves, 7
High winds, 12, 14, 15, 40, 41, 44, 51,
  55, 134
Highways, 9, 11, 12, 21, 51, 76, 116,
  128, 134, 164
"Hockey stick" growth, 68, 69, 80
Homeland Securities Doctrine (July
  2002), 101, 102
Homeland Security, 97, 101, 103–105,
  107–108, 122, 123, 125, 174
Homeland Security Act of 2002, 97
Homeland Security Advisory system
  (HSPD 3), 103
Homeland Security Council (HSPD 1),
  103
Homeland Security Presidential
  Directives (HSPD), 103–107,
  121–126
Hot-aisle/cold-aisle configuration, 71,
  157
Human intervention, 85. *See also*
  Terrorism
Human resources, role in site
  selection, 94, 95
Hurricane Katrina, 7, 53, 54, 96, 123
Hurricanes, 6–7, 9, 14, 40, 43, 53–56,
  96, 111, 112, 123
Hydroelectric power, 134, 151, 183

I

Immigration policies, 103
In-cabinet cooling, 140, 144
India, 65
Indian Point Nuclear Power Plant and
  Radiological Emergency
  Preparedness Plan, 128–131, 163
Indoor environmental quality, 159, 161
InfiniBand, 178
Information technology (IT), 139, 140
  and cyberterrorism, 171
  governance, 86
  internal controls, 97
Infrastructure, 3, 4, 8, 85, 97, 99, 100,
  102, 105–108, 120, 121
Inside plant (ISP) power, 85, 86, 155
Inspection of data center sites, 86, 92
Institute of Electrical and Electronics
  Engineers (IEEE), 136
Insurance, 48, 56
Intelligence, gathering, 86, 92–95,
  105, 106
Internal controls, 97, 98, 114, 115
International Building Code (IBC),
  135
Internet Protocol (IP), 108, 138, 172,
  179, 182

J

Japan, 3, 4
Just-in-time technology, 2, 48, 141

K

Kill zone, 15, 86, 117, 129, 130, 134,
  163, 165
Kyoto Protocol, 144, 185

L

Lab, 138
Landfills and dumps, 135, 167
Latency, 109, 110, 112, 178, 179
LeFrak, Richard, 2, 3
LeFrak, Sam, 2, 3

LeFrak Organization, 2, 3
Legacy systems, 1, 58, 69, 80, 85, 139–141, 189, 190
Lightning, 15, 39, 40, 134, 136, 137
Louisiana, 53, 54
Low energy electron diffraction (LEED), 144, 157, 159, 161, 187

M

Mainframes, 1–5, 58, 60, 142, 190
Maintenance, 7, 62, 65, 67, 76, 99, 133, 143–145, 157, 188–190
Man-made disasters, 9–13, 21, 41, 46, 121, 128, 134, 135, 163, 168
Management of Domestic Incidents (HSPD 5), 104, 122
Manhattan. *See* New York City
Maritime Security Policy (December 2004) (HSPD 13), 106
Mega-data centers, 57, 59, 67
Mines and quarries, 167
Mixed-use data centers, 184
Monitoring, 8, 106, 125, 130, 137, 154, 168
Moore, Gordon, 68
Moore's Law, 57, 61, 68, 75, 138, 143, 172–173
Multi-"U" topology, 61
Multiplexing, 8, 94, 138, 177, 180, 182

N

National Association of Securities Dealers (NASD), 97, 98, 113, 179
National Communication System (NCS), 108
National Electric Code (NEC), 136
National Fire Protection Agency, 97
National Fire Protection Association (NFPA), 113, 126–128
National Incident Management System (NIMS), 104
National infrastructure protection plan (2006), 97, 121, 122

National Infrastructure Security Council (NIAC), 107, 108
National Institute of Physical Protection (NIPP), 102, 103
National Institute of Standards and Technology, 106
National Intelligence Strategy of the United States, 102, 103
National planning scenarios, 123
National preparedness directive (HSPD 8), 105, 121–126
National Response Plan (NRP), 104
National Security Council, 108
National Security Telecommunications Advisory Committee (NSTAC), 108
National Society for Maritime Security, 102
National Strategy for Physical Protection of Critical Infrastructures and Key Assets (February 2003), 102
National Strategy to Combat Terrorism (February 2003), 102
National Strategy to Combat Weapons of Mass Destruction (WMD), 104
National Strategy to Secure Cyberspace (February 2003)
Natural disasters. *See* Acts of God
Natural gas, 13, 151, 153, 183–185, 187. *See also* Gas lines
Negative cascading of power, 58, 73, 96, 121, 154, 182
Negotiation with utilities and state/local entities, 168, 169
Network operating control center (NOCC), 67, 137, 138, 154, 168
New Jersey, 2, 3, 10, 12, 71, 83, 94, 165–167, 179
New Orleans, 53, 54
New York, 9, 14, 56, 78, 98, 128–131, 151
New York City, 3, 6, 53, 54, 58, 79, 83, 85–86, 108, 117, 118, 166, 186, 191

Newport Financial Center (NFC), 2, 3
North Carolina, 79, 85, 179
Nuclear facilities, 9, 15, 21, 79, 86, 117, 118, 122, 128–131, 134, 151, 153, 154, 163, 183, 185
Nuclear Regulatory Commission (NRC), 15, 86, 128, 130, 131

O

Office of Management and Budget (OMB), 108
Office of Science, Technology Policy (OSTP), 108
Office parks, 184
Offshoring, 144, 180
100-year storm, 51–53, 85
Operating expenses, 57–60, 65, 72, 76, 139, 140, 144, 151, 168, 185
Outside plant (OSP) infrastructure, 5, 15, 39, 71, 76, 81, 85, 86, 101, 120, 121, 135, 151, 154. *See also* Power outages

P

Pantry, 138
Patriot Act of 2002, 97, 179
Perimeter, 136
Personal knowledge, 92
Population growth, 158, 183, 185
Power consumption, 61–65, 67, 69, 71, 73, 75–81, 137, 140, 141, 147, 149, 155, 167, 182, 185
Power distribution units (PDUs), 6, 144, 155, 188, 191
Power grid, 76, 79, 111, 112, 154, 155, 158, 161, 182, 185–187
Power outages, 43–46, 73, 74, 76, 85, 86, 96, 119–121, 135, 155
Power plants, 134, 151–155. *See also* Hydroelectric power; Nuclear facilities
Pricing, 48, 49, 62, 65, 66, 126
Public Company Accounting Oversight Board (PCAOB), 84, 97

R

Radio-frequency (RF), 41, 108–110, 135, 157, 167
Radioactive "kill zone," 15, 86, 117, 129, 130, 134, 163, 165
Railroads, 9, 12, 13, 94, 111, 115, 128, 134, 190
Recruit, USA, 2–4
Risk assessment, 10, 11, 108, 114
Risk management, 42, 47, 179
Risk map, 21, 39
Roofs, 4, 15, 40, 42, 116, 135, 136, 157, 161
Russia, 154

S

Sales taxes, 60, 169, 181, 182
Sarbanes-Oxley Act (SOX), 48, 59, 84, 95, 97–99, 101, 110, 113–115, 179
Satellite technology, 52, 109, 110
Sea level, 52–55
Secure Cyberspace (February 2003), 97, 121
Securities and Exchange Commission (SEC), 84, 97, 98, 110, 113–115, 179
Securities companies, 118, 119
Security guidelines, 137
Security operating control center (SOCC), 137, 138
Seismic criteria, 136. *See also* Earthquakes
September 11, 2001 terrorist attacks, 57, 58, 83, 86, 95, 97, 101, 110, 116, 126, 130, 131, 139, 166, 175, 176, 179
Servers
  blade servers, 59, 61, 71, 141, 157, 159
  distribution, 71
  energy efficient, 67
  federal government, 75
  growth of market for, 67–69

infrastructure, 76
legacy, 1
rationalization, 58
security, 102
virtualization technology, 60, 61,
    69, 143, 182
voltage, 190, 191
waste and heat generation, 142, 188
Service-level agreements (SLAs), 4, 8,
    44, 126
Sewage. *See* Waste treatment facilities
Shared infrastructure, 3, 4, 8, 99, 100
Sinkholes, 54, 55
Smart buildings, 137
Snow storms and ice, 9, 11–14, 39,
    40, 42, 67, 111, 112, 134
Software, 47, 48, 58–60, 65, 67, 69,
    75, 120, 140, 143, 171, 174, 184
Software bombs, 171
Solar energy, 79, 152, 186
Solution providers, 60, 143
SONET. *See* Synchronous optical
    networks (SONET)
South Carolina, 79, 179
Spain, 153
Speed of light, 177, 178
Sporkin, Stanley, 110
Stand-alone data centers, 7, 85, 99,
    116, 185
Sustainable energy sources, 79, 152,
    183
Synchronous encryption, 83, 111, 112,
    115, 116, 163
Synchronous optical networks
    (SONET), 67, 108, 109, 111, 112,
    177

T

Targeted capabilities list (TCL),
    123–126
Tax incentives, 181, 182, 185
Tax maps, 51
Telecommunications, 5, 6, 76, 85, 108,
    109, 138, 179–180

Tennessee, 15, 79, 154
Terminology, 95
Terrorism, 9, 102, 103, 105, 106, 121.
    See also September 11, 2001
    terrorist attacks
Terrorist screening (HSPD 6),
    104–106
Texas, 9, 14, 15, 22–39, 55, 95, 154,
    171, 187
Thermal storage, 76, 145, 158, 182
Three "Cs," 115
Thunderstorms, 52. *See also* Floods
    and floodplains; Lightning
Tier 1, 61–64, 84, 98, 113
Tier 2, 62–64, 84, 98, 113, 114, 133
Tier 3, 61–64, 68, 76, 133, 188
Tier 4, 61–64, 68, 76, 133–138, 140,
    188
Tornados, 6, 9, 14, 15, 40, 43, 45,
    111, 112, 131, 134
Total cost of ownership (TCO), 2, 53,
    65, 67, 141–143, 145, 167, 168,
    179, 181, 183, 185, 187, 190, 191
Triangulation of data, 95, 116, 117
Trigeneration, 184
Tsunamis, 111, 112, 134

U

Uninterruptible power supply (UPS),
    8, 62, 68, 75, 76, 80, 99, 136,
    138, 141–143, 145, 186, 188,
    190, 191
United Kingdom, 79, 80, 144, 176
Universal task list (UTL), 123–125
Uptime Institute, 127, 133, 135
User efficiency, 60
Utility rates, 76, 78, 168, 169

V

Validus DC system, 189
Value-added resources (VARs), 61
Virtualization, 60, 61, 69, 143, 182,
    191
Volcanoes, 111, 112, 134

W

Waste treatment facilities, 54, 135
Water, 152, 153, 160, 166. *See also*
    Floods and floodplains
Water mains, 54
Waters, Charlie, 175, 176
Weapons of mass destruction (WMD),
    104, 135
Weather records, 52
White papers (SEC), 84, 85, 97, 98,
    111, 112, 177, 179
White space, 1, 57, 59, 62, 75, 138,
    146, 149, 158, 159, 163, 182

Wildfires, 14, 95, 111, 112, 134
Wind. *See also* High winds
    as power source, 79, 152, 186
World Trade Center, first attack, 11,
    85, 95

Y

Y2K, 57, 95, 100, 139, 140

Z

Z, 141, 143
Zoning and building department
    concerns, 41, 86, 92–94